DERIVING SYNTACTIC RELATIONS

A pioneering new approach to a long-debated topic at the heart of syntax: what are the primitive concepts and operations of syntax? This book argues, appealing in part to the logic of Chomsky's Minimalist Program, that the primitive operations of syntax form relations between words rather than combining words to form constituents. Just three basic relations, definable in terms of inherent selection properties of words, are required in natural language syntax: projection, argument selection, and modification.

In the radically simplified account of generative grammar Bowers proposes there are just two interface levels, which interact with our conceptual and sensory systems, and a lexicon from which an infinite number of sentences can be constructed. The theory also provides a natural interpretation of phase theory, enabling a better formulation of many island constraints, as well as providing the basis for a unified approach to ellipsis phenomena.

JOHN BOWERS is Professor in the Department of Linguistics at Cornell University. He has published two books, the most recent of which is *Arguments as Relations* (2010), published in the *Linguistic Inquiry Monographs* series. He has also published numerous journal articles and book chapters focusing primarily on the areas of predication, transitivity, argument structure, and control.

CAMBRIDGE STUDIES IN LINGUISTICS

General Editors

Deriving Syntactic Relations

In this series

Earlier issues not listed are also available

DERIVING SYNTACTIC RELATIONS

JOHN BOWERS

Cornell University, New York

CAMBRIDGE
UNIVERSITY PRESS

CAMBRIDGE
UNIVERSITY PRESS

University Printing House, Cambridge CB2 8BS, United Kingdom

One Liberty Plaza, 20th Floor, New York, NY 10006, USA

477 Williamstown Road, Port Melbourne, VIC 3207, Australia

314-321, 3rd Floor, Plot 3, Splendor Forum, Jasola District Centre, New Delhi - 110025, India

79 Anson Road, #06-04/06, Singapore 079906

Cambridge University Press is part of the University of Cambridge.

It furthers the University's mission by disseminating knowledge in the pursuit of
education, learning and research at the highest international levels of excellence.

www.cambridge.org
Information on this title: www.cambridge.org/9781107480650
DOI: 10.1017/9781316156414

© John Bowers 2018

First published 2018
First paperback edition 2020

A catalogue record for this publication is available from the British Library

Library of Congress Cataloging in Publication data
Names: Bowers, John S., author.
Title: Deriving syntactic relations / John Bowers.
Description: Cambridge, United Kingdom ; New York, NY : Cambridge
University Press, 2017. | Series: Cambridge studies in linguistics ; 151 |
Includes bibliographical references and index.
Identifiers: LCCN 2017017834 | ISBN 9781107096752 (hardcover :
acid-free paper)
Subjects: LCSH: Grammar, Comparative and general – Syntax.
Classification: LCC P291 .B678 2017 | DDC 415–dc23
LC record available at https://lccn.loc.gov/2017017834

ISBN 978-1-107-09675-2 Hardback
ISBN 978-1-107-48065-0 Paperback

Contents

Acknowledgments

My earliest attempt to develop a theory of syntax based on syntactic relations between words was inspired by a conversation with Chris Collins in early 2000 about his paper "Eliminating labels," during the course of which he suggested the possibility of eliminating constituent structure. I quickly produced an (unpublished) paper titled "Syntactic relations," followed by a longer manuscript with the same title (also unpublished), which was presented in talks and seminars at University College London and the University of Edinburgh in 2001 and 2002. Though I continued to work on the ideas in this manuscript over the next few years, I was not satisfied with the results and put it aside to pursue other interests.

Then, in the fall of 2012, partly as a result of the work in my monograph *Arguments as Relations*, I began to see the possibility of a radically different approach to the idea of replacing constituent structure with syntactic relations. I produced a draft of these new ideas that fall, which was presented in a seminar at Cornell in the spring semester of 2013. Thanks to the invaluable discussion and criticisms of the participants in that seminar, I was able to sharpen these initial ideas considerably, resulting in the first draft of *Deriving Syntactic Relations*, which was submitted to Cambridge University Press at the end of 2013. To this I eventually added two completely new chapters on syntactic variation and ellipsis, partly in response to the comments of two referees and partly as a result of further discussion in a seminar in the spring of 2015.

I am indebted to many people with whom I have discussed the ideas in this volume during its long gestation. I particularly wish to thank Neal Smith and Emmon Bach, both of whom read and commented on my early manuscript. I would like to single out for special thanks everyone who participated in my seminar in the spring of 2013. To the best of my recollection, they include (in no particular order): John Hale, Tim Hunter, Wayne Harbert, Ed Cormany, Sarah Courtney, Cara DiGirolamo, Nan Li, Todd Snider, Zachary Smith, and Miloje Despić. My apologies if I have inadvertently omitted anyone. I would also like to thank John Hale for his continuing encouragement during the last few years and for pointing me toward the highlights of the literature on Dependency Grammar. Finally, I would like to thank the participants in my seminar in the fall of 2016, Jacob Collard in particular, for a number of very helpful comments and suggestions.

Ithaca, New York
January 2017

Introduction

Background

Background

There have been a number of attempts in the modern era to argue that the primitives of syntactic theory should be relations (or dependencies) between words rather than constituents. Frameworks as diverse as Relational Grammar (Perlmutter 1983, Perlmutter and Rosen 1984) and its descendant Arc-Pair Grammar (Postal 1980), Dependency Grammar (Tesnière 1959, Hays 1964, Gaifman 1965, Robinson 1970, Abney 1995, Debusmann 2000, Covington 2001), Word Grammar (Hudson 1990), and Form Dependency (Manzini 1995, Manzini and Savoia 2011) have tried in various different ways to implement such a program.[1] By and large, however, these attempts have not been persuasive to mainstream generative syntacticians. I believe that there are at least five main reasons for this. The first is simply that quite a mass of important empirical and theoretical insights has built up over the last five decades within mainstream generative grammar, up to and including Minimalism. Existing relation-based theories thus tend to suffer in both empirical coverage and theoretical depth in comparison with mainstream theories based on constituent structure. The second reason is that relation-based theories have not generally come to terms with the problem of predicting the linear ordering of words at the phonetic level on the basis of syntactic representations. Instead, they have assumed linear order as a primitive of the theory (as was also the case in classical Phrase Structure Grammars), made do with *ad hoc* generalizations, or simply ignored the problem. The third reason is that proponents of relation-based theories have been primarily concerned with representation, leaving it unclear how relational structures are to be derived. Fourth, existing relational theories have not attempted to incorporate the most fundamental insight of X-bar theory

---

[1] See also Brody (1994) for an approach that includes both constituents and dependencies.

and Minimalism, namely, that syntactic structure is derived in bottom-up fashion from the most basic lexical units of language. Finally, the important idea that syntax must contain so-called functional heads as well as lexical heads, which plays a crucial role in most current work in syntax, does not figure prominently in the various versions of Dependency Grammar with which I am familiar.

Despite these problems, I believe that the time is ripe to consider seriously the idea that an optimal theory of syntax must in fact be based on relations between words rather than on constituent structure. One way of going about this is to utilize the logic of the Minimalist Program, which insists that it is necessary to examine critically the primitive concepts and operations of syntax, in order to eliminate anything that cannot be shown to be absolutely essential. Chomsky (2000) suggests that the irreducible minimum required by any theory of syntax are two interface levels, SEM and PHON, whose representations are "legible" to (can be "read" by) the conceptual-intentional (CI) systems and the sensorimotor (SM) systems, respectively. In addition there must be a lexicon LEX, consisting of a finite set of words or lexical items (LIs), from which an infinite set of sentences can be constructed. The fundamental minimalist question is: What else is needed?

Chomsky himself has already gone quite far in the direction of simplifying syntax, eliminating X-bar theory as well as unnecessary levels such as D-structure and S-structure entirely, leaving just the primitive operations of Merge, Move (partially reducible to Merge), and Agree. However, the resulting theory, though considerably simpler, is still firmly based on the notion of constituent structure. The Merge operation produces a new syntactic object which is simply a set consisting of just the two objects that are the input to Merge. The syntactic object produced in this way can in turn be part of the input to another application of Merge. The syntactic object produced by each application of Merge is thus carried along throughout the derivation, building up a full constituent structure for each sentence. The question is whether even a system this pared-down is still too rich. I believe that it is and that a still simpler theory in which the primitive objects are not constituents but relations (or dependencies) between words will suffice. If so, then the notions of constituent structure and movement can be eliminated entirely from syntactic theory and replaced with a set of asymmetric relations between words. Going a step further, I would argue that not only is a relational theory of syntax *possible* but that it comes very close to being the optimal solution to the problem of relating the representations of SEM and PHON, given the most basic legibility conditions imposed on those levels by CI and SM, respectively, and assuming that the only place that semantic, syntactic and phonetic information is stored is in a finite set of lexical items (LIs) contained in the lexicon (LEX) of each language.

Overview

The goal of this book is to achieve a radical simplification of syntactic theory by eliminating the notions of constituent structure and movement from narrow syntax, replacing them with asymmetrical dependency relations between words. In its final form, the theory proposed here generates such relations by means of a simple binary operation *Form Relation* (FR), which takes as input a pair of lexical items α and β and produces an ordered pair $<\alpha,\beta>$, where β satisfies a selection condition required by α. FR applies in strictly bottom-up fashion. Crucially, relational derivations are bottom-up not only in the obvious sense that each application of FR adds a new relation, but also in the sense that the item containing the selection condition (the head) is always lower than the selected item (the dependent). An important consequence of this approach is that the notion of an "extended projection" in the sense of Grimshaw (1990) is built directly into the structure of the theory without having to be stipulated.

Given a theory of this form, it can be shown that the appearance of constituent structure and movement simply arise from the incremental application of Spell-out, together with the most basic legibility requirements of phonetic representation. Minimally, these are (i) the phonetic representations of lexical items must be linearly ordered, and (ii) the phonetic representation of every head must be legible to SM. The illusion of constituent structure arises directly from requirement (i) together with the incremental nature of the Spell-out algorithm, which ensures that once a string is formed at PHON it cannot be disrupted by any later application FR. The illusion of head movement arises from (ii), via a general condition that permits a dependent containing an illegible symbol to be replaced by the phonetic form of its head. The illusion of constituent movement is more complex, arising from the fact that certain heads may have an athematic argument selection feature, combined with the legibility requirements of both PHON and SEM. In such a case, the linear ordering requirement of PHON, together with a requirement of SEM similar to the θ-Criterion, jointly require that the phonetic form of a previously selected head be displaced leftward. Finally, it turns out that Spell-out, given these assumptions, can be stated in the following maximally simple and general form without having to assume that order is a primitive of the theory as in Kayne

(2010): given a relation $<\alpha,\beta>$, the phonetic form of β must precede the phonetic form of α, i.e. dependents precede heads.

In the theory proposed here there are just three basic types of selection: (i) lexical projection, (ii) argument selection, and (iii) modification. Each is strictly and exhaustively definable in terms of inherent formal properties of heads. Furthermore, it turns out that the possible orders in which these three relation-types may be formed is automatically determined by FR together with a universal constraint, termed *Immediate Gratification* (IG), which requires that selection requirements of heads be satisfied immediately. This principle, which is independently needed in order to ensure that derivations operate in strict bottom to top fashion, also solves a fundamental problem that has plagued constituent-based grammars, namely, the fact that there is no way to determine, except by arbitrary stipulation, the order in which two selection requirements associated with the same head are to be satisfied.

A theory of this form leads naturally to a novel approach to adverbial and adjectival modification, based on the idea that it is the modifier that has a selection feature and the modified that is selected. Modifiers can then be precisely defined as a third type of head that has selectors of its own but which, in contrast to both arguments and lexical projections, is not itself selected as an argument by any other head. Hence the modification relation falls out in an entirely natural way from the structure of the relational theory.

Another fundamental problem that a relation-based theory is able to shed light on is how to account for the range of word order variation found in human language. It turns out that a very small set of simple word order parameters— some very general in application, others highly specific—are sufficient to account for the observed range of cross-linguistic variation, while maintaining, with varying degrees of transparency, the universal order of projection of syntactic heads.

Another welcome consequence of a relational approach to syntax is that the range of morphosyntactic phenomena found in natural language, such as Case (both inherent and structural), agreement, and applicative morphology, can be explained as simple reflexes in PHON of the restricted range of possible relations between heads and dependents permitted by the theory, without having to introduce a new primitive relation analogous to the Agree operation assumed in current minimalist theories. This makes it possible, I argue, to eliminate the minimalist assumption that derivations are driven by the need to value and delete uninterpretable morphological features, replacing it with the more natural assumption that Case and agreement features are simply a means of making syntactic relations visible at PHON. Ultimately, then, what drives relational derivations is simply and solely the need to satisfy the legibility requirements of both PHON and SEM.[2]

Similarly, the theory can accommodate the fundamental morphological and syntactic properties of A'-constructions without the addition of any new primitives, as well as providing a relational account of superiority, island effects, weak versus strong islands, factive versus non-factive complements, and multiple *wh*-movement. One particularly interesting result is that the well-known language-particular fact of English that lexical verbs fail to raise to T can be described in relational terms without having to assume either lowering operations or LF-movement. Likewise *wh*-movement can be interpreted in relational terms as a special case of selection that arises when an LI has one of a number of different operator features such as [wh].

Still another area illuminated by the relational approach is ellipsis. A novel approach to the phenomenon is proposed, based on the idea that identity of heads is the fundamental requirement for ellipsis, and it is shown that this approach solves a number of outstanding problems in the literature, while at the same time pointing the way toward a unified theory of ellipsis.

In the course of developing the approach to syntax proposed in this book, a number of important ideas in the minimalist literature are examined and reformulated in relational terms. It turns out, for example, that the notion of a "defective" category (such as TP), which has no real theoretical status apart from pure stipulation in theories based on constituent structure, is perfectly natural and expected in the relational theory. Likewise, the notion of a *v*-phase coincides with the "minimal category" (cf. Chapter 2, §2.1) needed to form a *v*-projection, while CP and DP phases can be identified as maximal *v*- and *n*-projections, respectively. Similarly, the fact that a head may "escape" from a phase under certain conditions is a consequence of the independently needed assumption *v*-phases are recursive.

In short, I hope to show that a relation-based theory of syntax developed along the lines proposed in this volume has both theoretical and empirical advantages over mainstream theories based on constituent structure, and, more importantly, that it suggests novel and fruitful lines of inquiry in a number of areas where the latter have been less than fully successful.

---

[2] See Manzini (1995: 329), for a similar idea embodied in the "Principle of Interpretation" that she formulates as follows: "All and only dependencies are interpreted."

1   *Relational Derivation*

Virtually all modern theories of syntax are based in one way or another on the two fundamental notions of constituent structure and movement. So, for example, the syntax of a sentence such as *What will John do?* is standardly derived roughly as follows:

(1)

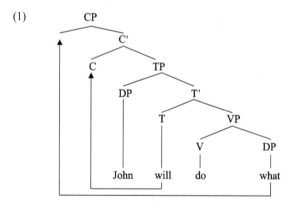

In a representation of this sort the subtrees [$_{VP}$ [$_V$ do] [$_{DP}$ what]], [[[$_{T'}$ [$_T$ will] [$_{VP}$ [$_V$ do] [$_{DP}$ what]]], etc. represent *labeled constituents*, projected in standard X-bar theory from basic lexical categories such as V, N, D, T, C, etc., while the arrows represent *movement* or *displacement* operations that create a copy of a constituent and merge it in an appropriate place in constituent structure. The questions that I will be concerned with in this work are the following. Where do these notions come from? How do they arise in the cognitive system of the human brain? Are these notions irreducible primitives? Or could they be derived from more fundamental concepts? And if the latter is true, how?

Let's start by considering some very basic properties of the human linguistic mechanism. Reduced to bare essentials, a language L is a cognitive system that

6

stores information about sound and meaning. The basic units of the system are words or lexical items (LIs) stored in a lexicon (LEX), each of which consists of a set of features [F] (linguistic properties). Minimally, there must be two interface levels SEM and PHON that provide information to the conceptual-intentional systems (CI) and the sensorimotor systems (SM), respectively. Then the computational system of human language C_{HL} must provide a recursive definition of a set of pairs of expressions Exp = <SEM, PHON>, based on the semantic and phonetic information contained in the LIs of L.

How did a system of this sort come into existence? Chomsky (2000, 2001) speculates that the strongest possible hypothesis would be the following:

(2)   *Strongest Minimalist Hypothesis*:
       Language is an optimal solution to legibility conditions.

Here the term "legibility conditions" refers to the conditions that must be met in order for other systems of the mind/brain to access the Exp of a language, i.e. to "read" them and use them as "instructions" for thought and action. Since the CI systems and the SM systems are independent of L, it makes sense to ask how well L satisfies the design specifications they impose. If the language system satisfies the legibility conditions in an optimal way and also satisfies all other empirical conditions, e.g. acquisition, processing, neurology, etc., then it could be said to be a perfect solution to minimal design specifications.

1.1   Relations between Words

Putting aside the question of whether the language system is perfect or not, let's focus on a more basic question: What is the minimal apparatus that must be assumed in order to derive the fundamental syntactic notions of constituent structure and movement from the legibility conditions imposed on PHON and SEM? I will show that given an operation *Form Relation*[1] (abbreviated henceforth as FR) that operates in sequential fashion to form networks of ordered pairs of LIs, the notions of constituent structure and movement can be derived from one of the most basic properties of PHON, namely, the requirement that lexical items be linearly ordered.

---

[1] This term is first used in Bowers (2000). Collins and Ura (2001) use the term "Establish Rel" for a similar operation. See also Manzini (1995) and Manzini and Savoia (2011), in which the term "Form Dependence" is used for essentially the same operation. See also Brody (1994), for work headed in this direction.

Before sketching out the form of the theory I intend to propose, some terminological clarifications are necessary. In mathematical parlance, an *ordered pair* is standardly defined in terms of sets as follows:

(3)   An *ordered pair* with *a* as *first coordinate* and *b* as *second coordinate*, denoted <*a,b*>, is equal to the set {{*a*},{*a,b*}}.

Once order has been defined in terms of the more primitive notion of a set, it can be used as if it were a primitive without having to go back to the definition at every point. Given any two sets *A* and *B*, the *Cartesian product of A and B*, denoted *A* × *B*, is defined as follows:

(4) $A \times B =_{def} \{<x,y> \mid x \in A \wedge y \in B\}$

A (binary) relation *R* that is a subset of *A* × *B* is said to be a relation *from A to B*, while one that is a subset of *A* × *A* is said to be a relation *in A*. I use the term "syntactic relation" in this work in a systematically ambiguous fashion to refer either to particular ordered pairs <α,β> of LIs α and β or to some subset of binary relations in LEX × LEX, where LEX is the set of LIs of a given language.

Given the operation FR and a set of LIs in LEX, the next question is how FR determines, for any two LIs α and β, whether it is possible to form a relation between them, and if so, which is the first coordinate of the relation and which the second. The standard answer to this question in the linguistic literature is that one of the LIs in a relation is the *head*. The head in turn is that LI which has a *selection* condition requiring that the other term of the relation meet some specific grammatical requirement. Let us assume, then, that FR may apply to a pair of LIs α and β to form the ordered pair <α,β>, just in case the second coordinate β has some specified set of syntactic properties that the first coordinate α requires it to have. Following standard practice, I assume that these properties are specified in the lexical entry of the LI in the first coordinate by means of *selection features* of the form [_X], where X is a categorial feature, some combination of categorial and other syntactic features, or a specific LI of some category. For example, a verb that selects an object DP has the feature [_D]; a verb such as *rely* has the selection feature [_on$_P$]; a verb that selects a finite complement has the selection feature [_that$_C$]; the complementizer *for* has a selection feature [_to$_T$]; etc. Any ordered pair of this sort, with head α and dependent β satisfying a selection condition of α, I will define as a *syntactic relation*. We may also refer to such an ordered pair as a *dependency relation*.

1.1.1   FR and the Head Principle

Let us assume, then, that there is just one basic operation FR in narrow syntax (NS). FR is a binary operation that applies to LIs α and β and forms an ordered pair <α,β> just in case β meets the requirements of a selection condition associated with α:

(5) $FR(\alpha,\beta) = <\alpha,\beta>$

Given this operation, a network of syntactic relations is built up in the following way. First, a selection of tokens of LIs is chosen from LEX to form a *lexical array* (LA).[2] Second, FR applies successively to pairs of LIs selected either from LA or from previously formed ordered pairs, continuing until all the selection features of every LI are satisfied and none are left unsatisfied. We assume also that the derivation is regulated by the following relational version of a principle of lexical access originally suggested by Chomsky (2000: 132):[3]

(6)   *The Head Principle* (HP):
       Suppose an LI λ, called the *head*, containing unsatisfied selection features, is selected from LA as input to FR. Then all the selection requirements of λ must be satisfied before a new head can be selected from LA as input to FR.

Utilizing the terminology of Collins (2002), an LI all of whose selectors have been satisfied is said to be *saturated*; if any of them have not been satisfied, it is said to be *unsaturated*.[4] The Head Principle thus rules out the possibility of an LI α forming a relation with an unsaturated LI β. As shown in Bowers (2000) and Collins and Ura (2001), this in turn imposes an inherent order on the process of forming a network of relations between LIs. Thus consider the phrase *Read the books*. Assume that *read* is a head that selects a word of category D and *the* is a head that selects a word of category N. Then the HP entails that the ordered pair <the,books> must be formed before the ordered pair <read,the>. If the latter were formed first, the HP would be violated, since *the* (selected from LA) would be unsaturated at that point. Note that the second coordinate of <read,the> is the (saturated) LI *the* constituting the first coordinate of <the,books>.

These assumptions will then produce a derivation of the following form:

---

[2] In §2.3 this step of the derivation will be refined to form a set of one or more *lexical subarrays*, to each of which FR applies independently.

[3] Essentially the same idea is embodied in Collins' (2002) "Locus Principle."

[4] The terms "saturated" and "unsaturated," as used here, are purely syntactic. Hence their use is related only indirectly, if at all, to the semantic (Fregean) sense of these terms as an expression required to "saturate" an incomplete expression, or in more modern terms, to assign a value to a function.

(7)   1 Select *the, books* from LA.
       Head: *the* (unsaturated); *books* (saturated).
       FR(the,books)=<the,books>

       2 Select *read* from LA; select *the* from <the,books> formed at step 1.
       Head: *read* (unsaturated); *the* (saturated).
       FR(read,the)=<read,the>

It is important to be clear that there are no syntactic constituents in a theory of this sort. In the example just discussed, there are no constituents {the, books} or {read,{the, books}} of the kind produced by Merge in NS, with or without labels.[5] Instead, there are simply two dependencies between words represented by the ordered pairs <the,books> and <read,the>. Though there is a superficial similarity between a theory based purely on the formation of ordered pairs and one that incorporates the operation Merge or its equivalent, due to the fact that both involve the construction of sets, the operation Merge goes far beyond what is required in a relational theory. In the example at hand, the output of the second Merge operation would be a new syntactic object of the form {read, {the, books}}. Despite the fact that the outputs of successive applications of Merge are only unordered sets, each operation results in a new syntactic object that incorporates the results of all the preceding operations. Hence it is clearly a theory that incorporates a notion of constituent structure. In a relational theory, on the other hand, no new syntactic objects of this sort are produced. Instead, there are just two sequentially ordered pairs <the,books> and <read,the>.[6] One could, of course, construct a set of constituents on the basis of FR plus the HP, if one wished. The point is that there is no need for a primitive operation such as Merge that forms constituents directly.

1.1.2   Dependency Trees

Before proceeding further, it is useful to introduce an equivalent way of representing derivations of the sort just described. A standard way of representing relations in graph form is by means of a directed arrow connecting two points: •→•. Since the basic elements of natural language are LIs, we may

---

[5] Collins (2002) argues that there are no *labels* associated with a constituent, apart from the features in the LIs that are themselves the input to Merge. In the present framework, this follows of course from the more fundamental fact that there are simply no constituents in syntax with which labels *could* be associated.

[6] As discussed above, the two relations <read,the> and <the,books> are reducible, by definition, to the sets {{read},{read,the}} and {{the},{the,books}}. However, neither of these sets incorporates the results of previous applications of FR.

simply replace the dots with the names of LIs. We may then represent the relation <the,books> between *the* and *books*, say, in the following way:

(8)   the → books

Obviously, the head is on the left side of the arrow and the dependent on the right. If we add to this the ordered pair <read,the> resulting from the application of FR to the LIs *read* and the (saturated) instance of *the* contained in the previously formed ordered pair <the,books>, the following graph results:

(9)   read → the → books

An alternative way of representing such a network of relations is to draw directed arcs connecting the linear succession of words:

(10)
         read   the   books

But the standard way of representing the output of a Dependency Grammar (DG) is by means of a tree in which heads are higher than dependents along the vertical dimension and the horizontal dimension represents linear order:

(11)   read
              \
               the
                   \
                    books

However, since we are adopting the minimalist assumption that the representations of NS do not incorporate linear order, it is sufficient to utilize the vertical dimension alone:[7]

(12)   read
          |
         the
          |
         books

If an LI (such as the predicate *read* in example (12)) has more than one dependent, then the two dependency relations are represented as follows, where left-to-right order is understood to be of no significance in NS:

---

[7] Perhaps not surprisingly, a diagram such as (12) is identical to what Tesnière (1959) termed a *stemma*, since he, in contrast to later proponents of DG, did not incorporate linear ordering into representations of dependency relations.

(13)

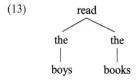

1.1.3   Linearization

Suppose a network of relations has been formed in the manner just described. In order to construct a representation at PHON legible to SM, the absolute minimum that must be done is to arrange the phonological forms of the LIs of the network in linear order. Hence there must be a Spell-out procedure that systematically maps a sequence of ordered pairs of LIs onto a linearly ordered string of phonetic representations of those LIs. Before discussing the operation of Spell-out, however, it will be convenient to introduce some notational conventions. Whenever it is clear from context, I shall use standard ortho-graphic forms such as 'the,' 'books,' 'read,' etc. in a systematically ambiguous fashion to refer either to the phonetic form of an LI or to the entire LI, consisting of a semantic representation, a set of syntactic features, and a phonetic representation. Where it is necessary in the text to distinguish expli-citly the name of an LI from its phonetic form, I will do so by italicizing the orthographic form in the former case and underlining it in the latter case. Thus *the* is the name of the LI: [the′, D, the], while the represents the phonetic form of *the*. In addition, I use the hyphen '-', when necessary, to make explicit the linear ordering relation between two phonetic forms.

Suppose $<\alpha,\beta>$ is an ordered pair produced by FR. Let us start by assuming that Spell-out operates in the simplest possible fashion, mapping the ordered pair $<\alpha,\beta>$ onto the linearly ordered string of phonetic forms $\underline{\alpha}\text{-}\underline{\beta}$:

(14)   *Spell-out*: $<\alpha,\beta> \Rightarrow \underline{\alpha}\text{-}\underline{\beta}$

Spell-out is thus a very simple and general algorithm that strips away the phonetic form of the first coordinate of an ordered pair (i.e. its head) and places it in a relation of immediate precedence with the phonetic form of the second coordinate (i.e. its dependent) at PHON. I assume in addition that the lineariza-tion algorithm operates simultaneously with each application of FR, an assumption I term *Immediate Spell-Out*.[8] Suppose a lexical item λ is picked

---

[8] Immediate Spell-Out is equivalent to what Collins and Ura (2001) term "incremental Spell-Out at the relation level." As Collins and Ura note, there are other possible theories of incremental Spell-out, e.g. Spell-out at the locus level, Spell-out at the phase level, etc. They argue, as I do, for

from the lexical array LA to serve as the head. FR then starts forming ordered pairs between λ and other lexical items in the array. Each time an ordered pair is formed, the linearization algorithm creates a corresponding phonetic form by arranging the phonetic forms of the two lexical items in the order specified by (14).

Stated in this fashion, the linearization algorithm will work fine for the first step of derivation (7), correctly spelling out the relation <the,books> as the-books:[9]

(15)   1 <the,books>   ⇒   the-books

If, however, we apply (14) to the second step of derivation (7), all we will get is a second PF string read-the, unrelated to the string produced at step 1 of the derivation:

(16)   2 <read,the>   ⇒   read-the

The output required for step 2 of the derivation is of course read-the-books. To obtain the correct result, the linearization process must not only be immediate, but also *incremental*. At each step of the derivation an ordered pair is produced, which is immediately mapped onto a linearly ordered string of phonetic forms of LIs. If, however, one of the LIs of this ordered pair is subsequently chosen as input to a later application of FR, then the entire string onto which Spell-out mapped that ordered pair must be taken as the phonetic form of that LI at the next step in the derivation. In example (16), because the saturated LI *the* is selected from the ordered pair <the,books> as partial input to the next application of FR, the entire string the-books produced by Spell-out at that stage of the derivation must be taken as the Spell-out of *the* in the next application of (12). If Spell-out works in the incremental fashion just described, then the output of step 2 of the derivation will be the correct string read-the-books, rather than merely read-the.

In order to reformulate the Spell-out algorithm, let us start by defining the *phonetic form* PF of a term α of a relation as follows:

(17)   *Definition*: The *phonetic form* PF(α) of a term α of a relation (irrespective of whether it is the head or the dependent term) is:
   (i) α, if α is an LI selected from LA;
   (ii) σ_α, where σ_α is the string produced by applying Spell-out to an earlier relation of the form <α,γ>.

the first of these, while Chomsky (2000, 2001) argues for the last. In the absence of strong arguments to the contrary, Immediate Spell-Out would seem to be the null hypothesis.

[9] Henceforth I simplify the statement of derivations by omitting everything except the outputs of FR (on the left) and Spell-out (on the right), as well as by refraining from underlining the phonetic forms of LIs in the latter.

Given this definition, we can now formulate the Spell-out algorithm straight-forwardly as follows:

(18)   *Spell-out*:   For any relation $<\alpha,\beta>$, PF(α) precedes PF(β) in PHON:
                          $<\alpha,\beta> \Rightarrow$ PF(α)-PF(β).

Derivation (7), combined with immediate application of Spell-out, will then proceed as follows:

(19)   1 Select *the* from LA; select *books* from LA:
            PF(the)=the; PF(books)=books
            FR(the,books)=<the,books> $\Rightarrow$ the-books

         2 Select *read* from LA; select *the* from <the,books>:
            PF(read)=read; PF(the)=the-books
            FR(read,the)= <read,the> $\Rightarrow$ read-the-books

At step 1, we start by choosing as head the lexical item *the*, which selects the noun *books*. This is the simplest possible case, where both coordinates of the relation are LIs selected from the lexical array. Therefore, by (17i) PF (the)=the and PF(books)=books, and by (18) Spell-out produces the string the-books in PF. To continue the derivation, a new head, the lexical item *read*, is selected from LA, together with the (now saturated) LI *the* from the previously formed relation <the,books>. By (17i) PF(read)=read and by (17ii) PF(the)=the-books, the output of Spell-out at step 1. Finally, Spell-out orders the former before the latter at PF, yielding the correct phonetic form read-the-books.

But now notice that the substrings the-books and read-the-books, produced at successive stages of the derivation, *are identical to the strings that would result from linearizing the constituents {the,books} and {read,{the,books}} in a grammar with the basic operation Merge*, despite the fact that no operation has at any point constructed such objects, either in NS or in PHON. The apparent existence of the constituents [the boys] and [read the books] in NS is thus simply an illusion caused by the incremental nature of the linearization proce-dure. The Merge operation is therefore unnecessary and can be eliminated from NS, because the simpler operation FR, combined with the legibility conditions imposed on PHON and the Spell-out algorithm, is sufficient to account both for the syntactic relationships between words and for the linear order in which their phonetic forms occur at PHON.

Consider next a more complicated case in which a single head has more than one selection feature—in X-bar terms, a head that requires both a complement and a specifier. I will first illustrate such a situation with the contrary to fact assumption that the subject of *read* is selected by a second selection condition. (A more refined analysis will be discussed very shortly in §1.1.4.) Applying the principles developed so far, the derivation in (19) would continue as follows:

(20)   3 FR(the,boys)=<the,boys> ⇒ the-boys
         4 FR(read,the)=<read,the> ⇒ *read-the-books-the-boys

Since the first coordinate *read* of the ordered pair in step 4 was taken from the ordered pair <read,the> produced at step 2 of the derivation, PF(read)=read-the-books, while PF(the)=the-boys, the output of (14) at step 3 of the derivation. Spell-out must then arrange these two strings in the linear order PF(read)-PF(the). Unfortunately, however, this produces the incorrect string shown in step 4 of (20). The problem is that the phonetic form the-boys of the second argument of *read* should be ordered to the left of read-the-books rather than to the right, as Spell-out incorrectly predicts. More generally, any head H which requires both a complement C and a specifier S will be linearized incorrectly as H-C-S, rather than S-H-C. This is not a new problem. In fact, it is at the heart of Kayne's (1994) Linear Correspondence Axiom (LCA), which was intended to derive the universal order S-H-C by applying general principles of linearization to constituent structure. I will not try to solve this problem now but defer until §1.3.3 a full discussion of the LCA. For the moment, I shall simply assume that Spell-out can somehow be formulated in such a way that the phonetic form of the dependent precedes the phonetic form of the head, whenever the second of two selection relations required by a given head is formed.

1.1.4   Eliminating Movement
I show next that in a relational theory of syntax there is no need for any type of movement operation, because the displacement phenomena that have been described by means of movement, understood as a special case of Merge, can be derived more simply from a combination of the selection properties of LIs, the operation FR (together with Spell-out), and the legibility constraints on representations at PHON imposed by SM. There are, however, two rather different kinds of displacement phenomena to be discussed. The first, generally referred to in the literature as "head movement," is usually formalized as a process of adjunction combining one X° category with another such category Y° to produce a new constituent of category Y°. The result is an

adjunction structure of the form $[_Y\circ\ X\circ\ Y\circ]$, though it has been claimed more recently in the minimalist framework that head movement can be described as a purely PF phenomenon. I shall argue here that the effects attributed to head movement arise simply as a consequence of the fact that LIs can be "defective," in the sense that they have no phonetic form of their own that can be automatically transferred to PHON by Spell-out. In such cases, FR automatically provides the defective LI with a phonetic form that will satisfy the requirements of Spell-out. The second type of movement is usually described in the generative literature as XP movement, or internal Merge in minimalist grammars. The displacement effects attributed to this type of movement, I shall argue, come about as a result of requirements at both SEM and PHON, together with the fact that the argument selection properties of certain LIs are inherently athematic, in the sense that they do not introduce a new argument relation at SEM.

1.1.4.1   Head Movement   It was noted in §1.1.3 that the analysis assumed there of transitive sentences such as *The boys read the books*, which treats both the subject and the object as arguments directly selected by the verb, is over-simplified. Following Larson (1988), Bowers (1993), and Chomsky (1995a, 1995b), it is now widely assumed in mainstream generative syntax that the subject of a transitive sentence is not actually selected directly by the lexical verb but rather by a "light verb" *v* whose complement is VP and whose Spec contains the subject DP. Following Bowers (1993, 2001a, 2002), I assume that *v* is actually just one of a number of LIs belonging to a broader category Pr whose phonetic form is usually null in English. Restating this analysis in relational terms, let us assume that the LI *v* first selects an LI of category V and then one of category D. Under these assumptions, derivation (19) would continue as shown in step 3, assuming that the LI *v* is contained in the lexical array:

(21)   1 <the,books>   the-books
       2 <read,the>   read-the-books
       3 <v,read>   ?-read-the-books

Let us also assume as a general condition that Spell-out is required to map every LI in a derivation onto a representation in PHON legible to SM, meaning that every LI must have a phonetic representation that is "readable" by SM. One way of thinking about such a condition is that it is simply a manifestation at the level of PHON of Full Interpretation. If at any point in a derivation Spell-out is unable to meet this condition, then the derivation crashes. Given this legibility condition, there is a problem at step 3 in derivation (21), as indicated by the question mark in the string on the right. The reason is that the LI *v* in English does not possess a phonetic form of its own that is legible to SM. Since Spell-out is unable to meet the general condition that every LI be readable at PHON, the derivation should crash.

Suppose that in a situation of this sort in which the head α of an ordered pair <α,β> does not have a legible phonetic form, FR automatically provides α with an occurrence (or token) of the phonetic form of the second coordinate β, if it has one. Assuming that β is itself legible, this makes it possible for Spell-out to map α onto a symbol at PHON that is legible to SM, namely β, thereby averting a crash of the derivation. In order to formulate more precisely this special case of FR, let us represent the internal structure of an arbitrary lexical item α in the more complete form [α:α]. An LI α that happens to lack a legible phonetic form will be represented as follows: [α:].[10] The operation of FR in the special case where the head of a relation lacks a legible phonetic form may then be stated as follows:[11]

(22)   FR([α:],[β:β]) = <[α:β],[β:β]> ⇒ β-β̶

Spell-out is then free to apply in a straightforward fashion to the output of FR, as indicated in (22).[12] I assume also as a general principle of phonetic inter-pretation that only the leftmost occurrence of two identical phonetic forms produced by Spell-out is actually pronounced. In the interests of perspicuity, I incorporate the operation of this principle into the output of Spell-out by automatically marking the right-hand occurrence of two identical phonetic

---

[10] An LI α that lacks a legible phonetic form altogether is distinct from an LI α that has the null phonetic form ∅. I represent the latter as [α:∅], where ∅ is a phonetic form legible to SM that can be thought of as an instruction to the SM systems to do nothing, whereas the former, represented, as suggested in the text, as [α:], is an LI that has no phonetic form at all legible to SM.

[11] This is the simplest case, in which the head of an ordered pair that is the input to Spell-out does not have a legible phonetic form of its own and must therefore assume the phonetic form of the dependent. If the head contains a bound morpheme, I will assume that it is ill-formed at PHON by virtue of being morphologically incomplete. In that case, the phonological form of the dependent must combine with the bound morpheme contained in the head to form a morpho-logically complete form at PHON. For example, the phonological form of T in French when it contains the features second person, plural, and present tense is *-ez* [e]. This is a bound morpheme, hence morphologically incomplete. Therefore if T selects *v* (which must itself have been assigned the phonetic form of a stem such as *aim-* [ɛm] in a previous step of the derivation), the phonetic form of *aim-* will combine with the phonetic form of *-ez* to produce the correct morphological form *aimez* [ɛme]. See Chapter 5 for further details.

[12] As formulated in the text, (22) is clearly too general, since it would apply to any kind of selection, including argument selection. A more constrained version will emerge from the revised theory to be proposed later in this chapter.

forms with a strike-through in representations at PHON. The strike-through may be interpreted as an instruction to the SM systems that the phonetic form thus marked is not to be pronounced.[13]

Given these principles, we can now formulate step 3 of the derivation in (21) as shown in step 3′ of (23), followed by formation of the relations <the,boys> and <v,the>, in order to satisfy the selection conditions of v:[14]

(23) 3′ <[v:read],[V:read>[15] ⇒ read-~~read~~-the-books
 4 <[D:the],[N:boys]> ⇒ the-boys
 5 <[v:read],[D:the]> ⇒ the-boys-read-~~read~~-the-books

At step 3′ the selection condition [_V] of v is satisfied by forming the ordered pair <v,read>, but by (22), the unreadable symbol v must also be provided with the phonetic form <u>read</u> of its dependent, enabling the output of Spell-out at step 2, namely, the string <u>read</u>-the-<u>books</u>, to be placed immediately to the right of <u>read</u>, yielding the string shown on the right in step 3′.

To appreciate fully why (22) is empirically necessary, consider how it works in the derivation of a ditransitive sentence such as *The boys read the books to her*. The derivation is as follows:

(24) 1 <to,her> to-her
 2 <read,to> read-to-her
 3 <the,books> the-books
 4 <read,the> the-books-read-to-her
 5 <v,read> read-the-books-~~read~~-to-her
 6 <the,boys> the-boys
 7 <v,the> the-boys-read-the-books-~~read~~-to her

As is evident, the operation of (22) is crucial here in ensuring that the verb *read* is actually pronounced immediately after the subject and immediately before the object rather than between the object and the PP complement.

---

[13] Alternatively, it could be stipulated that each time a new token of an LI (or substring of LIs) is created, the previous token is replaced with the null string *e* in PHON. See Bowers (2008) for discussion.

[14] It might be wondered what prevents operations 3′ and 5 in (20) from applying in the opposite order. More generally, given an LI α with selectors [_β] and [_γ], what determines the order in which these selectors must be satisfied? I take up this question in §1.3.2, showing that an adequate solution to the problem requires significant revision in our thinking about the way in which FR applies.

[15] Unless it is necessary for the sake of clarity to spell out precisely how (22) applies, I will generally exhibit the output of FR in such a case in the simplified form <v,read>.

I conclude that the apparent "movement" or "displacement" of the verb *read* to the left of the object DP *the books* is really just a consequence of the fact that FR operates in such a way as to guarantee that every LI in a derivation is mapped by Spell-out onto a representation at PHON that satisfies the legibility conditions imposed by SM. Consequently, there is no need to assume an operation of head movement in the syntax (however it might be formulated), since the correct result falls out as a consequence of the interaction of FR and Spell-out, together with the legibility requirements of SM.

1.1.4.2   Constituent Movement   In order to complete the derivation of the sentence discussed in §1.1.4.1, it is necessary to supply it with a marking of tense or modality. Avoiding for the moment the complications involved in producing the phonetic forms of simple present and past tense verbs in English,[16] I discuss the derivation of the sentence *The boy will read the books*, containing the modal auxiliary *will*. There is a mass of empirical evidence in the literature that tense morphology and modality are associated with a head T that selects the category *v*. Adapting the standard analysis to the relational framework, let us assume there is a category T that selects *v*. Then the derivation in (23) may continue as follows:

(25)   6 <will,v>   will-the-boys-read-~~read~~-the-books

The next question is how to explain the fact that subjects in English are pronounced before the auxiliary *will* rather than after it. Reinterpreting the usual "EPP" property in relational terms, let us assume that T simply has a second selection feature of the standard sort requiring that it form a relation with an LI of category D. In this case, however, we shall assume that it is an inherent property of the category T that its denotation, unlike that of argument heads such as V and *v*, does not introduce a semantic relation between a new argument and the event variable *e*. In other words, though T selects an LI of category D, D is not assigned a thematic relation at SEM. I shall refer to a selection feature of this kind as *athematic*.[17] Let us assume further the following relational version of the θ-Criterion:

---

[16] See §6.1 for a detailed discussion.

[17] It has been suggested in the minimalist framework (Chomsky 2000, 2001) that such a selection feature could be regarded as *uninterpretable*, in which case it would have to be deleted in order to satisfy Full Interpretation. It will be argued in Chapter 5, however, that just because a selection feature is athematic does not necessarily mean that it plays no role in interpretation.

(26)   *Relational θ-Criterion*:
Every (non-expletive) selected LI of category D must be interpreted as one and only one argument at SEM and every argument required at SEM must be realized as one and only one (non-expletive) selected LI of category D.[18]

Returning now to the derivation of the sentence *The boys will read the books*, consider first what would happen if the lexical array contained another token of the determiner *the* and a noun such as *girls* with which *the* could form a relation. Assuming that this instance of *the* forms a relation with the dependent *girl* after step 6 in (25), there would be nothing in the syntax to prevent the selection condition of T from being satisfied by applying FR to *will* and to the LI *the* which previously formed an ordered pair with *girls*. If, however, the selection feature of *will* were to be satisfied in this way, it would be impossible for *the girls* to be interpreted as an argument, since *will*, by hypothesis, does not assign a semantic relation to the D-element it selects. Therefore a sentence such as #*The girls will the boys read the books* violates condition (26), i.e. it is syntactically well-formed but semantically uninterpretable (see Bowers 2008 for supporting arguments). The only possible way for the selection feature of *will* to be satisfied, while at the same time respecting the θ-Criterion, is for it to form a relation with some LI of category D *that was interpreted as an argument at an earlier step of the derivation*. In this instance, the nearest such D-element available is the LI *the*, which was first introduced at step 4 of the derivation and subsequently selected at step 5 by *v*, thereby satisfying the θ-Criterion. By (14), the phonetic form the-boys must immediately precede the phonetic form will. This, however, seems to pose a problem, because the phonetic form the-boys was previously required to immediately *follow* will at step 6 of the derivation. A given (token of a) phonetic form α cannot both precede and follow another phonetic form β. How can this apparent contradiction be resolved?

To answer this question, we need to think more carefully about how Spell-out works. *A priori*, there are two possible ways that Spell-out might operate. First, it could strip away the phonetic forms of the LIs it applies to, leaving no phonetic forms at all in the syntax. Second, it could create copies of the relevant phonetic

---

I will also argue, contrary to what is assumed in the minimalist framework, that derivations are not driven by the need to value and delete uninterpretable features.

[18] The stipulation that (26) applies only to *selected* LIs of category D leaves open the possibility that DPs can function as predicate nominals. See Bowers (1993, 2001a) for discussion. Note also that the Relational θ-Criterion, as formulated here, rules out the relational analog of the movement theory of control. However, it is straightforward to restate it in such a way as to permit the relational equivalent of movement to a θ-position. See Bowers (1973, 2008) and Hornstein (1999, 2001) for discussion.

forms and transfer them to PHON, leaving the phonetic forms of the LIs intact in syntactic representations. If the first option is chosen, then once Spell-out has applied to a given LI, it will be impossible for it to apply to the same LI at a later stage of the derivation, because there will simply be no phonetic form available to be stripped away. If, however, the second option is chosen, then it will be possible to apply Spell-out more than once to the same LI, because the phonetic form of any given LI will remain available throughout the syntactic derivation.

Assuming, then, that the second mechanism is correct, there is nothing to prevent *will* from forming a new relation with the same LI *the* that was previously selected by *v*. Crucially, there is also nothing to prevent Spell-out from copying the substring the-boys, transferring it to PHON, and ordering it without contradiction immediately to the left of will:[19]

(27)   7   <will,the>   the-boys-will-~~the-boys~~-read-~~read~~-the-books

As shown in (27), an occurrence of the string the-boys, the output of step 4, is placed by Spell-out immediately to the left of the output of step 6. By the general principle of phonetic interpretation mentioned previously, the earlier occurrence of the substring the-boys immediately following will is unpronounced. Hence the apparent movement of the constituent [the boys] can be explained as nothing more than an artifact of the legibility conditions imposed by SM, together with general computational constraints on the application of FR and Spell-out. However, the appearance of constituent movement, in contrast to that of head movement, is forced by a combination of legibility conditions at *both* PHON and SEM.

I conclude that in a relational theory of the sort proposed here, there is no need to posit an independent operation of movement, internal Merge, re-Merge, or anything of the sort. Instead, the effect of movement is brought about automatically by the mechanisms of FR and Spell-out that are needed independently in any case. Nothing new has to be introduced into the theory, apart from the fact that certain LIs have an athematic selection feature, to account for the fact that under the right circumstances the phonetic form of an argument LI ends up being pronounced in a different position from the position where it was first selected.

---

[19] Representations at PHON are therefore *strings*, in the mathematical sense, rather than totally ordered sets (Wall 1972: 164–166). A string is a linear ordering of the *occurrences* or *tokens* of the members of a set, whereas in a totally ordered set each member occurs only once and occupies a unique place in the ordering. Note, however, that if all but one of the occurrences of a given substring are eventually deleted, reflecting the general principle that only the leftmost occurrence of a sequence of occurrences of strings is actually pronounced, the resulting string would in fact constitute a totally ordered set.

Utilizing the graphic display of dependency relations introduced in §1.3, steps 6 and 7 can be represented as follows:

(28)

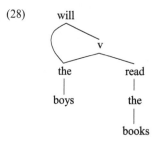

Here the LI *v* first forms a dependency relation with the LI *the* which previously formed a relation with *boys*. Subsequently, the LI *will* also forms a relation with this same LI *the*. Note, however, that because *the* is a dependent of both *v* and *will*, trees such as (28) violate a constraint, often assumed in formalized versions of Dependency Grammar, preventing a single node from being a dependent of more than one other node. This raises the question whether relaxing the ban on multi-attachment might lead to a catastrophic increase in the generative capacity of such systems. I believe that the answer to this question is negative as long as multi-attachment is suitably constrained.

Let us assume, as a first approximation, that a head such as *will* may only form a relation with the *closest* available instance of a required dependent such as *the*. This is simply the relational version of a locality condition of a familiar sort. Such a condition will permit *will* to form a relational link with the instance of *the* selected by *v*, but not with the instance of *the* selected by *read*. Formulated in derivational terms, *will* may only form a relation with the instance of *the* most recently introduced into the derivation, that is, it may form a relation with *the* introduced at step 4 of the derivation but not with *the* introduced at step 1. For the moment I will incorporate a locality condition of this sort into the system by reformulating part (ii) of the definition of PF in (17) to read: "The *phonetic form* PF(α) of a term α of a relation ... is: ... (ii) $\underline{\sigma}_\alpha$, where $\underline{\sigma}_\alpha$ is the string produced by applying Spell-out to *the most recently introduced* relation α of the form $\langle\alpha,\gamma\rangle$." In Chapter 2 I will examine this locality condition in greater depth and reformulate it in the light of revisions to the theory to be introduced shortly.

In terms of a graph representation such as (28), closeness can be measured by counting the number of links between *will* and the instance of *the* it selects. Let us imagine that the LI *will* searches for a previously introduced instance of *the* by traversing a path back through the links in the relational graph (28) until it finds an LI of the right kind. There are two links in (28) between *will* and the instance of *the* selected by *v*, whereas there are three links between *will* and the instance of *the* selected by *read*. The former instance of *the* is closest to *will*, hence must be selected by it.

I conclude that there is no need for a syntactic operation of constituent movement, or internal Merge, in a relation-based theory of the sort proposed here. The only operation needed in the syntax is FR. The appearance of XP movement of the internal subject to [Spec,T], as it is standardly formulated, is simply an artifact of the legibility conditions at PHON and SEM. Notice that no special conditions need be placed on the operation of FR: given an ordered pair $<\alpha,\beta>$, β can either be an LI drawn from the lexical array or an instance of β that was introduced by a previous application of FR to satisfy a selection feature of some other LI. In the first case, the resulting string will conform to the relational θ-Criterion just in case the selection feature satisfied is thematic (i.e. one whose head adds a semantic relation at SEM). In the second case, in contrast, the resulting string will only conform to the Relational θ-Criterion (and therefore have a well-formed representation at SEM) if the selection feature of α satisfied by the application of FR is athematic (i.e. one whose head does not add a semantic relation at SEM).[20] In short, FR can apply completely freely in the syntax, but not every ordered pair produced by FR will necessarily receive an interpretation at SEM.

1.1.4.3   Expletives   Before going on to formulate more precisely a relational version of minimality, it is useful to look at another instance of multi-attachment, familiar from the literature, and to discuss, at the same time, an alternative way of satisfying an athematic selection feature. Consider an intransitive sentence such as *An explosion occurred*. There is a mass of linguistic evidence in the literature supporting the claim that subjects of unaccusative verbs such as *occur* are selected by the verb and bear an argument relation to it. Hence the derivation of such a sentence must start out as follows:

(29)   1   <an,explosion>   an-explosion
        2   <occur,an>   occur-an-explosion

---

[20] Note that the relational equivalent of movement from a non-θ-position to a θ-position is also ruled out, because any LI α with which a head H has formed an athematic relation will either have picked up a θ-role earlier in the derivation or be an expletive. A violation of the Relational θ-Criterion will result in either case as soon as a new head H′ with a thematic selection feature tries to form a relation with α.

Let us assume, as before, that *v* has a selection feature requiring it to form a relation with an LI of category D. In this case, however, it will also be assumed as a lexical property of intransitive *v/occur* that its selection feature is athematic. Now suppose that the lexical array contained another determiner *an* and a noun such as *accident*, with which *an* could form a selection relation. There is nothing in the syntax that would prevent the selection condition of *v* from being satisfied by applying FR to *v* and the LI *an* which previously formed an ordered pair with *accident*. If, however, the selection feature of *v* were to be satisfied in this way, it would be impossible for *an accident* to be interpreted as an argument, since the selection feature of *v/occur* is, by hypothesis, athematic in this instance. Hence a sentence such as #*An accident occurred an explosion* is syntactically well-formed but uninterpretable. As in the case of T, the only possible way for the selection feature of *v* to be satisfied, while at the same time respecting the θ-Criterion, is for it to form a relation with some LI of category D that has already been interpreted as an argument at a previous step of the derivation. In this instance, the only such D available is the LI *an*, which selected *explosion* at step 1 of the derivation in (26) and which was subsequently selected at step 2 by *occur*. Therefore *v* must form a second relation with this instance of *a(n)* and Spell-out automatically orders its phonetic form an-explosion immediately before the token of occur that was substituted for *v*. The derivation will thus continue as follows:

(30)   3   <v,occur>   occur-~~occur~~-an-explosion
        4   <v,an>   an-explosion-occur-~~occur-an-explosion~~

At step 4 of the derivation, an occurrence of the string an-explosion, the output of step 1, must immediately precede the output of step 3. By the general principle of phonetic interpretation mentioned earlier, the original occurrence of an-explosion that immediately follows occur is unpronounced. Hence the apparent movement of a constituent [an explosion], can be explained once again as an artifact of legibility conditions imposed by SM, together with general computational constraints on the application of FR and Spell-out.

As it happens, there is direct empirical evidence in support of the claim that the subjects of unaccusative verbs such as *occur* are initially selected by the verb itself rather than by *v*. English has a special LI belonging to the category D, the expletive *there*, which has no semantic content and is therefore inherently incapable of being assigned a semantic role. Hence an alternative way for *v* to satisfy its athematic selection feature—assuming that *there* is present in the lexical array—is to form the ordered pair <v,there>, thus obviating the need for a second occurrence of the phonetic form of *an explosion* to precede that of *occur* in order to satisfy the legibility conditions of PHON and SEM.[21] The result is the sentence *There will occur an explosion*, in which the phonetic form of *an explosion* immediately follows that of the verb in PHON, while the phonetic form of *there* precedes it:

(31)   4'   <v,there>   there-occur-~~occur~~-an-explosion

In order to complete the derivation of this sentence, the LI *v* must be selected by an LI of category T such as *will*, whose athematic selection feature must also be satisfied. In this case, the nearest LI of category D is the expletive *there*. Since *there* has no semantic content and cannot be assigned a thematic role, it may be selected by *will*, permitting the derivation to be completed as follows:

(32)   5'   <will,v>   will-there-occur-~~occur~~-an-explosion
        6'   <will,there>   there-will-~~there~~-occur-~~occur~~-an-explosion

If, on the other hand, we had exercised the option of forming a relation between *v* and D, as in (27), then the following derivation would result:

(33)   5   <will,v>   will-an-explosion-occur-~~occur-an-explosion~~
        6   <will,an>   an-explosion-will-~~an-explosion~~-occur-~~occur-an-explosion~~

Represented graphically, these two derivations look as follows:

(34)   will

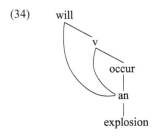

---
[21] Crucially, I assume, following Bowers (2002: 195–199), that expletive *there* may only be selected by *v* in English, not by T, thereby preventing sentences such as **There will an explosion occur* and **there will there occur an explosion*. Technically, this involves assigning *v* an optional athematic selection feature of the form [_there].

(35)

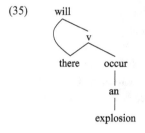

Example (34) is an instance of multi-attachment in which the article *a(n)* has been selected *three* times, once by *occur*, again by *v*, and a third time by *will*. In (35), in contrast, the expletive *there* is selected by *v*, leaving *an explosion* to be pronounced to the right of the main verb, but *there* is selected a second time by *will* in order to satisfy its selection requirements.

1.1.5   Minimality

Having analyzed a few very basic sentence types in relational terms, I now turn to the task of formulating a relational version of the *Minimal Link Condition* (MLC). I first recast the MLC as a very general constraint on derivations, concluding ultimately that such a constraint is still far too powerful. I then formulate an accessibility constraint on computations, which is basically a generalization of Chomsky's (2000) *Phase Impenetrability Condition* (PIC), and show that it is able to account for the data discussed so far.

1.1.5.1   The Derivational Minimal Link Condition (DMLC)   In theories that incorporate a level of constituent structure in NS, the MLC is standardly formulated in terms of a notion of distance based on the structural relation of c-command. In a relational theory of the sort that we are exploring here, however, there is no such structural relation available. There is only one possibility: the MLC must reflect some property of derivations. Let us therefore examine the derivation of *There will occur an explosion*, discussed in §1.1.4.3, which starts out as follows:

(36) 1 \<an,explosion\>   an-explosion
      2 \<occur,an\>   occur-an-explosion
      3 \<v,occur\>   occur-~~occur~~-an-explosion
      4 \<v,there\>   there-occur-~~occur~~-an-explosion
      5 \<will,v\>   will-there-occur-~~occur~~-an-explosion

At this point in the derivation, if there were no constraints placed on multi-attachment, we would have a choice of two continuations, only the first of which produces a grammatical sentence:

6   <will,there>   there-will-~~there~~-occur-~~occur~~-an-explosion

*6'   <will,an>   an-explosion-will-there-occur-~~occur-an-explosion~~

The only discernible difference between these two continuations is that in step 6 *will* has selected the LI of category D most recently introduced into the derivation, namely, *there* (at step 4), whereas in step 6' *will* has selected an LI of category D that was introduced into the derivation at a stage *before* the introduction of *there*, namely, at step 1.

It appears then that the MLC must be a purely derivational constraint on syntactic computations of the following form:

(37)   *Derivational Minimal Link Condition* (DMLC):
       Suppose that a head λ is introduced at the ith step of a derivation D with n steps $<1, 2, \ldots, i, \ldots n>$, where 1 is the first step and n is the final step of D, and that λ is searching for an LI α with which to form a relation $<\lambda, \alpha>$. Then if there are two potential candidates α' and α'', where α' was introduced at the $i-j^{th}$ stage of D and α'' at the $i-k^{th}$ stage, j<k, then the relation $<\lambda, \alpha'>$ must be formed.

The DMLC, thus formulated, requires that *will* form a selection relation with *there*, which was introduced into the derivation at the fourth step of the derivation rather than with *an*, which was introduced at the first step of the derivation. Formulated in terms of a graphic representation such as (35), the DMLC requires that *will* form a relation with the D-element that is "nearest" in terms of the number of relational links between *will* and the D-element in question. In the case of *there*, it is clearly 2, while in the case of *an*, it is 3. Hence *will* must form a relation with *there*, in this instance.[22]

The DMLC also works correctly in the case of a transitive sentence such as (28). At the stage of the derivation where *will* is searching for an LI with which to form a selection relation, the instance of the LI *the* that selects *boys* is nearer in derivational terms than the instance of *the* that selects *books*, since the former was introduced into the derivation more recently than the latter. In the graphic representation (28), there are two links between *will* and the first instance of *the*, whereas there are three links between *will* and the second instance of *the*.

---

[22] It might be wondered, given the incremental nature of Spell-out, why, when *will* forms a relation with *there*, the whole string there-occur-~~occur~~-an-explosion (the output of Spell-out at step 4 of the derivation) is not required to be placed to the left of *will*. The answer to this question will become clear in Chapter 2, where I further refine the manner in which nominal arguments are introduced into derivations.

1.1.5.2   Reducing Accessibility   Even if the DMLC is correct, however, it must be further strengthened to sharply limit the search space of FR. Otherwise, the entire derivation would have to be searched each time FR is applied—a computational nightmare. Chomsky (2000, 2001) argues that derivation must proceed by *phase*, a phase being a syntactic unit, some subpart of which becomes inaccessible to the computational mechanism once it has been constructed. Chomsky suggests that CP and *v*P (and perhaps DP) are the most natural syntactic units to be phases since they are (in a loose sense) propositional.[23] I shall consider this possibility in some detail in Chapter 2, but for the moment I will simply define the notion "phase" in terms of the Head Principle. Let us suppose that certain LIs have the property that once they are saturated, some part of the derivation is automatically "sealed off," so that any LIs introduced up to that point are rendered inaccessible to any further operations in the derivation. We must now survey the derivations outlined in the preceding sections to see whether any obvious candidates for phase-hood emerge. One thing that is immediately clear is that if λ_1 is a head and α is the second LI selected by λ_1, then both λ_1 and α must be available to the next head λ_2 that selects λ_1. Thus both the selected LIs *there* and *v* in *There will occur an explosion* (see derivation (36)) must be accessible to T, making it possible for *will* to select first *v* and then *there*. Similarly, both *an* and *occur* in the sentence *An explosion will occur* (see (30)) must be accessible to *v*. This immediately suggests the possibility of adapting Chomsky (2000, 2001) to the present framework in such a way that only the material satisfied by the first selector of a phase head is inaccessible, leaving the head itself and any material that satisfies a second selector still accessible to further operations. Supposing, then, that any head with two selectors is in fact a phase in the sense just indicated, the PIC can be formulated in relational terms in the following manner:[24]

(38)   *Relational Phase Impenetrability Condition* (RPIC):
Let λ be a head, α an LI satisfying the second selector of λ, and β an LI satisfying the first selector of λ. Then as soon as λ is saturated, β and all of the LIs that it selects are inaccessible to any further applications of FR, leaving α and λ accessible to further operations.

As each new head meeting the conditions in (35) is saturated, the RPIC automatically removes from the search space all but the Head itself and the LI

---

[23] See also Dobashi (2003) for arguments that Chomsky's notion of phase plays a crucial role in determining phonological phrases.

[24] See also Bowers (2010) for discussion. A similar constraint, developed in somewhat different terms, has been proposed independently by Collins and Ura (2001: 7).

satisfying its second selector, thus reducing to a bare minimum the set of LIs that must be searched through by the next head. To illustrate, consider derivation (35) again. As soon as v is saturated by forming the relation <v,there>, all other material selected by *occur* is "sealed off," hence unavailable to form further relations. In particular, the D *a(n)* is prevented from forming a selection relation with *will*, leaving *there* as the only possible LI of category D which *will* can select.[25] The RPIC can now replace the DMLC, since it not only limits the number of LIs that a head can select but restricts the search space as well.

Summarizing, suppose a head λ_{n-1} selects a head λ_n, which previously selected an LI α. If λ_{n-1} has a second selection feature that could be satisfied by α, then the RPIC permits it to form a relation with α. Suppose λ_{n-1} is in turn selected by λ_{n-2} and that λ_{n-2} also has a second selection feature that could be satisfied by α. If α were only selected by λ_n, then it would be inaccessible to λ_{n-2}. However, since it has also established a relation with λ_{n-1}, the RPIC will permit λ_{n-2} to select α as well. The RPIC thus permits a head to select a distant LI with the required properties, but only if the two LIs are connected to one another by a continuous "path" of intermediate selection relations, in the manner shown schematically as follows:

(39)

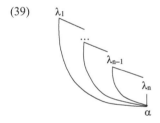

1.2 Problems

In the preceding sections I proposed a first approximation to a theory of syntax based on the formation of relations between words and I argued that it permits a significant simplification of narrow syntax. In particular, there is no need for a primitive notion of constituent of even the most minimal kind, since an incremental Spell-out procedure, mapping relations onto linearly ordered strings of phonetic representations of LIs at PHON, produces exactly the same set of substrings at PHON that would be produced by a constituent structure

---

[25] It will be shown in Chapter 2 (cf. §2.4.2) that the RPIC, as stated here, is too restrictive, requiring a relational version of phase theory. The RPIC would also prevent the relational equivalent of *wh*-movement from applying to any sentence containing a D-selection feature in T, a problem that will be addressed in §6.2.1.

grammar. Likewise, there is no need for syntactic movement operations of any sort, including both head movement and constituent movement. The appearance of head movement arises when a head happens to have no phonetic representation legible to the SM systems. In such a situation, FR automatically provides an occurrence of the phonetic representation of the LI selected by the head in order to satisfy the legibility requirements of PHON. The appearance of constituent movement, in contrast, comes about as a result of legibility conditions at both PHON and SEM whenever a head H_1 has an athematic selector. In order to meet the legibility requirements of PHON, while at the same time respecting the relational equivalent of the θ-Criterion, FR must select a head H_2 from a relation formed earlier in the derivation that has already been interpreted at SEM. Spell-out then automatically linearizes an occurrence of the phonetic form of H_2 to the left of the phonetic form of H_1.

Despite its initial plausibility, however, the tentative system proposed thus far suffers from a number of serious defects, some of which have been alluded to already. I discuss each of these difficulties in turn, concluding ultimately that the root of all of these problems can be traced to an uncritical acceptance of certain assumptions built into constituent-based theories of syntax. I then propose a revised version of the relational theory which, I claim, solves all of these problems.

1.2.1   S-H-C Order

The first major problem is that Spell-out, as provisionally formulated in §1.1.3, incorrectly orders the PF of the second of two arguments required by a given head to the *right* of the head rather than to its *left*. This is of course precisely the fact that Kayne's (1994) Linear Correspondence Axiom (LCA) was intended to explain. Kayne's original formulation of the LCA was stated in terms of the structural relation of *asymmetric c-command*, the basic idea being that if a nonterminal symbol A asymmetrically c-commands a non-terminal B, then the terminal string σ_A dominated by A must precede the terminal string σ_B dominated by B. This result, however, was only achieved at the expense of assuming that specifiers were adjuncts rather than arguments, and it required c-command to be defined in quite a complicated way in terms of the segment theory of adjuncts (May 1985). The upshot is that the LCA only works if it is assumed that a head H bears a *different syntactic relation* to its specifier S than it does to its complement C. This seems suspicious, since the selection properties of the head that drive Merge of specifiers and complements, respectively, do not appear to be fundamentally different in kind.

How does the LCA fare in the minimalist framework? The immediate problem is that if C and S are both branching constituents, then H asymmetrically c-commands C, but S does not even c-command H. Hence there is no way to determine a linear ordering relation between S and H, unless one is willing to add an *ad hoc* condition to the LCA. One might stipulate, for example, that α precedes β if and only if either α asymmetrically c-commands β or an XP dominating α asymmetrically c-commands β (cf. Hornstein et al. 2005). Notice that in the relational framework such a condition cannot even be formulated, since there is no constituent structure to refer to.

The most recent attempt to explain the universality of S-H-C order is that of Kayne (2010), who argues for reintroducing linear ordering into syntactic derivations. Specifically, Kayne proposes that the output of Merge(α,β) is not a set {α,β}, but an ordered pair <α,β>, interpreted as immediate (temporal) precedence. He also argues that Merge of H and C, for independent reasons that I discuss shortly, must produce the ordered pair <H,C> rather than <C,H>. Now suppose that H has a second selection feature requiring that it merge with a specifier S. The only way for Merge to ensure that H and S are in a relation of immediate precedence, Kayne argues, is to apply Merge to H and S in the order Merge(S,H), producing the ordered pair <S,H>. The order resulting from the application of first and second Merge is thus S-H-C.

Why must Merge of H and C result in the order <H,C>? Kayne suggests that it is because the probe–goal relation must follow the physical order in time in which speech is produced and interpreted. Then, since a probe is always located in a head and a goal in its complement, it follows that heads generally must precede complements. Why should it be the case that probes physically precede goals in time? Kayne's idea is that since both production and perception of speech take place in real time, it would be extremely inefficient—perhaps even impossible—for a probe to have to search for a goal in material that had already been processed, requiring at the very least storage of an indefinitely large amount of material which the probe would have to search through in order to find a matching goal.

There are, however, reasons to be skeptical of this approach. Taking the second assumption first, even if it could be demonstrated that the parsing mechanism of natural language is unable to deal with a situation in which a probe is required to locate a goal in previously parsed material—a claim for which there is no empirical evidence, as far as I am aware—it would not necessarily follow that *all* heads are subject to this constraint, for the simple reason that only a small subset of heads (at most two per clause under current assumptions) contain probes. Conceivably, a general condition requiring that

Spell-out apply to all head-dependent relations in a uniform manner could be invoked to ensure that a relation whose head lacks a probe is linearized in the same way as a relation whose head does happen to contain one. This, however, would be an additional theoretical assumption that does not follow in any way from parsing considerations. Since it also does not seem to follow from any formal property of heads themselves, it would have to stand as an independent postulate, unexplainable in either formal or performance terms.

As for the first part of Kayne's proposal, the main difficulty is that the linear ordering that results from second Merge does not actually follow from any inherent property of the head H which drives the Merge operation. In other words, there is no way to tell simply by looking at the properties of H and S whether the output of Merge should be <H,S> or <S,H>. There is thus a disconnect between the syntactic dependency relation that a head H bears to its specifier S, naturally representable (as suggested here) as an ordered pair <H,S>, and the order of Merge, which must produce the ordered pair <S,H>. Furthermore, the crucial assumption in this argument that both C and S must be immediately adjacent to H is, as far as I can see, simply stipulated, thus weakening the force of the LCA to the point of vacuity. Kayne's original conception of the LCA was theoretically interesting because it claimed that linear ordering could be *predicted* from the structurally definable relation of asymmetric c-command. The new version simply posits the *results* of the LCA as an axiom, hence is far less explanatory.

One of the virtues of trying to predict the correct linearization on the basis of a stripped-down theory of relations is that it makes it crystal clear that, absent the ability to appeal to the various kinds of formal tricks that constituent structure makes available, it is simply impossible to derive S-H-C word order from any obvious formal property of FR. It would be a big plus for a relation-based theory of the sort proposed here if it led naturally to a tight correspondence between syntactic relations and linear ordering along the lines originally envisioned by Kayne, but, as things now stand, that is not the case. I will show, however, that the fault lies not with the linearization procedure, but with other assumptions, unwittingly inherited from the standard theory based on constituent structure.

1.2.2   Order of Application of FR

Another problem facing the tentative theory outlined earlier is that there is no general way of deciding in what order the selectors associated with a head should be satisfied. Consider, for example the sentence *He put it there*. The verb *put* is a three-place predicate, requiring an agent, a theme and a goal. It was argued in §1.1.4.1, following mainstream work in generative syntax, that the agent is selected by *v*, rather than by the verb itself. However, *put* has two other selectors that must be satisfied. Assume, for the sake of discussion, that they are [_D] and [_P]. In what order should they be satisfied? Depending on the answer to this question, the derivation will yield either the correct linearization <u>he</u>-<u>put</u>-<u>it</u>-<u>there</u> or the incorrect linearization <u>he</u>-<u>put</u>-<u>there</u>-<u>it</u>. Yet there is no obvious way of determining which selector should be satisfied first and which second.

In fact, the problem is quite general. Thus *v* and T also have two selectors. In the first case, they would be [_V] and [_D]; in the second case, [_v] and [_D]. But in neither case is it possible to decide which selector should be satisfied first. We have been assuming without discussion that the verbal selector is satisfied first and the nominal selector second, but there is actually no theoretical reason why this should be so. In certain cases, one of the two possible orders of application can be ruled out on independent grounds. For example, if we tried to satisfy the [_D] selector of *will* before the [_v] selector, we would have to select a D-element (e.g. *she*) from LA to which no semantic interpretation could be assigned, violating the θ-Criterion. Only if the [_v] selector is satisfied first will there be an LI of category D available which has already been interpreted. In the case of *v*, however, there is no obvious way to prevent a derivation of the following sort:

(40) 1 <put,there>   put-there
      2 <put,it>   it-put-there
      3 <v,he>   v-he
      4 <v,put>   put-he-it-~~put~~-there

In English, it could perhaps be argued that derivation (40) is ruled out on the grounds that an illegible symbol such as *v* must be interpreted immediately in PHON, thus requiring that <v,put> be formed first. But what about a language in which *v* is lexically realized as a "light verb"? In that case there would be no obstacle to satisfying the selectors of *v* in the order indicated in (40).

The general problem revealed by this discussion is that there is an asymmetry between the selectors of a given head that is not in any way reflected in the theory. In particular, it seems that selectors responsible for producing some part of the "extended projection" in the sense of Grimshaw (1990) generally take precedence over selectors that are responsible for introducing arguments, though in the case of ditransitive verbs such as *put* it is far from clear how such a principle could decide in which order the two non-agentive arguments are to be introduced.

1.2.3   Taking Bottom-up Derivation Seriously

It was suggested at the outset that a relational theory of syntax should follow the lead of X-bar theory and the Minimalist Program in assuming that derivation is "bottom-up" rather than "top-down," reflecting the lexicalist view that the fundamental units of syntax are simply words. However, looking over the kinds of derivations proposed thus far reveals that though successive applications of FR do in fact take place in bottom-up fashion, it is not at all obvious that each application of FR is in an intuitive sense bottom-up. To clarify the issue, consider the following representation of the derivation of the sentence *She will kiss him*:

(41)

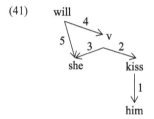

In this diagram the direction in which each application of FR takes place is explicitly indicated by directed arrows, while the order in which successive applications of FR take place is represented by numbering the arcs. The latter is clearly bottom-up, in the sense that each successive application of FR adds a new relation, starting with the most basic lexical items *kiss* and *him*. Equally clearly, however, each individual application of FR still retains a top-down character in the sense that the head is always higher in the tree than the dependent. One might imagine that in a relational theory that was truly bottom-up, derivations would start at the bottom with heads and build up structures by adding dependents.

   The representation in (41) also raises another fundamental question, which relates to the discussion in §1.2.2. In a relation between a head such as *kiss* or *v* and a D-element, it is clear that the former is the head and the latter the dependent. But what about the relation between *kiss* and *v*? Or between *v* and *will*? In such relations, which is the head and which is the dependent? It has been assumed thus far without discussion that in the first case *v* is the head and that it selects an LI of category V. Likewise, it has been assumed in the second case that *will* is the head and that it selects an LI of category *v*. It is far from obvious, however, that these assumptions are correct.

   In the remainder of this chapter, I propose a revised version of the relational theory in which both the order and the manner in which relations are formed by

FR are fully bottom-up. In such a theory, I claim, all the problems discussed can be resolved.

1.3   A Fully Bottom-up Relational Theory

As was hinted at in §1.2.3, in order to construct a truly bottom-up theory of relational syntax, it is first necessary to rethink the relation between functional heads and their complements. The conventional wisdom is that in the verbal system there are "functional" categories such as C, T, "light *v*," etc. and lexical categories such as V, N, A, and P. It is further assumed that C selects T, T selects *v*, and *v* selects V (Abney 1987). These assumptions were implicitly carried over into the relational theory proposed earlier. However, it is also widely assumed, following Grimshaw (1990), that functional categories should be, in some sense, part of an "extended projection" of the verb. There is a rather obvious conflict between the direction of selection that is standardly assumed, which is top-down, and the idea of an extended projection, which is clearly inherently bottom-up.

1.3.1   The Extended Projection

Let us start therefore by developing the notion of an extended projection in formally explicit terms. I propose, first, that *all* categories in the verbal system are nothing more than different "flavors" of the basic category *v*. Thus C is simply a *v* with complementizer features, T is a *v* with tense and agreement features, "light *v*" is a *v* with an [Ag] feature, etc. Second, I shall assume that the initial element of every extended projection is a lexical *root*, which must start by forming a relation with an LI belonging to one of the lexical categories *v*, *n*, *a*, or *p*. Finally—and this is the crucial step—I assume that selection proceeds in strictly bottom-up fashion, starting with the lowest "lexical" heads and proceeding to the topmost "functional" heads. The direction in which selection takes place, and hence the direction of the relations formed by FR, is thus exactly the reverse of that which is conventionally assumed. In particular, "light *v*" selects T, T selects C, etc. In graphic terms, a head is lower in the tree than its dependents.

   To illustrate, consider the derivation of a transitive sentence such as *She will kiss him*. I assume the following LIs in LA: the root √kiss; a "light *v*" with the feature [Th]; another with the feature [Ag]; a "functional" *v will* with the feature [T: future]; and a null LI ∅ with the feature [C]. To simplify notation, I shall henceforth write the features that characterize different "flavors" of a lexical category as subscripts of *v*, *n*, etc. or of a particular LI of the category in question, e.g. v_{th}, v_{ag}, *will*$_{tns}$, *she*$_{det}$, $\emptyset_{comp}$, etc. I assume in addition that v_{th} has selectors [_n_{det}] and [_v_{ag}]; v_{ag} has selectors [_n_{det}] and [_v_{tns}]; *will* has selectors [_n_{det}] and [_v_{comp}]; and $\emptyset_{comp}$ has no selectors at all.[26] (I discuss the selectors associated with a root such as √kiss in §1.3.5.) The direction of dependency relations will also be reversed in graphic representations, meaning that heads are lower in the tree and dependents higher, exactly the opposite of what was assumed previously. With these conventions in place, the derivation of the sentence *She will kiss him* can be represented as follows:

(42)

The steps of the derivation are as follows:

(43)　　1　　<√kiss,v_{th}>
　　　　2　　<v_{th},him$_{det}$>
　　　　3　　<v_{th},v_{ag}>
　　　　4　　<v_{ag},she$_{det}$>
　　　　5　　<v_{ag},will$_{tns}$>
　　　　6　　<will$_{tns}$,she$_{det}$>
　　　　7　　<will$_{tns}$,$\emptyset_{comp}$>

The vertical spine in (42) represents the extended verbal projection of the root √kiss, while the left branches represent argument relations. A relation-based theory is thus able to provide a precise formalization of the notion of an extended projection. Each element in the extended projection is necessarily selected by the one below it, starting with the lexical root, and every element, unless otherwise stipulated, belongs to the same lexical category *v*, differing only in their specific syntactic (and hence semantic) properties. The extended projection ends when an LI is selected that has no lexical projection feature that

---

[26] Note that selection is deterministic in the sense that it expresses a requirement that must be met. I assume, however, that a given head may have more than one possible selector, only one of which need (or can) be satisfied in a given derivation, or no selector at all. The latter possibility is discussed extensively in connection with so-called "defective" categories in §2.2. Thus v_{ag}, for example, may either have the projection feature [_v_{tns}] or not, producing a tensed clause in the first case and a verbal small clause, as in *I saw [him kiss her]*, in the second.

needs to be satisfied, in this instance the null complementizer $\varnothing_{comp}$. Constituent-based theories are unable to formalize the notion of an extended projection in a satisfactory manner for two reasons. First, every category in the extended projection, e.g. V, *v*, T, C, etc., is discrete and formally unrelated to the others, in the sense that there is no principled reason, apart from pure stipulation, why a selector and the maximal projection it selects as its complement or specifier should share any syntactic properties. In particular, there is no reason why complements should generally belong to the same category as the heads that select them, nor any reason why the opposite is generally true for specifiers. Second, each category in the extended projection can only project its own constituent structure, leaving no way for the relation between successive maximal projections of the extended projection to be formally expressed, other than by either resorting to f-selection or simply stipulating in *ad hoc* fashion the order in which complements are to be merged. In the relational theory, in contrast, it is straightforward to define formally the notion of an extended projection in terms of the fundamental selection properties of LIs, together with FR, the basic operation of syntax. I show in the following sections how each of the remaining problems enumerated earlier can be solved in the new version of relational theory. I then turn to a deeper consideration of selection, showing that there are just two fundamental types of relation, which can be formally defined in terms of the most fundamental selection properties of LIs.

1.3.2   Order of Selection

Consider next the problem posed by three-place predicates such as *put*. The order in which the theme and goal arguments are satisfied is no longer a problem because each argument is introduced by a separate argument head (cf. Bowers 2010) and because the order in which argument heads are introduced is determined by the intrinsic selection properties of the heads themselves. There are still empirical questions, of course, as to how many argument heads there are, what their selection properties are, whether there is a universal order of argument heads, and so forth (see Bowers 2010 for detailed discussion of many such questions), but the important point is that there is no longer a theoretical indeterminacy built into the theory itself.

It is still generally the case, however, that each head can have up to two selectors. For example, v_{th} in (42)/(43) has the two selection features (i) [_n_{det}]; (ii) [_v_{ag}]. Selection features of type (i) I refer to as argument features and those of type (ii) I refer to as lexical projection features. Won't this lead to exactly the same problem of deciding in what order the selection features should be satisfied in cases where an LI has both?

The answer, I claim, is no. To begin with, notice that the Head Principle (HP), assumed earlier to be the basic principle regulating derivations, can no longer be valid. The reason is that every lexical projection feature will violate it, since a lexical projection feature necessarily selects an LI that is unsaturated. What is needed in place of HP is a principle requiring that as soon as a new head is selected, its selectors must be satisfied immediately, i.e. before the selectors of any other head are satisfied. Such a principle is clearly necessary in any case in order to ensure that derivation proceeds sequentially from bottom to top, rather than by selecting pairs of LIs from LA and forming relations between them in random fashion. Let us call this principle *Immediate Gratification*:

(44)   *Immediate Gratification* (IG):
        If a head H is selected, its selectors must be satisfied immediately.

IG, together with the assumption that every extended projection must start with a lexical root, will ensure that FR applies in a fixed order from bottom to top. For example, the selectors of v_{th} must be satisfied before moving on to satisfy the selectors of v_{ag}, the selectors of v_{ag} must be satisfied before moving to satisfy those of v_{tns}, and so forth. The next question is why the argument selector $[\_n_{det}]$ must be satisfied first and the $[\_v_{ag}]$ selector second, as shown in derivation (43)?[27] IG answers this question as well. Suppose we tried to satisfy $[\_v_{ag}]$ first. The result would be as follows:

(45)

Now, however, IG will require that the selectors of v_{ag} be satisfied immediately, making it impossible to ever satisfy the $[\_n_{det}]$ selector of v_{th}. The only way the condition imposed by IG can be met for both v_{th} and v_{ag} is for the $[\_n_{det}]$ feature of v_{th} to be satisfied first, followed by satisfaction of its $[\_v_{ag}]$ feature, exactly as shown in derivation (42)/(43). Obviously, similar considerations apply quite generally, dictating that whenever a head has two selectors, one requiring an LI

---

[27] Note that there is actually nothing in the dependency graph (42) to indicate the order in which the dependencies between v_{th} and him_{det} and v_{th} and v_{ag} should be satisfied. I propose in §1.3.3 a modified form of dependency graph that incorporates this information.

of category D, another requiring a lexical projection category with selectors of its own, the former will have to be satisfied first and the latter second.

We have thus solved the ordering problem completely, since it follows directly from the properties of the selection features themselves, together with the principle of IG, which is independently needed in any case to ensure that derivations proceed in strict sequential order from bottom to top. One might still wonder, however, why there are just two types of selection features and why an LI can have at most two, one of each type. I come back to these questions in §1.3.4 and show that these properties also can be derived from the most fundamental syntactic properties of LI themselves.

1.3.3   Spell-out Revised

Consider next the difficulties with linearization discussed earlier. Recall that the basic problem was exactly that which the LCA tried to answer, namely, why the phonetic form of a complement C must *follow* the phonetic form of a head H, while the phonetic form of a specifier S must *precede* H. The difficulty with our first attempt to formulate the Spell-out algorithm was that it gave the right result for complements but the wrong result for specifiers. I will show now that the problem lies not with the Spell-out procedure but with the failure to implement a fully bottom-up theory of relational derivation.

In the revised theory we are now assuming, derivation proceeds in strict bottom-to-top fashion, starting with a lexical root and proceeding until an LI is selected that has no lexical projection feature that needs to be satisfied. I will show that given a model of this type, a slightly revised version of Spell-out will predict correctly the linear ordering that the LCA was intended to derive. Before reformulating Spell-out, however, it is first necessary to modify slightly the definition of the phonetic form PF of a term of a relation and also to restate the special case of FR that applies when one of the elements of the relation is not legible to the SR systems. The new definition of PF is as follows:

(46)   *Definition*: The *phonetic form* PF(α) of a term α of a relation (irrespective of whether it is the head or the dependent term) is:
   (i) $\underline{\alpha}$, if α is an LI selected from LA;
   (ii) $\underline{\sigma}_\alpha$, where $\underline{\sigma}_\alpha$ is the string produced by applying Spell-out to the most recently formed relation containing α as a term.

The main feature of this definition to be noted is that it is no longer necessary to stipulate in part (ii) that α is the *head* of the most recently formed relation containing α. Instead it is sufficient to find the most recently formed relation containing α as a term, regardless of whether α is the head or the dependent in that relation. As for the operation of FR when one of the terms of the relation is illegible, the direction in which it applies must also be reversed, so as to require that a dependent that is not legible at PHON be given the phonetic value of the head selecting it. Utilizing the notation introduced earlier, the operation of FR in such cases may then be revised as follows:

(47) $FR([\alpha{:}\underline{\alpha}],[\beta{:}]) = <[\alpha{:}\underline{\alpha}],[\beta{:}\underline{\alpha}]>$, β a lexical projection category.[28]

Principle (47) simply states that if a head α with phonetic form $\underline{\alpha}$ selects a lexical projection category β with no phonetic form of its own, then FR automatically supplies β with the phonetic form $\underline{\alpha}$ of the head α.[29] It actually makes more sense, intuitively, for a head to "rescue" a phonetically defective dependent than vice versa, since the head is the active term of the relation whose selection properties drive FR.

   Given the redefinition of PF in (46), together with (47), Spell-out can now be stated in maximally simple and general form as follows:

(48)   *Spell-out*:
         $<\alpha,\beta> \Rightarrow PF(\beta)\text{-}PF(\alpha)$

In other words, the phonetic form of a dependent must uniformly precede the phonetic form of a head. To illustrate, I show in (49) how Spell-out maps in incremental fashion each stage of the derivation (42)/(43) onto a phonetic form, culminating in the correct phonetic form of the sentence *She will kiss him* at the final step of the derivation:[30]

(49)   1 $<\sqrt{kiss},kiss_{th}>$ kiss-~~kiss~~
       2   $<kiss_{th},him>$ him-kiss-~~kiss~~
       3   $<kiss_{th},kiss_{ag}>$ kiss-him-~~kiss~~-~~kiss~~
       4   $<kiss_{ag},she>$ she-kiss-him-~~kiss~~-~~kiss~~

---

[28] I restrict (47) to the case where the dependent is a lexical projection category. It is possible, however, that extending it to the case where the dependent is an argument category could provide a way of accounting for cliticization.

[29] As observed in note 10, a lexical projection category with no phonetic form of its own, e.g. $[\beta{:}]$ in (47), is not the same as a lexical projection category whose phonetic form is $\varnothing$, e.g. $[\beta{:}\varnothing]$. (47) is not applicable in the latter case, since $[\beta{:}\varnothing]$ is an LI with phonetic content that happens to be interpreted gesturally as no movement, hence as silence acoustically. For example, lexical verbs in English at v_{ag} generally project $[v_{tns}{:}\ \varnothing]$, whereas in French they project $[v_{tns}{:}]$, explaining why lexical verbs are pronounced at the position of v_{ag} in English but at the position of v_{tns} in French. See §6.1 for further discussion.

[30] For the sake of perspicuity, I retain the informal notation introduced earlier in derivations rather than using the more explicit notation used in (47). Thus step 1 in derivation (49) is shorthand for the following:

   (i) $FR([\sqrt{kiss}{:}\underline{kiss}],[v_{th}{:}]) = <[\sqrt{kiss}{:}\underline{kiss}],[v_{th}{:}\underline{kiss}]>$

5	$<kiss_{ag}, will_{tns}>$	will-she-kiss-him-~~kiss-kiss~~
6	$<will_{tns}, she>$	she-will-~~she~~-kiss-him-~~kiss-kiss~~
7	$<will_{tns}, \emptyset comp>$	$\emptyset$-she-will-~~she~~-kiss-him-~~kiss-kiss~~

Each time FR applies, the phonetic form of the dependent element is ordered to the left of the phonetic form of the head. At step 1, the root $\sqrt{kiss}$ selects v_{th}, requiring Spell-out to order the new occurrence of <u>kiss</u> provided to v_{th} by FR to the left of the phonetic form <u>kiss</u> of the root $\sqrt{kiss}$. At step 2, v_{th} selects an *n* of category D such as *him*, whose phonetic form is ordered to the left of the output of Spell-out at step 1. Next, v_{th}, which has the phonetic form <u>him-kiss-~~kiss~~</u> as a result of step 2, selects v_{ag}, again ordering the copy of <u>kiss</u> required by (9) to its left. Then *she* is selected by v_{ag}, ordering its phonetic form to the left of the previously formed string. The rest of the derivation proceeds in similar fashion, alternately concatenating the phonetic form of *v* and D-elements on the left, producing ultimately the correct final string: $\emptyset$-<u>she</u>-will-~~she~~-<u>kiss</u>-him-~~kiss-kiss~~. Spell-out thus applies incrementally in a simple and uniform fashion to the output of FR, the most basic operation of syntax, and produces the correct linear ordering of the phonetic form of every LI in the derivation, thereby embodying the spirit that motivated Kayne's original conception of the LCA. In particular, every LI analyzed as a specifier in standard constituent-based grammars ends up to the left of the head that selects it, while every LI that would be treated as a complement ends up to the right of the head that selects it. Hence the LCA follows as a theorem from the Spell-out procedure proposed here.

Since the output of Spell-out is now completely predictable, given the order in which the operations of FR must apply, it is convenient to combine the results of FR and Spell-out in a single graphic representation from which it is possible to read off both the order of application of FR and the linear ordering in a transparent fashion. I therefore propose the following graphic representation of derivation (49):

(50)

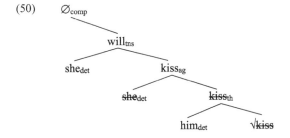

To see how a tree of this form is translated in uniform fashion into a derivation, consider the following abstract tree annotated so as to indicate (a) the direction of the dependencies (arrows), (b) the order in which they are to be formed (arabic numerals), and (c) the linear order, going from right to left, in which the phonetic forms of the nodes are to be arranged (lower case roman numerals):

(51)

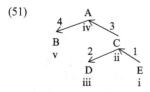

Following conventions (a), (b), and (c), this tree will be uniformly translated into the following sequence of applications of FR, mapped at each step by Spell-out onto the correct linear ordering of phonetic forms:

(52)   1   <E,C>   C-E
        2   <C,D>   D-C-E
        3   <C,A>   A-D-C-E
        4   <A,B>   B-A-D-C-E

For the reasons explained previously, whenever an LI such as C in (51) functions as the head in two successive applications of FR, the first must be an argument relation, while the second must be a relation of lexical projection. This general property of derivations is systematically represented in trees of this form in the following way: (i) lines going downward and to the left uniformly represent argument selection; (ii) lines going upward and to the left uniformly represent selection of a lexical projection. The order of application of FR can thus be derived from the tree by ordering the dependency lines from right to left and from bottom to top, starting from the rightmost arrow. Likewise, the linear ordering of the phonetic forms of the nodes can be read off from right to left in a similar fashion, as indicated by annotation (c):

(53)   B-A-D-C-E

This is exactly the linear order that results from the step-by-step application of Spell-out in the derivation (52).

In addition to these conventions, (50) incorporates the results of applying the special case of FR in (47). In particular, if a copy of the phonetic form of a head A has to be passed up to its dependent B in order to satisfy Full Interpretation at PHON, a copy of A is placed at the node representing the dependent and the phonetic form of A is represented with a strike-through. Likewise, if a copy of the phonetic form of a subtree is required at PHON because a head A selects a dependent B that was previously selected by C, then a copy of B is shown as the dependent of A and the original occurrence of B is represented with a strike-through.

It can easily be verified that the application of these algorithms to (50) will yield precisely the order of operations of FR shown in derivation (49), as well as the linear ordering of the phonetic forms shown in the final step of derivation (49). Trees of this form thus provide a convenient graphic representation of all the information contained in a derivation consisting of ordered applications of FR to LIs, accompanied by immediate, incremental application of Spell-out to each relation formed by FR.

Since it is completely predictable that only the last copy of a sequence of phonetic forms passed up through a projection is pronounced, it is redundant to show all the previous copies with a strike-through. Likewise, since only the last copy of a sequence of athematically selected arguments is pronounced, it is also unnecessary to show all the copies of previously selected arguments with a strike-through. I therefore propose to further simplify the canonical graphic representation of a derivation such as (50) as follows:

(54)

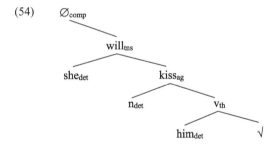

Here the projections v_{th} and $\sqrt{}$ are to be understood as containing (unpronounced) copies of the phonetic form <u>kiss</u>. Similarly, the argument n_{det} selected by $kiss_{ag}$ is to be understood as containing an (unpronounced) copy of the phonetic form <u>she</u>. Henceforth this notational convention will be followed quite generally, though there will be cases where it is more perspicuous, for one reason or another, to revert to the practice of spelling out a sequence of copies in full.

1.3.4   Types of Selection: Arguments versus Lexical Projections

Eliminating constituent structure in favor of a syntactic theory based on relations between words has revealed the important fact that there are two fundamentally different types of selection. One type requires that a head form a relation with an *argument*, while the other type requires that a head form a relation with some part of the *extended projection* of a lexical category. The next question is how to characterize formally these two types of selection. The problem with theories based on a notion of constituency is that there is no principled way of distinguishing them in formal terms, since both involve selection of maximal projections. In practice, what linguists have done is tacitly assume that selection of the second type (sometimes referred to as "f-selection," following Abney 1987) is satisfied by first Merge, whereas selection of the first type is satisfied by second Merge. This, however, is pure stipulation and does not follow from any general principle of grammar or from any legibility conditions imposed on representations at either PHON or SEM. Furthermore, in any theory that assumes that more than one argument may be contained in the projection of a lexical category such as V, there will be no non-arbitrary way of deciding which of two arguments selected by V is merged first. The preliminary relational theory sketched out at the beginning of this chapter inherited the same difficulty, for the reasons discussed earlier.

It should perhaps be mentioned in passing that another possible way of distinguishing the two kinds of relation, sometimes suggested in the literature of Dependency Grammar, is simply to label them differently, thereby treating them as distinct primitive relations of the theory. However, this approach is not very interesting, for the same reason that distinguishing the subject relation from the object relation in a constituent structure grammar by simply labeling branches as either *subject* or *object* is not, because it fails to derive these notions from more primitive elements of the theory. In this case, it would also fail to provide any explanation why argument relations must always be formed before lexical projection relations.

A fully bottom-up relational theory of the sort proposed in this chapter, in contrast, provides a formally simple and straightforward way of defining the two kinds of relations in terms of the inherent properties of selected LIs. A selected LI that has *no* unsatisfied selectors will be defined as an *argument*, whereas a selected LI that *does* have unsatisfied selectors will be defined as a *lexical projection*.[31] In other words, arguments are saturated, whereas lexical projections are unsaturated. As shown earlier, it follows from these definitions, together with the principle of IG, that a head that selects both an argument and a lexical projection must always form the argument relation first and the lexical projection relation second. A head may of course select only an argument, only

---

[31] Notice that a potential indeterminacy arises in the case of a root projection such as v_{comp}, which is similar to an argument in having no lexical projection features of its own. This problem will be resolved in Chapter 2, cf. §2.3, note 21.

a lexical projection, or neither. But in all of these cases the ordering problem simply does not arise. Furthermore, it cannot be the case that a head selects more than one argument or more than one lexical projection. The second possibility is ruled out because the resulting structure would not have a single root, hence would not be a tree. The first possibility is ruled out by the general principle that each argument is introduced by one and only one head (Bowers 2010). This principle could be regarded as the relational equivalent of Baker's UTAH principle under the reasonable assumption that each argument relation is mapped onto a fixed semantic role (or perhaps set of semantic roles). It can also be ruled out by a general principle governing FR, namely, that the initial occurrences of any two LIs α and β must be uniquely ordered with respect to one another. If a head H had more than one argument selector, there would be no way of determining which of the two selectors should be satisfied first. Hence there would be nothing to prevent either derivation, resulting in a non-unique linear ordering of the initial occurrences of the (phonetic form of the) arguments at PHON.

It follows, then, from general principles that every head selects a maximum of one argument and/or one lexical projection, where an argument is a head that has no unsatisfied selectors, while a lexical projection is one that does. In addition, we may define a head with no lexical projection selectors of its own as the *root* of a derivation/tree. Similarly, a head that has unsatisfied selectors but is not selected by any other head must be a *lexical root*. Given these definitions, in Chapter 2 I shall proceed to discuss in more detail what kinds of categorial projections other than *n* may serve as arguments and what sorts of lexical projections are required by each of the lexical categories *v, n, a*, and *p*. Before doing so, however, it is first necessary to provide a means of expressing the lexically idiosyncratic distributional properties of roots.

1.3.5   The Lexicon: Categorial and Lexical Selection Properties of Roots
As mentioned earlier, I adopt the assumption of Distributed Morphology (Halle and Marantz 1993) that derivations uniformly begin with lexical roots. However, following Ramchand (2008), Bowers (2010), and others, I stop short of the radically constructionalist view of Marantz (1997) and Borer (1998, 2005) that roots contain no syntactic information at all, assuming instead that roots are classified in terms of syntactic categories and purely syntactic selection properties.[32] In particular, roots are classified in terms of the lexical

---

[32] Later on, in Chapters 5 and 6, I further modify this assumption, arguing that every derivation starts with a fully inflected morphological form of a lexical item.

features v, n, a, and p plus a set of lexically idiosyncratic *a(rgument)-selection* features such as $[\_v_{th}]$, $[\_v_{ag}]$, $[\_v_{aff}]$, etc.[33] Thus an unaccusative root of category v such as *die* will have only the first of these, a transitive verb root such as *kill* will have the first and the second, while a ditransitive verb root such as *put* will have all three. I assume that when a root such as *kill* selects a lexical projection such as v_{th}, its a-selection feature $[\_v_{th}]$ is deleted and any remaining a-selection features are automatically transferred to the selected lexical projection, in this case the v_{th} head. If the v_{th} head in turn selects a lexical projection such as v_{ag}, then the a-selection feature $[\_v_{ag}]$ is also deleted, leaving no a-selection features to be satisfied. All a-selection features of roots must be deleted in the course of a derivation in order for the derivation to terminate.

Some roots, however, restrict not only the set of lexical projections that they may occur with but also restrict the argument *type* that a given lexical projection may select. For example, the thematic argument of a verb such as *believe* may be either nominal or sentential, e.g. *They believed the story, They believed that he left*, whereas *insist* may only have a sentential theme, e.g. **They insisted the plan, They insisted that he leave*. For a root of the first kind it is only necessary to specify the a-selection feature $[\_v_{th}]$. Then, since the head v_{th} is itself quite generally free to select either n_{det} or v_{comp} arguments, both types of thematic argument will be permitted. To restrict the distribution of √*insist*, on the other hand, it is necessary to specify an a-selection feature of a slightly more complex form:

(55)   √insist
     [$\_v_{th}$]
      [$\_that_{comp}$]

The lexical entry in (55) states that the root √*insist* may only a-select a lexical projection v_{th} that is itself restricted to selecting a finite sentential argument headed by *that*. Obviously, a wide variety of restrictions on the distribution of specific roots can be represented in this fashion.

The virtue of this approach is that it clearly distinguishes between distributional properties that are idiosyncratic to particular LIs and those that are more general properties of the syntactic system. The former are represented as a-selection restrictions associated with roots, while the latter are represented as selection properties associated with lexical projection categories.

---

[33] Like all syntactic heads, roots have semantic, syntactic, and phonetic properties. The phonetic properties of roots may include both segmental and suprasegmental information, permitting pairs such as [√object$_N$: [ˈabdʒɛkt]], [√object$_V$, [əbˈdʒɛkt]] to be distinguished.

However, the selection mechanism that drives FR is the same in both cases. There is thus no radical dissociation between syntax and lexicon. It is therefore not surprising to find that words, in addition to being lexical roots, can belong to a wide variety of different "flavors" of lexical categories, including those that are often thought of as "functional" categories such as v_{comp}, v_{tns}, n_{det}, etc. At the same time, however, lexical roots occupy a somewhat special status since every extended projection must start with a lexical root.

1.4 Conclusion

I have argued in this chapter that syntactic theory can be radically simplified by eliminating the notions of constituent structure and movement from narrow syntax, replacing them with asymmetrical dependency relations between words. Syntactic relations are generated by means of a simple binary operation *Form Relation* (FR), which takes as input a pair of lexical items α and β and produces an ordered pair <α,β>, where β satisfies a selection condition required by α. FR applies in strictly bottom-up fashion.

In a theory of this form, the appearance of constituent structure and movement arise from the incremental application of Spell-out, together with the most basic legibility requirements of phonetic representation. Minimally, these are: (i) the phonetic representations of lexical items must be linearly ordered; (ii) the phonetic representation of every head must be legible to SM. The illusion of constituent structure arises directly from requirement (i) together with the incremental nature of the Spell-out algorithm, which ensures that once a string is formed at PHON it cannot be disrupted by any later application of FR. The illusion of head movement is a consequence of (ii), which requires that a dependent containing an illegible symbol be provided with the phonetic form of the head that selects it. The illusion of constituent movement is more complex, arising from the fact that certain heads may have an athematic argument selection feature, combined with the legibility requirements of both PHON and SEM. In such a case, the linear ordering requirement of PHON, together with a requirement of SEM similar to the θ-Criterion, jointly require that the phonetic form of a previously selected head be displaced leftward.

Crucially, relational derivations are bottom-up not only in the obvious sense that each application of FR adds a new relation, but also in the sense that the item containing the selection condition (the head) is always lower than the selected item (the dependent). An important consequence of this approach is that the notion of an "extended projection" in the sense of Grimshaw (1990) is built directly into the structure of the theory without having to be stipulated.

Another important consequence of a strictly bottom-up theory is that Spell-out can be stated in a maximally simple and general form without having to assume that order is a primitive of the theory as in Kayne (2010): given a relation <α, β>, the phonetic form of β must precede the phonetic form of α, i.e. dependents precede heads.

The two most basic types of relations discussed in this chapter are lexical projection and argument selection, to which a third, namely, modification, will be added in Chapter 3. Each is strictly and exhaustively definable in terms of inherent formal selection properties of heads. It turns out that the possible orders in which these three relation-types may be formed is automatically determined by FR together with a universal constraint, termed *Immediate Gratification* (IG), which requires that selection requirements of heads be satisfied immediately. This principle, which is needed in any case in order to ensure that derivations operate in strict bottom-to-top fashion, also solves a fundamental problem that has plagued constituent-based grammars, namely, the fact that there is no way to determine, except by arbitrary stipulation, the order in which two selection requirements associated with the same head are to be satisfied.

In the remainder of this book I draw out the consequences of a theory of syntax of the basic form outlined in this chapter for a wide variety of syntactic phenomena, arguing that a relation-based approach is at least as descriptively and explanatorily adequate as one based on constituent structure, and in many crucial respects demonstrably superior.

2 Types of Lexical Projections and Arguments

Having outlined in Chapter 1 the basic principles of a relational approach to syntax, I turn next to a more detailed discussion of both the substance and the architecture of relational derivation. This chapter is divided into two parts. In §2.1 and §2.2, I flesh out in more detail the extended lexical projections of each of the basic lexical categories *v, n, a*, and *p* and consider what types of projections may function as arguments in natural language. It is first shown that for each type of lexical category there is exactly one projection which is (a) obligatory in all projections of that type, and (b) constitutes the absolute minimum required in order for a lexical root to form a projection of that type. This unique projection of each lexical category I term the "minimal category" of that category type. I then discuss what types of projections may be selected as arguments in natural language, arguing that the existence of so-called "defective categories" for arguments of every lexical category provides a major argument in support of a theory of syntax based on relations rather than constituents. In the second part, §2.3 and §2.4, I discuss in further detail the architecture of relational derivations and the constraints governing them. It is first shown that sentences are derived not by applying FR to a single monolithic LA but rather by applying FR independently to a set of lexical subarrays, whose outputs must then be integrated with one another. This in turn leads to further refinement of the accessibility constraint and, ultimately, to the conclusion that the best empirical results are provided by a relationally defined version of phase theory.

2.1 Types of Lexical Projections

As previously indicated, I assume that there are four basic types of syntactic categories, *v, n, a*, and *p*, each with its own characteristic set of lexical and

49

functional categories that are selected in a fixed order to construct an extended projection.[1] In order for a lexical root of a given syntactic category type to form a lexical projection at all, there must be a unique projection, required in every projection of that category, with which it must minimally form a relation. It is important to note that the minimal category of a given type is not necessarily always the *first* category that is projected—quite the contrary, as will be discussed shortly. Crucially, however, it is obligatorily projected. It is an empirical question whether there are any other lexical projections of each syntactic category that are universally obligatory or whether all projections, apart from the minimal projection for each syntactic category, are optional, either within a given language or varying parametrically across languages. In the following sections I discuss the minimal projection of each of the basic syntactic category types, followed by a brief survey of other lexical projections for each type that have figured prominently in the literature.

2.1.1   *v-projections*

For v-projections, the minimal category is v_{pred}, where the feature [pred] is intended to indicate that the primary property of v-projections is predication. In Modern English, v_{pred} has no phonetic form of its own legible to SM, hence it is the position where all lexical verbs, apart from *be* in finite clauses, are pronounced. Root clauses, as well as finite and non-finite complement clauses (except for so-called "defective" infinitive complements, which are discussed later in this chapter), must also project at least the category v_{tns}, containing the features of tense and modality, and the clause-typing head v_{comp}. However, v-projections functioning as arguments can be found that consist of v_{pred} alone without any other arguments or lexical projections. These are the bare infinitival complements with 0-place predicates such as *rain, snow, hail*, etc. that appear in examples such as the following:

(1)   a. John made/had/let *(it) rain.
         b. We saw/heard/felt *(it) rain.

Such minimal v-projections are derived simply as follows:

---

[1] Henceforth I drop the term "extended projection," which is now somewhat redundant, and simply refer to the *lexical projection* of one of the basic syntactic types *v, n, a*, and *p*, or to a *v*-projection, *n*-projection, etc.

(2)

Notice that these minimal v-projections must have an expletive subject *it*. To account for this, it must be assumed that v_{pred} has an obligatory athematic argument selector. Since there is no other n_{det} available that was previously interpreted as an argument, this selector can only be satisfied in the case of 0-place predicates by forming a relation with the expletive *it*. Independent evidence in support of this assumption can be derived from the fact that in unaccusative sentences either the theme argument or a special expletive form *there* must be pronounced to the left of the verb. This can be explained under the assumption that the obligatory athematic selection feature of v_{pred} may be satisfied either by forming a relation with the expletive *there* or with an n_{det} previously selected by v_{th}, as argued in Chapter 1 (see also Bowers 2002, 2010 for details). For the moment, I will also follow Bowers (2002) in assuming that v_{pred} may optionally have an [ag] feature as well, in which case its argument selector will of course be thematic. It is this argument that functions as the subject of transitive and unergative verbs.[2] For further discussion of the structure of bare infinitive complements as well as other types of "small clause" complements, see §2.2.1.2.

Below v_{pred} are various categories, all optional, that select arguments and quasi-arguments of different kinds. Following Bowers (2010), I assume, in addition to v_{ag} (which may or may not be identified with v_{pred}: cf. note 2), the core thematic categories v_{th} and v_{aff}, as well as a variety of non-obligatory argument-like categories such as v_{goal}, v_{source}, v_{instr}, v_{ben}, and others. As for the lexical projections above v_{pred}, I will argue in Chapter 3 (cf. §3.1.3) that v_{tns} must be split into two distinct projections v_{tns} and v_{inf}. Below these categories,

---

[2] But see Bowers (2010) for an alternative view according to which the agent argument of transitives and unergatives is selected by a separate v_{ag} head projected earlier than all other thematic argument heads. I do not have space here to pursue this line of inquiry, but if it is correct, then either the agent-argument in actives or the theme-argument in passives must be pronounced at v_{pred} because of its athematic selection feature, depending on whether the sentence is active or passive. (See §2.4.1.4 for further discussion of this possibility.) More generally, it could either be the case that every minimal projection has only an athematic selection feature and that all arguments are introduced by argument projections below the minimal head, or, alternatively, that every minimal projection has either an athematic selection feature or a characteristic thematic selection feature. I will have to leave it to future research to determine which of these possibilities is correct.

but above v_{pred}, is at least one head containing the perfect auxiliary *have*, about which I will have more to say in §2.2.1.3.

2.1.2   n-*projections*

Following Bowers (1991, 2010), I designate the minimal obligatory category in the *n*-projection as n_{nom}, the feature [nom] being intended to indicate that *n*-projections refer to entities. In contrast to v_{pred}, n_{nom} never requires any kind of expletive such as *it* or *there*, hence does not have an athematic argument selector, though, as will be shown shortly, it can have a thematic selection feature. Below n_{nom} may appear the same range of arguments and quasi-arguments that appear in *v*-projections.[3] Above n_{nom} it has been standard since Abney's (1987) influential work to assume at least the determiner category n_{det}. Whether or not all languages must project n_{det} has been the subject of lively debate in recent years, and even in languages such as English that clearly project n_{det}, there is evidence that it is not required in all *n*-projections. I return to this issue in §2.2.2.1.

There is also strong cross-linguistic evidence supporting the existence of another nominal projection associated with the feature [number], which is located below n_{det} and above n_{nom}. I will designate this projection $n_{\#}$. As many researchers have observed, $n_{\#}$ is associated with the weak quantifiers *many, few, some* (unstressed), *a few*, etc., as well as the numerals *1,...,n* (cf. Bowers 1991, Picallo 1991, Ritter 1991, Valois 1991). Furthermore, it has been noted by Bowers (1991) and Higginbotham (1987) that these quantifiers behave like adjectives. Hence it may be assumed that they are minimal *a*-projections of the category a_{prop} to be discussed shortly (cf. §2.2.1.2) selected by $n_{\#}$:[4]

(3)

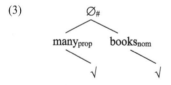

It has also been frequently noted that $n_{\#}$ is associated with indefiniteness and that the indefinite article *a(n)* in English is in complementary distribution with

---

[3] But see Bowers (2010: 167–172) for arguments that there exists at least one category n_{prtv} that appears to have no direct counterpart in *v*-projections.

[4] I assume, following most of the recent literature on nominals, that lexical nouns in English are pronounced at the n_{nom} position, never at the position of $n_{\#}$ or n_{det}. Hence n_{nom} in English must project $\emptyset_{\#}$ rather than $n_{\#}$.

the weak quantifiers and numerals, suggesting (following Perlmutter 1970) that it is also a weak quantifier selected by $n_\#$. Finally, noun classifiers, in languages that have them, are associated with $n_\#$ and typically follow weak quantifiers and numerals, as in the following example from Chinese:

(4)   jei   san-ben   shu
        this   3-CL   book
        'these three books'

suggesting that classifiers occupy the head position of $n_\#$.

Nominals differ from sentences in that all the arguments below n_{nom} must be headed by prepositions. Even so, they clearly correspond to the same argument categories that can be selected in *v*-projections, as has been shown in the extensive literature stemming from Chomsky (1970). Furthermore, given the systematic possibility of derived nominals such as *The enemy's destruction of the city*, it would appear that n_{nom} is parallel to v_{pred} in being able to select an agent nominal. This nominal must, however, be pronounced at n_{det} and marked with structural genitive Case (see Chapter 5 for further discussion), as can be seen when the noun is modified by a weak quantifier or prenominal adjective, e.g. *John's many books, the enemy's recent destruction of the city*, but **the many John's books, *the recent the enemy's destruction of the city*. Hence n_{det} must have an athematic argument selector just in case it has the null phonological form $\varnothing_{\mathrm{det}}$. These assumptions will result in the following derivation for *the enemy's destruction of the city*:

(5)

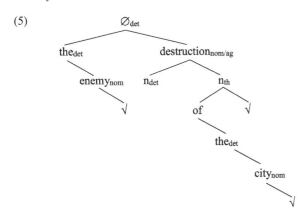

If the nominal is non-eventive, n_{nom} may optionally select an argument interpreted as a possessor, as in *the enemy's bombers*:

(6)

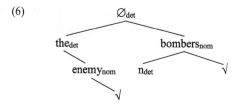

Parallel to the agentive argument in derived nominals, possessives must be selected by $\varnothing_{det}$, as shown by the fact that they also must appear to the left of prenominal adjectives and elements such as weak quantifiers associated with $n_\#$, e.g. *the enemy's many new bombers,*(the) many new the enemy's bombers.*

As is well known, prenominal possessives in English are in complementary distribution with demonstratives and articles:[5]

(7)   (*that/*this/*these/*those/*the) the enemy's (*that/*this/*these/*those/*the) bombers

This can be accounted for by assuming that demonstratives and the definite article *the* are themselves *n*-projections (cf. §2.2.2.1 for discussion) selected by v_{det}:

(8)

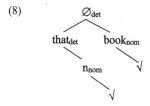

Supporting evidence comes from the fact that demonstratives are inflected for the nominal feature of number, as well as by the fact that the demonstratives can be used alone as arguments:

(9)   a. This/these is/are nice.
         b. That/those is/are horrible.

Neither property is true, of course, of the definite article in English, though both are true of articles in many languages, suggesting that *the* is simply a defective noun lacking even the feature of number, though still selected by n_{det}. Alternatively, *the* could simply be a n_{det} head lacking any selection features, rather than a lexical root. I will not try to decide between these two alternatives here.

---

[5] In fact, of course, demonstratives and articles can co-occur with possessives but only if the possessive is postposed, e.g. *that book of John's, those bombers of the enemy's*, etc. See Bowers (2010: 174–179), who uses this observation, among others, to argue that possessives ultimately derive from a subtype of the affectee argument.

In languages such as Danish the definite article is postnominal, e.g. *hund-en* 'the dog,' unless preceded by an adjective, in which case it is prenominal, e.g. *den store hund* 'the big dog.' Such observations can be accounted for by assuming that n_{det} may be realized either as a suffix *-en*, in which case it requires that the noun be pronounced in n_{det} in order to be morphologically well formed, or as $\emptyset$, in which case it must select the freestanding article *den* and must be selected by an intervening adjective selecting head n_{φ} (cf. §3.2.2 and §4.2 for motivation and discussion of this projection). Further evidence in support of the hypothesis that demonstratives and the definite article are selected by n_{det} will be discussed in §4.1, where it will be shown that it is crucial for explaining the attested range of word order variation found in nominals.

To conclude this brief overview of the *n*-projection, I will make one additional assumption, namely, that the highest possible head in the *n*-projection is not in fact n_{det} but a category I will designate as $n_{K(ase)}$. This category is manifested overtly in languages with pre- or postnominal Case-markers, and perhaps even marginally in English, which arguably has the postnominal genitive marker *'s*. However, I shall defer further discussion of this category until Chapters 4 and 6. Also, in order to save space, I will generally omit reference to n_K unless it is directly relevant to do so.

2.1.3   a-*projections*

The minimal projection of the lexical category *a* is a_{prop}, the feature [prop] intended to reflect the fact that *a*-projections refer to properties. Parallel to v_{pred}, examples can be found of a minimal a_{prop} projected from a 0-place adjectival root without any other arguments or lexical projections. In such cases, a_{prop} shares with v_{pred} the property of having an obligatory athematic argument selector that can only be satisfied by forming a relation with the expletive *it*:

(10)   a. I want *(it) cool (today).
        b. The furnace is making *(it) hot (in here).
        c. They have/keep *(it) (too) warm (in their house).

Such minimal *a*-projections are therefore derived as follows:

(11) $cool_{prop}$

Also parallel to v_{pred}, a_{prop} may have a thematic argument selection feature, yielding 1-place APs such as the following:

(12)   a. I want the house clean.
        b. The stove made the kettle hot.
        c. We have/make books available.

Similarly, *a*-projections share with *n*-projections the property that arguments below the minimal projection a_{prop} must be headed by prepositions:

(13)   a. John is fond *(of) Mary.
        b. Everyone is angry *(at) Hubert.
        c. They are all interested *(in) linguistics.

There is at least one projection above a_{prop} to which belong the set of degree elements such as *so, too, as, -er/more*, and *-est/most*. Following standard terminology, I will notate this projection a_{deg}. Hence the adjectival phrase in a sentence such as *I don't want him too fond of Mary* would be derived as follows:

(14)

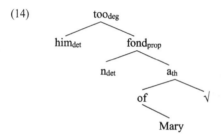

Notice that since the subject of adjectival predicates is pronounced before the degree word, the degree head a_{deg}, just like v_{tns} and n_{det}, must have an athematic argument selector which, as shown in (14), selects the argument *him*, previously selected by a_{prop}.

2.1.4   *p-projections*
It has been clear since early work by Emonds (1969) and Jackendoff (1977) that even the minor category preposition has a lexical projection. The minimal prepositional projection is p_{rel}, where the feature [rel] is meant to reflect the fact that prepositions generally express spatial and temporal relations between entities. Examples of the minimal *p*-projection are what Emonds (1969) called "intransitive" prepositions, that is, prepositions without an object:

(15)   a. John ran out/in/by/through/over/etc.
        b. The plane went up/down/away/etc.

Hence the minimal projection of p in such cases would be derived simply as follows:

(16)   out$_{rel}$

         √

An interesting question is whether PPs have subjects, as suggested by Bowers (1993, 2001b). If they do, then we might expect to find cases where p_{rel}, like v_{pred} and a_{prop}, has an athematic argument selector. Though it is not easy to find PPs with expletive subjects, there do seem to be a few:[6]

(17)   a. We can't have/we don't need/they don't want/etc. it out of control (in here).
         b. They want/they should have/they can't get/etc. it under control (out there).

There are also expressions such as *have it out (with someone), hash it out, cut it out, screw it up*, etc. where the pronoun *it* could be analyzed as the expletive subject of an intransitive preposition.

    Prepositions may also select a thematic subject, producing a phrase such as *send him out*, derived with a PRO subject as follows:

(18)   send$_{pred}$

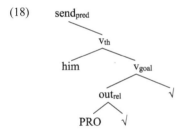

In examples such as *they want him out*, in contrast, the "subject" of *out* is lexical and the minimal projection p_{rel} is the thematic object of √want:

(19)   want$_{pred}$

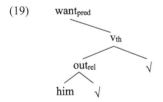

Below p_{rel} there can be a thematic argument, yielding "transitive" PPs such as *in the room*:

6 Thanks to Zac Smith for suggesting these examples.

(20)

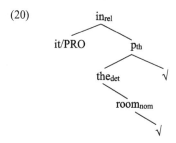

The "subject" of the preposition is either a lexical n_{det} or PRO, depending on whether it is the goal/locative argument of a raising predicate such as *want* or of a control predicate such as *put*, respectively. Prepositions such as *down* may also select a goal/locative argument, yielding expressions such as *down in the basement, out beyond the shack, up to the attic*, etc.:

(21)

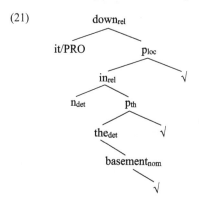

These selection processes can be embedded indefinitely, like other arguments, yielding complex PPs such as *He came up out from behind the basement steps.*

Finally, it has been argued that there is at least one projection above p_{rel} for adverbial qualifiers specific to the category *p* such as *right, straight, precisely, directly*, etc. Let us call this category p_{qual}. Then the *p*-projection in a sentence such as *We want them right on the table* would be derived as follows:

(22)

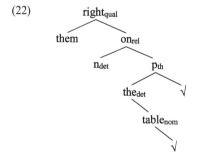

Note that the p_{qual} projection must have an athematic argument selection feature, since the subject *them* is pronounced to its left. Thus the "determiner" projection of every lexical category must have an athematic selection feature in English. Whether this property is universal or a parameter specific to English I leave as a question to be decided by future research.

2.1.5 Summary

Summarizing briefly, it has been shown that in order for lexical roots to be projected at all, there must be a minimal projection for each of the lexical categories *v, n, a, and p*. Each minimal projection apart from *n* must have at least an athematic selection feature, as shown by the fact that an expletive is required in the case of 0-place predicates. As mentioned in note 2, it may or may not be the case that each minimal projection also has a thematic selection feature, but in any event all thematic argument selecting heads, apart from possibly the minimal projection itself, are projected below the minimal projection, while above the minimal projection are projected a set of "functional" heads that differ in number and content depending on the category.[7]

2.2 Types of Arguments

I discuss next the range of possible projections that can be selected as arguments. The canonical type of argument is of course the noun phrase, or DP, as it is widely assumed to be in the recent literature. However, it is generally taken for granted that the extended projections of other categories, such as CP, PP, and AP, for example, can also be selected as arguments. In addition, there are so-called "defective" complements such as infinitival TP, as well as so-called "small clause" complements (including participial phrases), that are widely assumed in the literature to be able to function as arguments, despite the fact that the standard theory really provides no clear way to license them. I will show next that the existence of such defective categories is not merely possible but predicted by the theory proposed here. This in turn leads to a firmer theoretical grounding for certain kinds of parametric variation that have been argued for in recent work.

---

[7] It is possible that the *v*-projection is itself divided into two subdomains, a core domain whose highest projection is v_{pred} and an Infl/C domain whose highest projection is v_{comp}. Though intriguing, serious exploration of this idea is beyond the scope of this work.

2.2.1   Clausal Arguments

As is well known, nominal projections are not the only categories that can function as arguments. For example, the complement sentence headed by *that* in an example such as *they believe that he will eat* functions as the theme argument, as shown by the fact that it can be passivized, e.g. *That he will eat is believed by them*. Why should it be the case that v-projections as well as n-projections can be selected as arguments? The relational theory proposed here provides a straightforward answer to this fundamental question. The category v_{comp}, like n_{det}, does not have a lexical projection feature to be satisfied. Hence it is, by definition, an argument. Assuming, then, that *believe* may select the lexical projection v_{th}, and that v_{th} in turn may select v_{comp}, the following derivation for the example immediately results:[8]

(23)

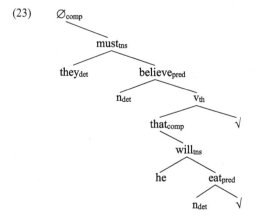

The fact that v_{comp}, as well as n_{det} (or n_K), can be selected as an argument thus follows directly from the axioms of the theory by virtue of the fact that it is saturated.

2.2.1.1   Defective TP Complements

Consider next so-called "defective" TP complements of the kind that have been argued to occur in exceptional Case-marking (ECM) structures such as *He seems to like cheese, I believe him to like cheese*, etc. How, one might ask, is it possible for a sentential complement obviously lacking any complementizer at all to function as the argument of a verb? This is actually quite a serious problem for the standard theory of f-selection. Given that the topmost category in the extended projection of V is C

---

[8] Henceforth I simplify derivations by omitting the internal structure of nominals and omitting category labels when it is clear from context what they are.

and that C selects T, T selects v, etc. it is not at all obvious what makes it possible for CP to be omitted from the extended projection of V. The theory simply provides no mechanism that licenses a TP projection lacking a CP layer to function as a complement. Hence all that can be said about such a TP complement is that it is a "defective" version of a (presumably) "normal" CP complement and it must simply be stipulated that certain verbs "exceptionally" select TP as a complement.

The relational theory proposed here, in contrast, provides a straightforward explanation for the existence of defective TP complements. In this theory, selection as well as derivation is fully bottom-up, so that v_{tns} selects v_{comp}, rather than vice versa. It is therefore not in the least surprising to find that certain types of v_{tns} elements have the option of either projecting v_{comp} or not. In particular, suppose that non-finite v_{tns} in English, realized lexically as *to*, has precisely the property that its lexical projection feature [__for$_{comp}$] is *optional*. But now observe that an instance of non-finite v_{tns} lacking a projection feature is, by definition, an argument! Once its argument selection feature has been satisfied, it has no lexical projection features remaining to be satisfied. It is therefore saturated, hence by definition an argument. There is thus nothing to prevent a root such as √seem or √believe from projecting a v_{th} with the argument selection feature [__to$_{tns}$], producing derivations of the following sort:[9]

(24)

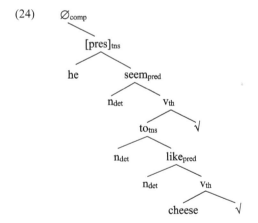

[9] I argue in Chapter 3 (cf. §3.1.3) that infinitival *to* is actually the head of a projection v_{inf} which is below v_{tns} and above v_{pred}. This revision does not materially affect the points made here concerning "defective" categories. See also §6.4.1 where it is argued that finite complements lacking a complementizer *that* are instances of v_{tns} that do not project v_{comp}.

Whether or not a given language makes use of this possibility is of course a language-specific property that simply has to be learned and, as is well known, not every language permits ECM complements of this kind. Notice, incidentally, that *he*, the agent of *like*, must be selected successively by *to* (in the *v*-projection of √like), by v_{pred} (in the *v*-projection of *seem*), and by *[pres]*$_{tns}$ (in the same projection), since all three projections have an athematic argument selection feature. As usual, however, only the leftmost occurrence of *he* is pronounced, thereby accounting for the appearance of raising of the infinitival subject into the matrix clause.

The general point is that in a relational theory of the kind proposed here, in which lexical projection categories are selected in strict bottom-up fashion, not only is it possible for so-called defective categories to exist, but that is precisely what one expects to find. The standard theory of c-selection, in contrast, fails to provide a principled reason for the existence of defective categories. The only connection between the sequence of maximal projections that constitute the extended verbal projection, in Grimshaw's sense, is f-selection. But f-selection is a downward relation: it tells us that C must select TP, T must select *v*P, etc., but there is no formal property of a maximal projection such as TP, for example, that tells us when it must function as an argument and when it must be part of the extended verbal projection. The standard theory of c-selection thus fails to explain why maximal projections such as TP are available for selection as arguments.

In a strictly bottom-up relational theory, in contrast, it is possible in principle for *any* lexical projection from the minimal projection on up to either project a higher lexical category or not. This in turn leads one to predict the existence of a wide variety of even smaller defective categories. In that light, it is illuminating to consider the much discussed issue of so-called "small clauses."

2.2.1.2   Small Clauses   It has been assumed thus far that v_{pred} selects v_{tns}, and that v_{tns} in turn selects v_{comp}. Now suppose that just as the lexical projection feature [_v_{comp}] may be optional for v_{tns}, so the lexical projection feature [_v_{tns}] may be optional for v_{pred}. Such an instance of v_{pred} that does not select v_{tns} is then, by definition, an argument, since it has no lexical projection features remaining to be satisfied, hence is saturated. There is thus no reason why such a non-projecting v_{pred} cannot be selected as an argument by projections such as v_{th}, v_{goal}, etc. Returning now to the minimal *v*-projections discussed in §2.1.1, suppose that a verb such as *make* is specified in the lexicon to select the argument category v_{th} with the argument selection feature [_v_{pred}]. This will automatically produce the following derivation for an example such as (1a):

(25)

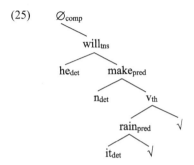

Similarly, there is no reason why the lexical projection feature of the minimal *a*-projection a_{prop} cannot be optional. Suppose the root √make selects v_{th} with the argument selection feature [_a_{prop}]. The result will be a sentence such as (10a) containing the "small clause" complement *it cool*:

(26)

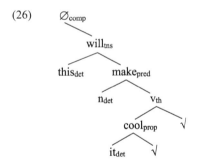

Similarly, if v_{th} selects the minimal *a*-projection of one-place adjectival predicates such as *strange*, then the relational structure of an ECM small clause complement such as that in *John considers him strange* will be derived:[10]

---

[10] The derivations of (27) and (28) are somewhat simplified. A full derivation would include selection of *him* by v_{tr}, accompanied by assignment of ACC Case. See Chapter 5 for details.

(27)

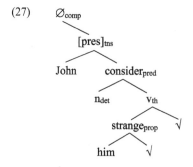

On the other hand, if the minimal *a*-projection of a root such as *drunk* is selected as an argument of a transitive verb such as *see*, then a control small clause complement such as that in *John saw him drunk* will be derived:[11]

(28)

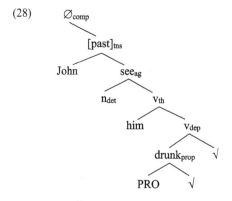

I assume, following Bowers (2010: 86–87), that there is a category v_{dep} ("dep" a mnemonic for "depictive") below v_{th} that selects a small clause as an argument.

Similarly, consider resultative constructions such as the following:

(29) a. John ran his Nikes threadbare.
   b. John watered the tulips flat.

Bowers (1997, 2001b) has shown that both of these examples contain a small clause functioning as a goal-argument, the difference between them being that

[11] See Bowers (1993, 1997, 2001b) for discussion of raising versus control in small clause constructions. Alternatively, rather than positing a PRO subject, the Relational θ-Criterion could be relaxed so as to permit the subject of the small clause to be selected by the thematic argument selection feature of a category such as v_{th} in (28). See Bowers (1993, 2008) and Hornstein (1999, 2001) for discussion.

(29a) is a raising construction, whereas (29b) is a control construction. Viewed in relational terms, then, a resultative construction results when a_{prop} is selected by v_{goal}. If the main verb is a raising predicate such as *run*, (29a) is derived:

(30)

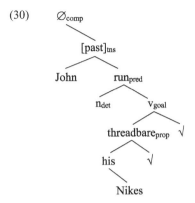

If, on the other hand, the main verb is a control predicate such as *water*, (29b) is derived:

(31)

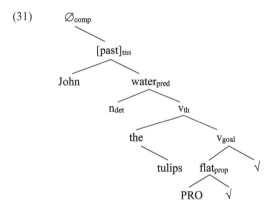

Further, *p*-projections can be selected as arguments, producing contrasts parallel to (2a) and (29b) such as the following:

(32)   a. They consider John in the know.
        b. They put John in the dungeon.

In (32a), a raising construction, the minimal p_{rel} projection *John in the know* is selected as a v_{th} argument, while in (32b), a control construction, the minimal *in*$_{rel}$ head with a PRO subject is selected by *put*$_{loc}$.

Despite the fact that there is widespread agreement in the literature that small clauses must exist, linguists have been hard put to find a reasonable and well-motivated constituent structure to assign to them. As often as not, they are simply represented as a constituent with the *ad hoc* label "SC," though there have been attempts to account for their structure in a more principled way.[12] In the relational theory proposed here, however, a small clause is nothing more than a minimal lexical projection lacking any further lexical projection features that need to be satisfied. Such non-projecting v_{pred}, a_{prop}, and p_{rel} heads are therefore by definition arguments, hence able to be selected by argument heads, if the language in question so permits. The vexing question of what type of constituent to assign small clauses to and how to label it simply does not arise.

2.2.1.3　Participial Small Clauses　It has been assumed thus far that there is just one type of v_{pred} that can be selected as an argument, namely, bare infinitival complements. There are, however, participial forms of the main verb in English expressing perfect aspect, progressive aspect, and passive voice, which must be accompanied by the verbal auxiliaries *have, be*, and *be*, respectively:

(33)　　a. He has eaten the bagel.
　　　　b. He is eating the bagel.
　　　　c. The bagel was eaten.

As is well known, these forms of the verb can be combined with one another as long as the fixed order perfect-progressive-passive is preserved:

(34)　　a. He has been eating bagels.
　　　　b. The bagels have been eaten.
　　　　c. The bagels are being eaten.
　　　　d. Bagels have been being eaten.

One way of accounting for this data is to assume that each type of participle projects a specific v-head of the appropriate phonetic form. Suppose, for example, that the progressive auxiliary *be* is the lexical realization of a projection v_{prog} which is selected by the progressive participial form of v-ing_{pred}. An example such as *He should be eating bagels* could then be derived as follows:

---

[12] For one such line of research, see Bowers (1993, 1997, 2001b) and related work, especially Bailyn (1995a, 1995b, 1995c).

(35)

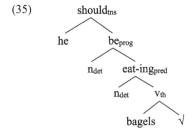

In parallel fashion the corresponding passive sentence could be derived as follows:

(36)

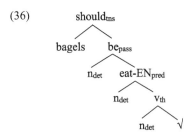

There are, however, a number of major problems with this approach.

First of all, in order to produce passive progressive sentences such as (34c), it will be necessary to assume that $v\text{-}ing_{pred}$ can be selected by be_{pass}, thereby making v_{pred} a recursive projection. Then, in order to prevent massive overgeneration, it will be necessary to impose an array of highly specific selection features. For example, the opposite order of selection, namely, selection of $v\text{-}EN_{pred}$ by be_{prog}, must be ruled out. Similarly, though the perfect participle $v\text{-}EN_{pred/perf}$ may be selected by either be_{prog} or be_{pass}, neither $v\text{-}ing_{pred}$ nor $v\text{-}EN_{pred}$ may be selected by $have_{perf}$. And so forth.

A second problem is posed by the distribution of the existential expletive *there*. As is well known, *there* may occur in progressive, passive, and progressive passive sentences, but in the last of these it may only be associated with the first instance of *be* that accompanies the progressive participle:

(37) a. There is someone eating bagels.
  b. There were some bagels eaten.
  c. There are some bagels being eaten.
  d. *There are being some bagels eaten.
  e. *There are there being some bagels eaten.

It was proposed in Chapter 1 that *there* may be selected by v_{pred} just in case it has an athematic selection feature. In order to account for the data in (37), however, it will be necessary to stipulate that *there* may be selected by be_{prog} and be_{pass}, as well, making it impossible to characterize the occurrence of *there* in a simple and unified fashion. Worse yet, there will be no way of preventing *there* from being selected by either be_{prog} or be_{pass} in passive progressive sentences, producing both the grammatical (37c) and the ungrammatical (37d). For that matter, *there* could be selected by both be_{prog} and be_{pass}, producing (37e).

A third problem arises from the fact that both progressive and passive phrases may appear as subjects in English, parallel to Locative Inversion:

(38)   a. On the table are three books.
        b. Sitting on the fence was a crow.
        c. Arrested for larceny were several linguists.
        d. Being arrested at this very moment are several protestors.

Adapting the analysis of Bowers (2002) to the relational framework, I propose to account for Locative Inversion by specifying that the athematic argument selection feature of v_{pred} may select either a *p*-projection or an *n*-projection or *there* (see §2.4.2.1 for more detailed discussion of Locative Inversion). Now suppose we try to extend this analysis to progressive and passive inversion by giving be_{prog} and be_{pass} the option of selecting the progressive or passive participial v_{pred} heads, respectively, from which they are projected. The problem is that this will produce incorrect examples such as the following:

(39)   a. *A crow sitting on the fence was.
        b. *Several linguists arrested for larceny were.
        c. *Several protestors being arrested at this very moment are.

The reason is that the v_{th} argument is contained in the *v-ing*$_{pred}$ and *v-EN*$_{pred}$ heads that project be_{prog} and be_{pass}, respectively. Worse yet, such an operation is not even well defined in this framework, for reasons that will be made clear in §2.3, because the heads in question are not arguments but part of the *v*-projection itself.[13]

It seems clear, then, that treating progressive and passive participles as auxiliary verbs contained in the main *v*-projection simply will not work. A clue to a better approach is provided by the observation that both progressive and passive participles can serve as small clause arguments of lexical verbs other than *be*:

---

[13] In standard Minimalism, the required operation could be ruled out as a violation of anti-locality, a condition that has been proposed to prevent a complement from recombining with a projection of its selecting head: cf. Abels and Neeleman (2008: 22–23) and the references therein. In the relational framework, anti-locality need not be stipulated as a separate condition, since the same result follows trivially from general principles.

(40)   a. I saw/had/want him eating bagels.
        b. I saw/had/want bagels eaten (by them).
        c. I saw/had/want bagels being eaten (by them).

Suppose we now simply include *be* in the set of verbs that may select such participial small clauses.[14] Then progressive sentences can be derived as follows:[15]

(41)

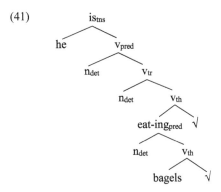

Passive sentences are derived in a parallel fashion:

(42)

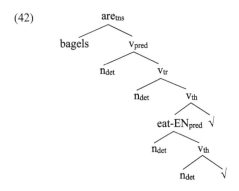

This analysis solves all the problems. First, the restrictions on the occurrence of expletive *there* are explained by the fact that v_{pred} can only select *there* if it is the

---

[14] For similar reasons, copular sentences with predicate adjectives and nominals, e.g. *he is interested in linguistics, Mary is an interesting person*, etc. should also be analyzed as small clause arguments of main verb *be*, predicting correctly that both can undergo inversion, e.g. *interested in linguistics are several undergrads, an interesting person is Mary*, etc. (cf. Bowers 2002 for details). It follows, as argued extensively in Bowers (1993, 1997, 2001b), that such small clause complements are v_{pred} projections.

[15] In this derivation, as in the ones that follow, I anticipate the treatment of transitivity discussed in Chapter 5. There, following Bowers (2002), I posit a head v_{tr} with an athematic selection feature, which is also responsible for selecting structural ACC Case in transitive sentences.

main verb in a v-projection, i.e. if it is non-participial. This restriction is independently motivated, since participial v_{pred} can never select *there*, even if the verb is unaccusative or passive:

(43)   a. *I saw/had/want there rolling a ball down the hill.
        b. *We saw/had/want there being bagels eaten.

The fact that *there* can only be selected by the first instance of *be* in passive progressive sentences (cf. (37c,d)) then follows automatically because the lower instance of *be*, namely *be-ing*$_{pred}$, is participial, hence unable to select *there*.[16]

(44)

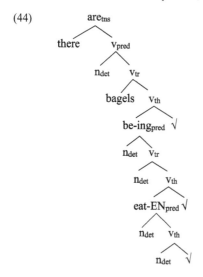

It is also necessary to specify that progressive participial *be* can select passive participial *be*, but not vice versa. This assumption is independently needed in order to account for examples such as (40c) containing passive participial complements of lexical verbs such as *see, have, want*, etc. Hence the fact that the progressive auxiliary must precede the passive auxiliary reduces to a simple matter of selection.[17]

This analysis also explains why progressive and passive inversion are possible. Since progressive and passive participial heads are analyzed as

---

[16] Anticipating the discussion of morphology in Chapter 5, I assume that fully inflected forms of roots are listed in LEX and that morphological features (in this instance, [prog] or [pass]) may be built into the selection features of verbal roots and their projections, as spelled out below. See also the discussion of the lexical realization of v_{tns} in §6.1.

[17] Technically, progressive *be-ing* projects a v_{th} head that itself selects a passive participle: cf. the discussion of lexical selection properties of roots in §1.3.5.

small clause arguments rather than as a part of the lexical projection of the main verb, they can optionally be selected by be_{pred} in derivations (41), (42), and (44) in place of *there* or the thematic argument, producing examples such as (38b–d). Furthermore, the subject of the displaced participle will no longer be incorrectly pronounced along with it, as it was in the first analysis, because the thematic argument is selected independently of the participial small clause.

In the light of this proposal, consider the fact that perfect participles, in contrast to progressive and passive participles, can never be selected as small clause complements:

(45) *I saw/had/wanted him eaten the bagels.

Similarly, $have_{perf}$ can never select *there* or undergo inversion:

(46) a. *There has someone eaten the bagels.
    b. *Eaten the bagels has someone.

These systematic differences can be explained if it is assumed that perfect *have*, in contrast to progressive and passive *be*, actually is a true auxiliary verb projected above v_{pred}:

(47)

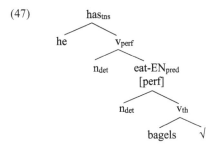

This shows, incidentally, that perfect and passive *-EN* should not be treated as the same morpheme, contra Collins (2005), since they have totally different selection properties. The former must select the lexical projection $have_{perf}$, whereas the latter has no further projection features, hence must itself be selected as an argument.

2.2.2 *Nominal Arguments*

As was mentioned earlier, the canonical type of argument is the *n*-projection. If a root projects the highest nominal category n_{det} (or n_K), then it is by definition an argument, since it has no lexical projection features to be satisfied. It was shown previously, however, that there are at least two nominal projections

below n_{det}, namely $n_{\#}$ and n_{nom}. In a bottom-up theory of lexical projection
there is no reason why the lexical projection features of these lower categories
could not be optional. From the point of view of the standard theory of
selection, it would simply have to be stipulated that such defective nominal
categories can exceptionally be selected as arguments. In the theory proposed
here, in contrast, such "small nominals" are, by definition, arguments since
they are saturated. We therefore predict that languages should not only have
small nominal arguments with all the properties of $n_{\#}$ projections, but that
even the minimal n-projection n_{nom} should be able to be selected as an
argument in certain cases. I show next that both predictions are borne out
by the facts.

2.2.2.1   Small Nominals: $n_{\#}$ Pursuing this line of investigation, let us
consider first whether it is ever possible for defective $n_{\#}$ categories that lack
the projection feature [_n_{det}] to function as arguments. In fact, objects of just
this sort exist in many languages. In particular, Pereltsvaig (2006) provides
extensive argumentation in support of the claim that there are two kinds of
subject nominal in Russian, which she terms "agreeing" and "non-agreeing."
Despite the fact that a phrase such as *pjat' izvestnyk aktërov* 'five famous
actors' is phonetically identical in the two cases, the two types of subject can
be systematically distinguished by a series of syntactic and semantic properties, starting with contrasts in agreement such as the following (Pereltsvaig
2006: 438–439):

(48)   a. V ètom   fil'me   igrali   pjat'   izvestnyk   aktërov.
         in this   film   played.PL   five   famous   actors
         'Five famous actors played in this film.'

        b. V ètom   fil'me   igralo   pjat'   izvestnyk   aktërov.
         in this   film   played.NEUT   five   famous   actors
         'Five famous actors played in this film.'

Pereltsvaig shows that the subject in (48a) has an individuated (i.e. non-group,
non-mass) interpretation, whereas (48b) has a non-individuated or group
interpretation. Similarly, agreeing subjects can have specific reference, hence
are compatible with adjectives denoting specificity such as *opredelënnye*
'certain,' whereas non-agreeing adjectives are not. There is also a correlation
between agreement patterns and the availability of a partitive interpretation,
only agreeing subjects allowing the latter. Likewise, there are scopal
differences between agreeing and non-agreeing subjects, the former at least
permitting non-isomorphic scope, while the latter do not. Similarly, only

agreeing subjects can take wide scope with respect to negation. Agreement also correlates with the possibility of control and anaphor binding. On the other hand, there is a construction termed "approximative inversion" in the Slavic literature that is possible only with non-agreeing subjects. Finally, agreeing subjects can be replaced with personal pronouns, whereas non-agreeing subjects can only be replaced with *stolk'o* 'that much/many' and *skolk'o* 'how much/many.'

Pereltsvaig argues that this array of differences in syntactic behavior and semantic interpretation between agreeing and non-agreeing subjects can be explained if the former have a null D head that projects DP containing φ-features, whereas the latter are bare QPs that lack a DP projection and hence lack φ-features as well. Transposed into the relational theory proposed here, non-agreeing subjects project only to $n_\#$, i.e. are small nominals, whereas agreeing subjects project to the highest nominal head n_{det} (ultimately to n_K). Pereltsvaig goes on to show that both DPs and QPs can occur in object position as well and, furthermore, that the latter can be selected by certain heads, for example, the perfectivizing cumulative prefix *na-*, which has a perfective interpretation:

(49)   a. Džejms Bond skopiroval čerteži.
               James   Bond copied   blueprints.ACC
               'James Bond copied {some/the} blueprints.'

          b. Džejms Bond **na**kopiroval čertežej.
               James   Bond CUM-copied blueprints.GEN
               'James Bond copied (many) blueprints.'

Crucially, the genitive Case-marked objects of verbs with cumulative *na-* cannot project n_{det}, because they cannot contain elements of that level, including demonstratives, pronouns, and proper names.

I cannot do justice here to the full range of data and persuasive argumentation presented by Pereltsvaig, for which I refer the interested reader to her paper. Suffice it to say, she provides convincing evidence that Russian nominals come in two sizes that correspond precisely to what I have termed the n_{det} projection and the $n_\#$ projection. I would only like to supplement her arguments with some discussion of a well-known construction in English which I believe can be shown to select an $n_\#$ small nominal. I refer to the famous "definiteness effect" in the existential expletive construction, first noted and extensively discussed by Milsark (1974). As the following data shows, the only quantifiers that can occur in the nominal associated with the expletive *there* in the existential construction are weak quantifiers selected by $n_\#$, demonstratives and strong quantifiers being excluded in this position:

(50)   a. There is/are a/one/3/many/few/no/some/∅/etc. book(s) on the table.
　　　b. *There is/are the/this/that/these/those/all/most/each/etc. book(s) on the table.

(51)   a. There is some/little/much/no/∅/etc. milk in the pitcher.
　　　b. *There is the/this/that/all/most/etc. milk in the pitcher.

The definiteness effect can thus be explained, at least in part, if one of the syntactic conditions for selection of expletive *there* by v_{pred} is that the associated argument selected by v_{th} must be a small nominal $n_\#$ (and may not be a full n_{det}/n_K projection). This, then, is a clear case in English where a small $n_\#$ nominal is selected under certain well-defined syntactic conditions. Some further cases of this sort will be discussed shortly.

2.2.2.2   Smallest Nominals: n_{nom} The next question is whether even smaller projections such as the minimal projection n_{nom} can be selected as arguments. The answer appears to be affirmative. One systematic example discussed by Pereltsvaig (2006) is that of bare singulars in languages such as Norwegian (cf. Kallulli 1999, Borthen 2003, Julien 2004, 2005 for discussion), as in the following example:

(52)   Jeg   bruker   ikke   nakent   nomen.
　　　I   use   not   naked   nominal
　　　'I don't use bare nominal.'

Pereltsvaig shows that bare singulars have all the properties listed in §2.2.2.1 for small nominals in Russian, namely, lack of specific and partitive interpretations, non-isomorphic wide scope, inability to control PRO or antecede anaphors, and lack of agreement with the predicate. In addition, bare nominals can only be replaced with the pronominal form *det* 'that. NEUT' whereas a full n_{det} nominal must be replaced with *den* 'it.MASC.' It is clear, however, that bare nominals are even smaller than small nominals in Russian, since they cannot select even weak quantifiers or numerals and only occur in the singular. I propose therefore that a bare nominal is simply a n_{nom} head that projects no further.[18]

Pereltsvaig notes further that in many languages, including English, German, French, Spanish, and Italian, bare n_{nom} nominals can be selected by prepositions:[19]

---

[18] Note, however, that bare nominal in Norwegian can have prenominal adjectival modifiers, as in
　　　(52) above. I discuss prenominal adjectives in Chapter 3: cf. §3.2.2.
[19] McIntyre (2001) refers to these as "Small PPs."

(53)   a. They put him in (*the/*this/*a/*one/etc.) prison(*s).
        b. The children went to (*the/*that/*a/*one/etc.) school(*s).

Smallest nominals can also occur as objects:

(54)   a. He took (*the/*this/*a/*one/*much/etc.) charge(*s) of the company.
        b. The general took (*the/*this/*a/*one/*much/etc.) command(*s) of the regiment.

What does not seem to have been noticed, however, is that constructions of this type contrast with superficially similar ones in which the object is clearly an $n_\#$ projection rather than an n_{nom} projection:

(55)   a. They paid (*the/*this/*most/etc.) much/little/some/no/$\varnothing$/etc. attention to him.
        b. I give (*the/*this/*most/etc.) much/little/some/no/$\varnothing$/etc. credence to his claims.
        c. We took (*the/*this/*most/etc.) much/little/some/no/$\varnothing$/etc. pleasure in his discomfort.

These are all examples in which the selected nominal is a mass noun rather than a count noun (which explains why the noun cannot be plural), but examples of the latter sort can be found as well:

(56)   I took (*the/*this/*every/etc.) a/few/a few/$\varnothing$/etc. picture(s) of Mary.

We thus find minimal pairs consisting of a verb and thematic object where the n-projection selected must in one case be $n_\#$ and in the other n_{nom}.

    I conclude that just as verbal arguments come in a variety of different sizes, so nominal arguments do as well, lending further support to a strictly bottom-up relational theory of the sort proposed here in which it is not only possible but entirely natural to find that intermediate projections of virtually any size can simply fail to project any further, thus qualifying, by definition, as arguments.

2.2.3   *Parametric Variation in Lexical Projection*

Once the possibility of selecting a whole range of defective argument categories is opened up, it becomes perfectly reasonable to entertain the idea that such options might be systematically parameterized. Thus it has been suggested in the recent literature (cf. Bošković 2005, 2008, 2009, Despić 2011, 2013) that there are languages lacking a DP projection altogether. In such languages all nominals are in effect small nominals. From the point of view of the standard top-down theory of selection, such a notion makes little sense, because a bare NumP or NP would simply be an anomaly, a nominal projection that is defective in the same way that TP complements and small clause complements are said to be defective relative to CP. It would therefore be quite strange to argue that a language could exist in which *all* projections of a given category are defective. From the viewpoint of the theory proposed here, in contrast, such cross-linguistic parameterization is not at all odd. At the same time, it is an empirical question whether or not there is any natural language that does in fact completely lack one or more levels of projection such as n_{det}. It might still be the case that all languages project all the lexical projections made available by universal grammar, even though projections of different sizes can be selected under particular conditions. Establishing the even stronger claim that there exist languages in which n_{det}, for instance, is never projected at all entails a good deal of complication. For example, it would have to be claimed that demonstrative elements in such a language have quite different properties from demonstratives in a language that does project n_{det}.

The same kind of considerations apply to v-projections. Languages such as Chinese, for example, have no complementizers at all: whatever evidence there is, if any, to support the existence of a v_{comp} level is necessarily indirect. It would therefore be perfectly reasonable to entertain the hypothesis that Chinese uniformly fails to project v_{comp}, in other words, that the v_{tns} head in Chinese systematically lacks the lexical projection feature [_v_{comp}]. Whether such an analysis is viable is not a question I will try to decide here. As in the case of nominal projections, however, difficulties immediately arise. If, for example, as will be shown in Chapter 6, v_{comp} is an island for extraction, would it follow that in a language lacking v_{comp} altogether there are no island effects?

2.3   *Relational Derivation Refined: Selection of Lexical Subarrays*

Returning now to more general considerations, the discussion of lexical projection and argument selection in the preceding sections opens the way to further clarification of the difference between argument selection and lexical projection, as well as to further refinement of the architecture of relational derivation. Recall that in Chapter 1 the final form of the definition of the phonetic form PF of a term α of a relation was as follows:

(57)   *Definition*: The *phonetic form* PF(α) of a term α of a relation (irrespective of whether it is the head or the dependent term) is:
    (i) $\underline{\alpha}$, if α is an LI selected from LA; or
    (ii) $\underline{\sigma}_\alpha$, where $\underline{\sigma}_\alpha$ is the string produced by applying Spell-out to the most recently formed relation containing α as a term.

Now consider the following derivation of the sentence *The boy will eat*:

(58)   1 $<\sqrt{}eat,eat_{ag}>$ eat-~~eat~~

    2   $<\sqrt{}boy,boy_{nom}>$ boy-~~boy~~

    3   $<boy_{nom},the_{det}>$ the-boy-~~boy~~

    4   $<eat_{ag},the_{det}>$ the-boy-~~boy~~- eat-~~eat~~

    5   $<eat_{ag},will_{tns}>$ will-the-boy-~~boy~~- eat-~~eat~~

    6   $<will_{tns},the_{det}>$?

    7   $<will_{tns},\varnothing_{comp}>$

It is immediately evident that there is a problem at step 6 of the derivation. Applying part (ii) of the definition of PF in (57) to the second term of the relation in step 6 will yield the string produced at step 4: PF(the)= the-boy-~~boy~~-eat-~~eat~~, which, combined with the output of step 5, will yield nonsense: the-boy-~~boy~~-eat-~~eat~~-will-the-boy-~~boy~~-eat-~~eat~~. Obviously, the correct output can only be produced by ordering the output of step 3, rather than step 4, to the left of the output of step 5, yielding the string: the-boy-~~boy~~-will-~~the~~-boy-~~boy~~-eat-~~eat~~. The difficulty is that there is no obvious basis for selecting *the* from the relation formed at step 3, rather than from the relation formed at step 4. In fact, the minimality constraint built into part (ii) of the definition of PF in (57) would seem to require that step 4 be preferred, since it is closer.

The problem with the derivation in (58) is that it conflates two separate projections, namely, the *v*-projection of the root √eat and the *n*-projection of the root √boy. Rather than trying to produce a single monolithic derivation for the entire sentence, what we need to do is to derive the *n*-projection separately and then integrate its output with the output of the *v*-projection at the appropriate point in the derivation of the latter. But what *is* the appropriate point? Is it possible to predict where in the derivation of a lexical projection LP_1 the phonetic output of another derivation LP_2 should be integrated with the phonetic output of LP_1? In fact, the theory already provides the answer to this question: LP_2 must be integrated with LP_1 whenever a projection α of LP_1 has an argument selection feature that can be satisfied by forming a relation $<α,β>$ with the highest projection β of LP_2. Recall that an argument, by definition, is a saturated LI. Obviously the highest category in an *n*-projection is saturated. Hence an argument selection feature can be satisfied just in case there is an independently formed, lexical projection available whose highest projection meets its requirements.[20]

---

[20] Satisfaction of an argument selection feature is thus reminiscent of the generalized transformations that embedded an independently formed subtree into another one in the pre-*Aspects* version of generative grammar.

In order to make this idea more precise, let us assume that every derivation begins, not by forming a single lexical array LA, but by forming a set of one or more *lexical subarrays* SA_i, each of which consists of a lexical root $\sqrt{R_i}$ and a set of lexical projections $\lambda^i_{1, \ldots, n}$. FR then applies independently to each SA_i, forming a lexical projection LP_i. Each time there is a lexical projection feature to be satisfied in the course of forming LP_i, a new LI must be drawn from the lexical subarray SA_i. Each time there is an argument selection feature to be satisfied, on the other hand, the highest LI in another projection LP_k formed from separate subarray SA_k must be selected.

In the case at hand, there would be two SAs: (i) $SA_1=\{\sqrt{boy}, n_{nom}, the_{det}\}$; (ii) $SA_2=\{\sqrt{eat}, v_{ag}, will_{tns}, \varnothing_{comp}\}$. FR applies to each SA separately, forming the two projections LP_1 and LP_2:

(59)

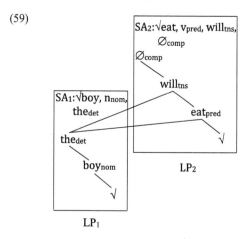

Each time a link is added to the lexical projections LP_1 or LP_2, a new LI is picked from SA_1 or SA_2, respectively. If, however, an LI, e.g. v_{pred} in LP_2, has an argument selection feature to be satisfied, then it must select a saturated LI from a different lexical projection such as LP_1. The reason is that by hypothesis all the LIs available in SA_2 are unsaturated. The only place that v_{pred} can find a saturated LI to form a relation with is in a separate n-projection such as LP_1. Assuming that the closest saturated LI in any given lexical projection is always the highest one (see §2.4 for further discussion), v_{pred} in LP_2 must then form a relation with the highest projection the_{det} in LP_1. Likewise, after v_{pred} projects $will_{tns}$ in LP_2, the athematic argument feature of the latter can only be satisfied by forming a relation with the same LI the_{det} in LP_1.

The derivation in (58) can now be reformulated in terms of two subderivations as follows:

(60) $SA_1 = \{\sqrt{boy}, n_{nom}, the_{det}\}$ $SA_2 = \{\sqrt{eat}, v_{pred}, will_{tns}, \emptyset_{comp}\}$.

  1 $<\sqrt{boy},boy_{nom}>$ boy-~~boy~~   1 $<\sqrt{eat},eat_{pred}>$ eat-~~eat~~

  2 $<boy_{nom},the_{det}>$ the-boy-~~boy~~   2 $<eat_{ag},the_{det}>$ the-boy-~~boy~~-eat-~~eat~~

    3 $<eat_{ag},will_{tns}>$ will-the-boy-~~boy~~-eat-~~eat~~

    4 $<will_{tns},the_{det}>$ the-boy-~~boy~~ will-~~the-boy-boy~~-eat-~~eat~~

    5 $<will_{tns},\emptyset_{comp}>\emptyset$- the-boy-~~boy~~ will-~~the-boy-boy~~-eat-~~eat~~

With this refinement in place, the problem with derivation (58) pointed out earlier simply does not arise because the lexical projection features of a given head can only be satisfied by forming a relation with an LI chosen from the SA containing that head, while an argument selection feature can only be satisfied by forming a relation with the highest (saturated) LI of a projection formed from a different SA.[21] In short, the point at which one projection must be integrated with another one is completely determined by the general constraints developed in Chapter 1, together with the specific properties of the lexical roots and LIs contained in the respective SAs. That being the case, there is no harm in continuing to use the canonical projection trees developed in Chapter 1 without having to mark explicitly the fact that each argument is projected from a separate subarray.

  Finally, let us reformulate the definition of PF that provides the input to Spell-out. There are three cases to be covered. First, for any LI α drawn directly from a lexical subarray SA_i, PF(α) is simply $\underline{\alpha}$. Second, for any α selected from a relation previously formed in the derivation of SA_i, PF(α) is the string σ_α resulting from the application of Spell-out to the most recent relation containing α in the derivation of SA_i. Third, for any α selected from an independent subarray SA_j, where α is the highest projection of SA_j, PF(α) is the string σ_α resulting from applying Spell-out to the projection formed from SA_j. The definition may thus be formulated as follows:

(61) *Definition*: The *phonetic form* PF(α) of a term α of a relation formed in a subarray SA_i is:
  (i) $\underline{\alpha}$, α an LI selected from SA_i; or
  (ii) σ_α, the string produced by applying Spell-out to the most recent relation in SA_i containing α; or
  (iii) σ_α, the string produced by applying Spell-out to the projection formed from an independent subarray SA_j, whose highest projection is α.

---

[21] This also resolves the ambiguity of root projections mentioned in note 31 in Chapter 1. An LI with no selection features left to be satisfied is an argument if it is contained in a different projection from that of the head λ that selects it, whereas an LI selected by λ is a (root) lexical projection, even if it has no selection features to be satisfied, if it is contained in the same projection as λ.

The formulation of Spell-out remains in the final form arrived at in Chapter 1:

(62)   *Spell-out*:
        $<\alpha,\beta> \Rightarrow PF(\beta)\text{-}PF(\alpha)$

As is evident from the derivation in (60), Spell-out will produce, in essentially the same way as suggested in Chapter 1, the correct linear ordering of phonetic forms at PF.

In order to produce a complete sentence, a relational derivation must form a tree, i.e. there must be only one highest LI that is not selected as an argument by any other LI. Obviously, this can only be guaranteed if there is one and only one subarray whose highest projection is not selected as an argument by any LI. We may call this designated subarray the *root* subarray SA_{root}. In order for a derivation to be complete, every subarray must be selected as an argument at some point by an LI in SA_{root} or by an LI in some other subarray.

2.4   Limiting Accessibility: The RPIC Revisited

I conclude this chapter by reconsidering the Relational Phase Impenetrability Condition (RPIC), tentatively put forward in Chapter 1. I first show that given the final version of the theory proposed there, together with the refinements discussed in this chapter, the RPIC can be eliminated and replaced with a much simpler Accessibility Condition (AC) that limits access to argument projections, while all the remaining effects of the RPIC can be derived from the fundamental axioms of the theory. I then consider a less stringent version of the AC based on a relational interpretation of the minimalist notion of derivation by phase, which I term the *Phase Accessibility Condition* (PAC). I conclude by discussing a number of novel empirical arguments in support of the PAC.

2.4.1   The Accessibility Condition

Suppose that λ is a head, β is the LI that λ forms a relation with first (i.e. its complement), and α is the LI that λ forms a relation with second. The RPIC states that as soon as λ is saturated, neither its complement β nor any heads contained in β are accessible to FR, leaving just α and λ itself accessible to further operations. This formulation, however, is based on the standard assumption that selection is top-down. Given the revised theory in which selection is fully bottom-up, together with the revisions proposed in §2.3, the constraints embodied in the RPIC can be separated into three cases: (i) constraints on the application of FR *within* a given subarray SA_1; (ii) constraints on the application of FR within any subarrays $SA_2, \ldots, SA_n$, which satisfy the argument selection features of $LI_2, \ldots, LI_n$, respectively, in SA_1; (iii) constraints on which subarrays $SA_2, \ldots, SA_n$ can be selected by which heads $LI_2, \ldots, LI_n$ in SA_1. I will show now that cases (i) and (ii) follow directly from the axioms of the theory, while case (iii) can be accounted for by all that remains of the RPIC, namely, a simple and general constraint governing the accessibility of argument projections.

To illustrate (i), consider the derivation of SA_2 in (60). There are two subcases. First, it is necessary to ensure that the head eat_{pred} of the relation formed at step 3 of the derivation is taken from the relation formed at the previous step 2, not from the relation formed at step 1. Second, the head $will_{tns}$ at step 5 must be taken from the relation formed at step 4, not from the one formed at step 3. To illustrate (ii), consider the selection of the_{det} in SR_1 by eat_{pred} in SR_2. The question here is why eat_{pred} could not form a relation with boy_{nom} at step 1 of SR_1 rather than with the_{det}, assuming that eat_{pred} had an argument selection feature $[\_n_{nom}]$. Both (i) and (ii) are explained by IG. Taking (i) first, the reason the term eat_{pred} of the relation formed at step 3 can only be eat_{pred} at step 2 is that the latter has a lexical projection feature that must be satisfied immediately. If we tried to take eat_{pred} from the ordered pair produced at step 1, then the selection feature of eat_{pred} at step 2 would fail to be satisfied immediately, violating IG. The same reasoning applies to $will_{tns}$ at step 5. More generally, as soon as an LI is selected from a given subarray, IG requires that its selection features be satisfied immediately, making it impossible to go back to any earlier relation in which that LI appeared. As for (ii), it is also explained by IG. The LI boy_{nom} in SR_1 is unsaturated, since it still has selectors that must be satisfied. Therefore, it cannot be selected to satisfy an argument selection feature.[22] The LI the_{det}, in contrast, is fully saturated and may therefore satisfy an argument selection feature. More generally, it will always be the case that only the topmost LI in the derivation of any given subarray will be available to form a relation with an LI in another subarray with an unsatisfied argument selection feature. We have thus succeeded in deriving cases (i) and (ii) of the RPIC from general principles.

To illustrate (iii), we need to look at a derivation containing at least two *n*-projections that could potentially satisfy an argument selection feature of an LI in a *v*-projection. Consider, for example, the following derivation of the sentence *The boy will kiss the girl*:

---

[22] Note, however, that if SR_1 was a "small nominal" whose highest projection was n_{nom}, then n_{nom} would of course be saturated and could therefore be selected as an argument by an LI in SR_2 with the selection feature $[\_n_{nom}]$.

(63)

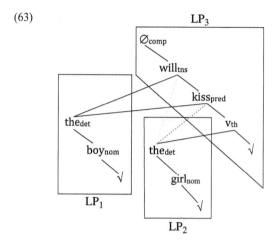

Let us assume that *kiss*th selects *the*det in LP2 to satisfy its argument selection feature. The next head with an argument selection feature that needs to be satisfied is *kiss*pred. The question is why *kiss*pred in LP3 must form a relation with *the*det in LP1 rather than with *the*det in LP2 (the offending relation is shown by the dotted line in (63)). In this case the correct result can be derived from the Relational θ-Criterion proposed in Chapter 1, since the latter derivation would result in *the girl* being assigned two θ-roles. However, we cannot appeal to the same principle to explain why the next head *will*tns with an argument selection feature must form a relation with *the*det in LP1 rather than with *the*det in LP2, since no violation of the Relational θ-Criterion would result in either case. (The offending relation in this instance is shown by the dashed line in (63).)

One way of thinking about this, as pointed out in Chapter 1, is in terms of distance. There are three links connecting *will*tns to *the*det in LP2, whereas there are only two links connecting *will*tns to *the*det in LP1. Thus we might formulate a minimality constraint requiring that a head satisfy an argument selection feature by forming a relation with the closest available argument projection. The problem with this approach is that every argument projection in the derivation that matches the selection features of the head in question is still accessible, requiring that the whole derivation be searched. A better approach, therefore, would be to formulate the constraint as an accessibility condition making it impossible for a head to even consider any argument projection but the nearest one. Refining the process of relational derivation in terms of lexical subarrays, as proposed earlier, makes it possible to formulate a very simple and general accessibility condition governing relational derivation:

(64)   *Accessibility Condition* (AC):
         Let λ_1 be a projection in a subarray SA_i that satisfies its argument selection
         feature by forming the relation $\langle\lambda_1,\alpha\rangle$, where α is the highest projection of a
         subarray SA_j. Then, as soon as the next projection λ_2 in SA_i satisfies its
         argument selection feature by forming the relation $\langle\lambda_2,\beta\rangle$, where β is the
         highest projection of a new subarray SA_k, α becomes inaccessible to any
         further applications of FR.

Returning to derivation (63), the AC ensures that as soon as a relation is formed
between *kiss*$_\text{pred}$ in LP$_3$ and *the*$_\text{det}$ in LP$_1$, *the*$_\text{det}$ in LP$_2$ becomes inaccessible to
further applications of FR. Hence *will*$_\text{tns}$ may only satisfy its argument selection
feature by forming a relation with *the*$_\text{det}$ in LP$_1$.

The AC is thus a simple and general derivational constraint that allows an
argument projection to be accessible only until the next argument relation is
formed, thereby dramatically reducing the search space of FR by imposing a
stringent locality condition on the relation between an LI and its selected argument.
Crucially, however, the AC, as formulated in (64), only renders an argument
projection inaccessible when a *new* argument projection is selected. Hence there
is nothing to prevent an argument projection from remaining accessible indefinitely, as long as it is only selected by a sequence of uninterpretable selection
features. This explains the well-known fact that under the right conditions an
argument projection can be pronounced indefinitely far away from the position
where it was initially selected. It seems clear that there are two reasons why this
systematic departure from strict locality is tolerated. The first is that uninterpretable
argument selection features do not add semantic content to the sentence; the second
is that there is a sequence of strictly local relations connecting the initial link
between an LI and its selected argument to the position where its phonetic form is
ultimately pronounced. Hence the interpretation associated with the phonetic form
of an argument can easily be computed, despite the fact that it is pronounced in a
position far removed from where it was initially selected as an argument.

2.4.2   The Phase Accessibility Condition

The AC, as formulated in §2.4.1, is about as stringent a locality condition as
could be imagined. Basically, an argument LP is only available until the next
argument in the derivation is selected, at which point it, along with everything
contained in it, becomes completely inaccessible to FR. It is possible, however,
to imagine a weaker version of accessibility, utilizing a notion similar to that of
a *phase* proposed in the minimalist literature (Chomsky 2001). The idea here is
that the units that become inaccessible as the derivation proceeds are somewhat
larger than a single argument projection. In particular, Chomsky proposes that

at least the "propositional" categories vP and CP (and most likely DP, as well) are phases. Accordingly, I shall next consider how a relational version of phase theory might be formulated. I then look at some empirical evidence that could potentially decide between strictly local versus phase accessibility. I focus here on the relational equivalent of the vP phase, leaving for Chapter 6 a detailed discussion of the CP phase.

Conceived of in relational terms, a phase is simply a designated projection λ_P which has the property that once it is saturated, all arguments selected up to that point, apart from the one selected by λ_P itself (if there is one), become inaccessible to further applications of FR. Thus we might formulate a *phase accessibility* constraint as follows:

(65)   *Phase Accessibility Condition* (PAC):
   Suppose v_P is a phase projection and α is an LI selected by v_P to satisfy its argument selection feature. Then as soon as v_P is saturated, all previously selected arguments apart from α become inaccessible to further applications of FR.

If every projection that had an argument selection feature were a phase projection, then the PAC would reduce to the AC. Suppose, however, that only certain projections are designated as phase projections. In particular, let us assume that v_{pred}, the nearest equivalent of "light v" in the framework proposed here, is a phase projection. Then the effect of the PAC can be represented, schematically, as follows:[23]

(66)

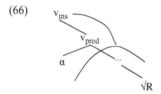

As soon as v_{pred} is saturated, that is to say, as soon as it has selected both an argument α and the lexical projection v_{tns}, all previously selected arguments apart from α itself become inaccessible. Note that it is crucial that the arguments below the phase head v_{pred} not become inaccessible until v_{pred} is fully saturated. Otherwise, nothing inside v_{pred} could ever be selected by v_{pred}, contrary

---

[23] The notation in (66), which I use henceforth as an informal representation of the effect of the PAC, is intended to indicate that the barrier below v_{pred}, which renders inaccessible all arguments introduced up to that point apart from α, goes into effect as soon as v_{tns} is projected. Note that α could either be a new argument satisfying a thematic selection feature or a previously selected argument satisfying an athematic selection feature.

to fact. As formulated, however, it is perfectly possible for v_{pred} to satisfy its argument selection feature by selecting some argument α below v_{pred} before α becomes inaccessible.

In the minimalist version of phase theory, it simply has to be stipulated rather arbitrarily that the contents of a phase do not become inaccessible until the next head up has been maximally projected, leaving it unexplained why a phase does not become inaccessible as soon as it is maximally projected, or for that matter why inaccessibility is not delayed until the second head up is merged. However, in a fully bottom-up theory of the sort proposed here, it is entirely natural to assume that the PAC goes into effect precisely when the phase head is saturated, i.e. as soon as v_{pred}, in the case at hand, satisfies its projection feature by selecting v_{tns}. In fact, the point at which accessibility goes into effect can be viewed as yet another consequence of IG: once the phase head is selected, its selectors must be satisfied immediately, only after which the PAC may go into effect.

Another question that can be answered more satisfactorily by formulating phase theory in relational terms is why the particular heads v_{pred} and v_{comp} are phase heads. Chomsky has suggested that vP and CP are phases because they are the two projections that are in some sense "propositional," but it is far from clear what this means, precisely. In contrast, in the relational theory proposed here, it is entirely natural to hypothesize that v_{pred} is a phase because it is the *minimal v-projection*, in the sense discussed earlier in this chapter, while v_{comp} is a phase because it is the *maximal v-projection*.

Let us consider next how the AC and the PAC differ in their empirical predictions. Suppose we have an LP of the following sort with two projections v_α and v_β below v_{pred}, each of which selects an argument:

(67)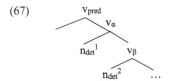

If the AC were correct, the only n_{det} argument available to the athematic selection feature of v_{pred} would be n_{det}^1. As soon as n_{det}^1 is selected by v_α, v_β and everything below it should become inaccessible. In contrast, the PAC predicts that both n_{det}^1 and n_{det}^2 should be available to the selection feature of v_{pred}, because at that point in the derivation v_{pred} has not yet been saturated, hence nothing below the phase projection v_{pred} is yet inaccessible. The question then is whether data can be found that confirms one or the other of these two predictions. I discuss four such cases.

2.4.2.1   Locative Inversion   Going back, first of all, to the phenomenon of Locative Inversion, discussed briefly in §2.2.1.3, consider the following data:

(68)   a. A genie will appear on the table.
       b. There will appear a genie on the table.
       c. On the table will appear a genie.

It is argued by Bowers (2002, 2010) that Locative Inversion sentences such as (68c) are derived by moving the locative-PP successively into [Spec,Pr] and [Spec,T]. This analysis accounts neatly for the fact that Locative Inversion, like existential *there*, can only occur in English with unaccusative verbs:

(69)   a. Someone put the book on the table.
       b. *There put someone the book on the table.
       c. *On the table put someone the book.

It also accounts for the fact that existential *there* and Locative Inversion cannot co-occur, under the assumption—also argued for in Bowers (2002, 2010)—that expletive *there* can only merge in [Spec,Pr]:

(70)   a. *On the table will there soon appear a genie.
       b. *There will on the table soon appear a genie.

In addition, cross-linguistic data from a variety of languages (cf. e.g. Bresnan and Kanerva 1989) confirms that the preposed locative-PP in Locative Inversion behaves like a subject with respect to agreement processes rather than a topic. Sentences involving Locative Inversion are thus quite different in structure from sentences with a topicalized locative such as the following:

(71)   a. On the table a genie will appear.
       b. On the table there will appear a genie.

Notice, however, that some kind of locality constraint must be in effect because nothing can move into [Spec,T], crossing over whatever happens to occupy [Spec,Pr]:

(72)   a. *On the table will a genie appear.
       b. *On the table will there appear a genie.

Rather, whatever moves into [Spec,Pr] *must* move further into [Spec,T].
Now consider the relational structure of Locative Inversion sentences:

(73)

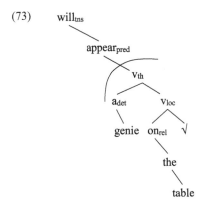

In order to account for all three examples in (68), it must be the case that the
athematic argument selection feature of v_{pred} can select either a_{det} in the
argument projection selected by v_{th}, on_{rel} in the argument projection selected
by v_{loc}, or expletive *there*. The AC predicts only the first and third of these,
while the PAC predicts that all three should be possible. Furthermore, the PAC
also correctly predicts that the *only* argument accessible to v_{tns} is whatever has
been previously selected by v_{pred}, since as soon as v_{pred} is saturated by projecting v_{tns}, everything but the argument selected by v_{pred} becomes inaccessible. In
short, if the proposed analysis of Locative Inversion is correct, then phase
accessibility must be preferred to strictly local accessibility, because it predicts
precisely the pattern of data observed.

2.4.2.2   Dative Alternations   Consider next the well-known fact that dative
phrases in English can either appear as PPs headed by the prepositions *to* or *for*,
in which case they follow the thematic object, or as indirect objects DPs, in
which case they precede the theme-DP:

(74)   a. John will give books to Mary.
         b. John will give Mary books.

(75)   a. John will buy books for Mary.
         b. John will buy Mary books.

Bowers (2010) argues on the basis of numerous syntactic arguments that the
simplest way to account for these alternations is to assume: (i) the dative phrase
in all these examples is the realization of a relation *affectee* (Aff) which is projected

above the theme (Th) relation; (ii) Aff may select either a DP or a PP; (iii) Th may select either a DP with unvalued Case or a DP marked with inherent ACC Case; (iv), following Bowers (2002), there is a functional category Tr, located above Aff but below Pr, containing an uninterpretable argument selection feature, which may or may not contain a probe that assigns structural ACC Case. If the Aff-DP has a Case feature that needs to be valued, it will be Case-marked and moved to [Spec,Tr]. If the Th-DP, on the other hand, has this property, then it will be Case-marked and moved to [Spec,Tr]. Translating this proposal into relational terms, we would then have the following two possible derivations:[24]

(76)

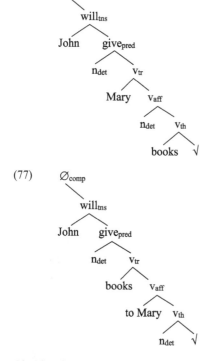

(77)

Clearly, the AC will permit derivation (76) but rule out (77). The PAC, in contrast, will permit both, since at the point where the athematic argument feature of v_{tr} is to be satisfied, both *books* and *Mary* will still be accessible to the

---

[24] I ignore here the role of Case in these derivations. That will be discussed in detail in Chapter 4.

selection feature of v_{tr} by virtue of the fact that the phase head v_{pred} has not yet been saturated.

2.4.2.3   Pseudopassivization   Another well-known phenomenon suggesting that accessibility must be stated in terms of phases is pseudopassivization, illustrated in examples of the following sort:

(78)   a. Mary should pay (more) attention to John.
        b. (More) attention should be paid to John.
        c. John should be paid (more) attention to.

There are quite a few quasi-idiomatic expressions such as *pay attention to, take advantage of, pay heed to*, etc. that have the property that either the object, i.e. *attention, advantage, heed*, etc., can be passivized or the object of a PP following it. Assuming that the small nominal object is the theme argument and the PP is an affectee argument, the relational structure involved would be as follows:

(79)

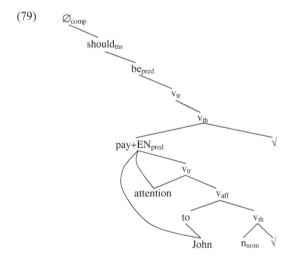

In order to produce both (78b) and (78c), both *attention* and *John* must be accessible at the point where the athematic argument feature of *pay+EN*_{pred} is to be satisfied. Under the AC, only the former is accessible, whereas under the PAC, both are accessible until the phase head *pay+EN*_{pred} is fully saturated by virtue of selecting one or the other of them.

2.4.2.4   Active versus Passive   It is argued by Bowers (2010) that the subject of an active sentence and the *by*-phrase of the corresponding passive are derived from a position lower than any other argument position. Let us call this projection v_{ag}. If the athematic selection feature of v_{pred} is satisfied by selecting the v_{ag} argument, an active sentence is derived, whereas if it is satisfied by selecting the v_{th} argument, a passive is derived. Omitting irrelevant details, the proposed derivations in relational form are as follows:[25]

(80)

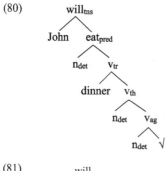

(81)

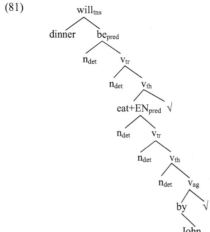

If, however, derivations are constrained by the AC, active sentences such as (80) will be ruled out, since the v_{ag} projection will already be inaccessible at the point where the selection feature of v_{pred} is to be satisfied. On the other hand, if derivations are constrained by the PAC, then both the v_{ag} argument and the v_{th}

[25] See Chapter 5 for further details, including explicit discussion of the role of structural NOM and ACC Case.

argument are accessible to the selection feature of v_{pred}, permitting both active and passives to be derived. Furthermore, once an argument projection has been selected by v_{pred}, the PAC predicts correctly that it will be the only argument henceforth available to the uninterpretable selection of feature of v_{tns}. As Bowers (2010: 26–29) observes, the interaction of Locative Inversion and *there*-expletivization with passivization, together with this crucial property of the PAC, predict correctly the following pattern of data:[26]

(82) a. On the table will be (*a book) placed a book by John.
  b. By John will be (*a book) placed a book on the table.
  c. *A book will be on the table placed by John.
  d. *A book will be by John on the table placed.
  e. There was a book placed (*a book) on the table by John.
  f. *On the table was there (a book) placed (a book) by John.
  g. *By John was there (a book) placed (a book) on the table.
  h. *On the table will John place a book.
  i. *A book will John place on the table.

Once v_{pred} has selected some projection α to satisfy its athematic selection feature, the PAC will ensure that only α is available to satisfy the selection feature of any higher *v*-projections, including both v_{pass} and v_{tns}, from which follows all the data in (82).

2.4.3   Summary

Recapitulating briefly, a strictly local accessibility condition such as the AC, proposed as a more stringent constraint on relational derivation than the RPIC, is too strong. The PAC, in contrast, appears to make exactly the right predictions in a wide range of cases. Within a phase such as v_{pred}, any argument is available to satisfy its athematic selection feature. Once v_{pred} has been saturated, however, the only argument henceforth available to a higher projection with an athematic selection feature is whatever projection was selected by v_{pred}. I leave it to the reader to verify that similar arguments can be constructed to support the claim that n_{nom} is a phase in *n*-projections. Clearly, what v_{pred} and v_{nom} have in common is that both are minimal projections and both mark the boundary between argument projections, projected below them, and "functional" heads, projected above them. Phase heads thus "seal off" the

---

[26] Bowers (2010) attempts to account for this data by distinguishing "pure" EPP-driven movement from movement driven by EPP in conjunction with Agree, suggesting these two types of movement are orthogonal to one another and that only the latter is subject to a locality condition equivalent to the AC. The approach suggested here is far more straightforward, as well as being independently motivated.

propositional part of a projection from the higher part of the projection, only allowing whatever projection has been selected by the phase head itself to be available to satisfy higher projections with an athematic selection feature.

2.5   *Conclusion*

It has been argued in this chapter that the existence of "defective" categories of varying sizes from the minimal projection upward is a natural and predictable consequence of a strictly bottom-up relational theory, since any projection can, in principle, have the option of not projecting further. In a constituent-based theory, in contrast, the existence of defective categories can only be stipulated in *ad hoc* fashion, since there is no principled reason, given the standard theory of selection, why such entities should exist. Similarly, the notion "phase" and the constraints on accessibility embodied in the PAC, arise quite naturally within the relational framework. A phase may be either the minimal category required to form a lexical projection or the maximal possible category in a lexical projection. Furthermore, the cut-off point for access to the head that projects a phase head is naturally defined as the point at which the phase head is saturated, whereas in standard phase theory it must be arbitrarily stipulated that the contents of a phase do not actually become inaccessible until the next head up has been maximally projected. I conclude that a theory based on relations between words is not only at least as successful in terms of empirical coverage as standard constituent-based theories, but is superior to them in terms of descriptive and explanatory adequacy.

3   *Modification*

Next I take up modification, a relation that has posed major difficulties for theories of constituent structure. It will be shown that the relational theory developed in the preceding chapters is sufficient to account for the fundamental properties of modification without introducing any new primitives. I consider first adverbial modifiers and then show that the same basic ideas can be extended to postnominal adjectival modifiers. I then turn to the question of prenominal adjectival modifiers, arguing that a different approach altogether is required to explain their properties—one that involves an extension of the notion of selection. I conclude by showing that the same approach is needed—somewhat surprisingly—in order to describe correctly the properties of adverbial modifiers of adjectives and adverbs.

3.1   *Adverbial Modification*

To see the problem that adverbial modification poses for theories of constituent structure, consider the two expressions *walk slowly* and *eat lunch*. Both are phrases consisting of two words and both are projections of the verb, hence standardly assumed to form a VP constituent. Yet the relation between the words in the two cases is entirely different. Traditional grammars typically describe the difference in intuitive terms by saying that whereas *lunch* is an argument of *eat, slowly* is a modifier of *walk*. An attempt to account for the difference in more formal terms was made in X-bar theory by permitting a node X^i of bar-level i to project a node of the same bar-level X^i rather than projecting a node of the next higher bar level X^{i+1}. The relation between such a node and its sister was defined as *adjunction* and it was assumed that this notion was sufficient to provide a formal characterization of the various kinds of modification relations found in natural language. That idea, however, has turned out to be problematic for many reasons. Thus VP-adjuncts, to mention only one, are incorrectly predicted to c-command all the arguments within VP (Pesetsky 1995, Bowers 2010).

If anything, the problem becomes even more acute in the minimalist framework. In Chomsky (2000: 133), the Merge operation is said to form *unordered sets* of elements when driven by selection (*set-Merge*), but to form *ordered pairs* in the case of modification (*pair-Merge*). Essentially, this approach deals with modification by introducing a new primitive operation into syntactic theory, with the result that syntactic representations become a mixture of sets and ordered pairs. Such representations are far more complex than representations in terms of either sets alone or relations alone, and are far more difficult to interpret at either PHON or SEM.[1] This idea is also conceptually quite strange, because it is clear, thinking in terms of relations, that the simplest way to account for the difference between *eat slowly* and *eat lunch* is to represent the latter as a relation between *eat* and *lunch* and the former as a relation between *slowly* and *eat*. In other words, in *eat lunch*, the verb *eat* is the head of a binary relation <eat,lunch> and *lunch* is the dependent, whereas in *eat slowly*, the adverb *slowly* is the head of a binary relation <slowly,eat> and *eat* is the dependent.[2] Given the notion of an ordered pair, there is no simpler way of representing the difference between selection and modification than this.

A strong argument in support of this approach derives from the fact that adverbs are naturally classified in terms of the kind of head they are required to modify (Bowers 1993, 2001a, 2002, 2010, Cinque 1999). I therefore propose, following Bowers (1993, 2001a, 2002, 2010), that just as verbs contain features indicating the category of LI they select, so adverbs contain selection features specifying the category of LI they modify. Thus a manner adverb such as *perfectly* has the selector [_V], indicating that in an ordered pair of the form <perfectly,α>, it must be the case that α belongs to the category V. An adverb such as *probably*, in contrast, has the selector [_T], while an adverb such as *reluctantly* has the selector [_v]. Notice that this immediately accounts for the otherwise puzzling fact that adverbial modifiers are always optional. Whether

---

[1] An earlier version of this approach (cf. Chomsky 1995a, 1995b) incorporates the ordered pair notation into the label assigned to the output of Merge. While avoiding the problem of "mixed" representations containing both sets and ordered pairs, this still amounts to introducing a new primitive into the theory, this time built into the labeling function. If labels are eliminated, as suggested by Collins (2002), then a theory of this sort is obviously ruled out. See Oseki (2014) for a recent critique of pair-Merge as a means of representing adjunction.

[2] Assuming that the modifier is the head and the modified the dependent is also consistent with the standard view of the semantic relation between modifiers and their hosts, namely, that the modifier takes the host as an argument.

or not an adverb occurs in a given sentence simply depends on whether or not it is present in LA. If it is, then it occurs; if not, not. The relational theory thus accounts in the simplest possible way for the difference between modification and selection, while at the same time accounting for the fact that modifiers are always optional.

Next we must ensure that the notion of a modifier can be formally defined within a relational theory solely in terms of the inherent properties of heads and their selectors. Recall that in Chapter 1 an argument was defined as a selected head that has no unsatisfied selectors, while a lexical projection was defined as a selected head that does have unsatisfied selectors. It was tacitly assumed, however, that both arguments and lexical projections are heads *that are themselves selected by other heads*. This leaves open the possibility of a third type of head, namely, one that has unsatisfied selectors but which *is not itself selected as an argument by any other head*.[3] It is precisely a head with these properties that I shall define as a *modifier*. Following traditional terminology, we may further define a modifier that selects a head of category *v* as an *adverbial* modifier and one that selects a head of category *n* as an *adjectival* modifier. Note that I have not excluded the possibility of a modifier itself being selected *as a lexical projection*. This is essential, since modifiers, like all syntactic expressions, are projected from roots. Indeed, if we were to exclude the possibility of a modifier being selected as a lexical projection, only bare roots would ever be capable of being modifiers.

Recalling now the tree representation of relational derivations proposed in Chapter 1, I propose as a first approximation (to be modified shortly, however: cf. §3.1.1.1) to integrate modifiers into such structures in the following manner:

(1)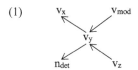

As indicated in the diagram, the arrow connecting the modifier v_{mod} to the lexical projection v_y is directed downward and to the left, parallel to argument selection, though the two relations differ in that a modifier selects a lexical projection rather than being selected by it.

---

[3] The fourth possibility, namely, a head that has unsatisfied selectors but is not selected *as a lexical projection* by any other head, defines a root, as observed in Chapter 1.

3.1.1   *Manner Adverbs*

To be more concrete, let's consider next the empirical properties of various classes of adverbs,[4] starting with the type of adverb generally referred to in the literature as a *manner* adverb. As discussed in Chapter 2, every type of projection must have a minimal category. Let us designate the minimal adverbial modifier as a_{mod}, in order to distinguish it from the minimal adjectival projection a_{prop}.[5] Noting that adverbial modifiers are regularly derived from adjectival roots by adding the suffix *-ly*, let us also assume that a_{mod} may be lexically realized as the bound morpheme *-ly*, whose phonetic form combines at PHON with the phonological form of an adjectival root. To illustrate, if the adverbial category a_{mod} is selected by the root √slow, then a phrase such as *he walk slowly* would be derived as follows:

(2)

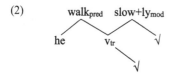

I assume, anticipating the discussion of transitivity in Chapter 4, that all sentences project the category v_{tr}[6] and that manner adverbs are modifiers of v_{tr} in both transitive and intransitive sentences. Since *walk*$_{tr}$ is the dependent and *slowly* the head, the former will be correctly linearized before the latter: he-walk-~~walk~~-√~~walk~~-slow+ly-√~~slow~~. The derivation of a transitive sentence such as *He ate dinner slowly* is derived similarly, except that the v_{tr} head modified by *slowly*, being transitive in this case, also selects the v_{th}-argument *dinner*:

(3)

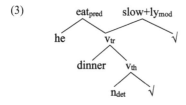

---

[4] I discuss here only a small selection of the most basic types of adverbs. See Cinque (1999) for an exhaustive listing of adverb types, together with arguments in support of the view that each type of adverb is generated in the specifier of a distinct head and that these heads are arranged in a fixed universal hierarchy.

[5] Technically, a_{mod} is simply a_{prop} with a modifier selection feature. Since prepositional phrases can also be modifiers, we may also designate p_{mod} as a p_{rel} projection with a modifier selection feature.

[6] See also §5.4.4 for further arguments in support of this claim.

As indicated in diagram (3), the principles of linearization established in Chapter 2 produce the correct linear order he-eat-dinner-slowly.

3.1.1.1 Linearization of Manner Adverbs At this point, it is necessary to come to grips with the fundamental fact that manner adverbs are not restricted to clause final position, but may also occur to the left of a variety of non-core arguments such as v_{goal}, v_{ben}, v_{instr}, etc. (cf. Bowers 1993, 2001a, 2002, 2010 for discussion):

(4)   He kicked the ball (perfectly) into the goal (perfectly).

In fact, it is true quite generally of -*ly* adverbs that they can occur either in some clause-internal position or at the right edge of a clause (Bowers 1993, 2001a):

(5)   a. He (inadvertently) kicked the ball into the goal (inadvertently).
        b. He will (probably) kick the ball into the goal (probably).
        c. He (unfortunately) must have kicked the ball into his own goal (unfortunately).
        d. (Frankly,) he is not a first rate footballer(, frankly).

How is it possible to explain this systematic variability in the linear ordering of adverbial modifiers and the heads they modify? It seems that there must be some fundamental difference between modifiers and arguments that is in need of further explanation.

   The solution to this problem lies in the fact that adverbial modification is essentially independent of argument selection and lexical projection. In diagram (1) the modification relation was simply added to a two-dimensional graph representing the relations of projection and argument, but I will argue now that such a representation is misleading. Suppose instead we interpret the graph notation quite literally as a two-dimensional space in which the vertical dimension represents the relation of lexical projection and the horizontal dimension represents the relation of argument selection. If that is the right way of thinking about these graphs, then the modification relation cannot simply be added to the plane representing lexical projection and selection. Rather, we must imagine that modifiers are represented in a third dimension orthogonal to the plane containing the heads they modify.[7] The modification

---

[7] In a somewhat similar fashion, Chomsky (2004) proposes that the objects produced by pair-Merge are placed in a separate "plane" from the objects produced by set-Merge, though the terminology seems to be purely metaphorical: cf. Oseki (2014). Such complex objects must then be undone by the operation SIMPL, an optional part of TRANSFER which converts

relation may then be represented by a directed arrow connecting a modifier in this third dimension to a head in either the lexical projection dimension or the selection dimension. Visualizing the modification relation in this way provides a graphic representation of the fact that modifiers are fundamentally independent of the heads they modify. Thinking in terms of derivation, this implies that a modifier projection, like an argument projection, is first built from an independent subarray and then integrated into sentential structure by selecting a head in the projection/argument dimension and forming a modification relation with it.

Let us consider next how the linearization properties of modification discussed earlier can be accounted for. Suppose that the basic Spell-out algorithm proposed in Chapter 1 applies to modification in exactly the same way that it does to projection and argument selection, except that it leaves the direction of linearization free, rather than specifying (in the unmarked case) a fixed direction. One reason for thinking this might be the case is that lexical projections and arguments are obligatory, whereas modifiers are always optional. Hence it makes sense to suppose that there is a fixed direction of selection for the former but not the latter. If the direction of linearization of modifiers is simply left unspecified by the Spell-out algorithm, it follows that the phonetic form of a modifier is free to be ordered either to the left or the right of the phonetic form of the head it modifies. Once a modifier selects a head and forms a relation with it, their respective phonetic forms must of course be arranged in *some* linear order, since phonetic forms are only legible to the SM systems if they are linearized. If the approach proposed here is correct, the choice of direction is simply free, reflecting at the level of PHON the fundamental fact that the relation between a modifier and the head it modifies is independent of the argument selection and projection properties of the latter.

There is, however, a possible alternative to free ordering of modifiers, namely, language-specific parameterization, arbitrarily imposing a fixed ordering between a modifier and the head it modifies. Such language-specific parameters can be quite general, applying uniformly to all modification relations in a given language, or they can vary idiosyncratically from one type of modifier to another. A language can also combine free ordering of some modifiers with parameterization of others. Empirically, all of these

ordered pairs back into unordered sets, prior to being linearized. See also Bobaljik's (1999) suggestion that adverbs should be on a separate tier from argument relations and extended projections.

possibilities are found in the world's languages. In this chapter, I focus mainly on what I take to be the unmarked case, namely, free ordering, leaving for Chapter 4 some discussion of the range of parameterization found cross-linguistically.

To illustrate free ordering, consider first what happens if the modifier *perfectly* in example (4) is ordered to the right of the phonetic form of v_{tr} at step 6 of the derivation:[8]

(6)

1	$<\sqrt{kick},v_{goal}>$	kick-~~kiek~~
2	$<v_{goal},into>$	into-the-goal-kick-~~kiek~~
3	$<v_{goal},v_{th}>$	kick- into-the-goal-~~kiek-kiek~~
4	$<v_{th},the>$	the-ball- kick-into-the-goal-~~kiek-kiek~~
5	$<v_{th},v_{tr}>$	kick-the-ball-~~kiek~~-into-the-goal-~~kiek-kiek~~
6	$<perfectly,v_{tr}>$	kick-the-ball-~~kiek~~-into-the-goal-~~kiek-kiek~~-perfectly
7	$<v_{tr},the>$	the-ball-kick-~~the-ball-kiek~~-into-the-goal-~~kiek-kiek~~-perfectly
8	$<v_{tr},v_{pred}>$	kick-the-ball-~~kiek-the-ball-kiek~~-into-the-goal-~~kiek-kiek~~-perfectly
9	$<v_{pred},he>$	he-kick-the-ball-~~kiek-the-ball-kiek~~-into-the-goal-~~kiek-kiek~~-perfectly

The phonetic form of v_{tr} after step 5 is the string kick-the-ball-~~kiek~~-into-the-goal-~~kiek~~-$\sqrt{kiek}$. If at the point where *perfectly* selects v_{tr}, the phonetic form of the adverb is ordered to the right of the phonetic form of v_{tr}, it will end up at the end of the entire sentence.

Consider, in contrast, what happens if the phonetic form of *perfectly* is ordered to the left of the phonetic form of v_{tr} at step 6:

(7)

6'	$<perfectly,v_{tr}>$	perfectly-kick-the-ball-~~kiek~~-into-the-goal-~~kiek-kiek~~
7'	$<v_{tr},the>$	the-ball-perfectly-kick-~~the-ball-kiek~~-into-the-goal-~~kiek~~-$\sqrt{kiek}$
8'	$<v_{tr},v_{pred}>$	kick-the-ball-~~kiek~~-perfectly-~~the-ball-kiek~~-into-the-goal-~~kiek~~-$\sqrt{kiek}$
9'	$<v_{pred},he>$	he-kick-the-ball-~~kiek~~-perfectly-~~the-ball-kiek~~-into-the-goal-~~kiek~~-$\sqrt{kiek}$

The result is that the phonetic form of the adverbial modifier *perfectly* ends up between the object *the ball* and the v_{goal} argument *into the goal*.

Notice, however, that it is crucial that *perfectly* forms a relation with v_{tr} *before* the argument selection feature of the latter is satisfied. If the relation $<v_{tr}, the>$ at step 7' of derivation (7) was formed first, followed by the formation of the relation $<perfectly,v_{tr}>$, i.e. if the order of steps 6' and 7' were reversed, the

---

[8] I ignore details of the internal derivation of argument expressions such as *into the goal* and *the ball*.

result would be *he kicked perfectly the ball into the goal*, which, as is well known, is robustly ungrammatical in English. This leads to the conclusion that a modifier may only select a head *none of whose selectors have been satisfied*. In other words, modifiers may only select completely unsaturated heads. This constraint is not arbitrary but reflects a fundamental property of the modification relation, namely, that the content of a modifier is combined with that of the head it modifies, irrespective of whatever arguments or lexical projections the latter may be required to select. In other words, the relation between a modifier and the head it modifies is not dependent in any way on satisfaction of the selection properties of the latter.

The next step is to show that this constraint can be derived from the selection properties of modification, together with the general principles of the theory. Recall that IG states that the selection features of a head must be satisfied immediately. It follows from IG that given two unsaturated heads α and β, where β selects α, the selection features of β must be satisfied first. Otherwise, it would never be possible for β to satisfy IG. In the case of projection, IG thus ensures that projection starts from the lowest possible head and proceeds upward, rather than permitting a derivation to start somewhere in the middle. In the case of modification, IG implies that the selection feature of a modifier head must be satisfied *as soon as a head of the required kind is projected in another subarray*. In the case at hand, for example, a manner adverb such as *perfectly* must form a relation with v_{tr} as soon as the latter is projected, i.e. before any of the projection and selection features of v_{tr} itself are satisfied. If v_{tr} projected another head before the selection feature of *perfectly* was satisfied, that head in turn would have to project a further head, which would itself be required to satisfy IG, and so forth, making it impossible for the selection feature of the modifier to be satisfied immediately, hence violating IG. More generally, it follows from IG that a selected head must either be fully unsaturated or the maximal fully saturated head in a projection. This prevents argument selection features from being satisfied by selecting an intermediate saturated head in some projection. At the same time, it prevents both projection features and modifier selection features from being satisfied by selecting anything but a fully unsaturated head. Notice, however, that nothing prevents a modifier from having projection and selection features of its own, quite independent of its modifier selection feature, that are required to satisfy IG *within* the modifier subarray.

It is important to stress that the hypothesis that modifier heads are represented in a separate "dimension" from argument heads and lexical projection

heads is not mere stipulation. Rather, it is forced by the special formal properties of the modifier relation itself, together with IG.[9] Likewise, the fact that the
modification relation is linearized differently from other relations—being
basically free, unless parameterized—is also a reflection of its special formal
properties. There have been other attempts in the literature to account for the
distinctive linearization properties of modifiers, such as Keyser's (1968) suggestion that adverbs bear a feature [+transportable] that allows them to precede
or follow their sister. Such an approach, even if descriptively adequate, clearly
fails at the level of explanatory adequacy since the transportability property is
simply stipulated *ad hoc* without being derived in any way from fundamental
principles. Other approaches suggested in the literature, such as the
Government–Binding notion that modifiers are not "visible" to certain operations by virtue of being added at a later stage of derivation, though somewhat
less *ad hoc* than positing a feature [+transportable], are nevertheless not
derivable in any way from the basic properties of adjuncts but simply man-
dated. In addition, there are empirical problems with the notion of an adjunct, as
mentioned earlier (cf. also §3.1.7).

In order to incorporate modification into the canonical tree notation introduced
in the preceding chapters in a manner that accurately reflects these properties, I
propose now to place a modifier vertically above the head it modifies, intending
by this to represent graphically the fact that the modifier is actually in a third
dimension relative to the plane of selection and projection. At the same time,
since the modifier occurs neither to the left nor to the right of the head it modifies,
this notation will serve to indicate that there is no fixed linear ordering between
the two, leaving it to be freely assigned or specified by language-specific
parameters. Abstractly, relational trees will thus have the following canonical
form:

(8)

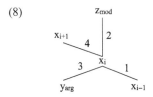

---

[9] Note that though every type of relation, i.e. argument selection, projection, and modification, is
uniformly formed by the same syntactic operation FR, each relation is defined differently in
terms of the primitives of the theory and therefore has its own distinctive formal properties.

Here x_i is a lexical projection which is selected by x_{i-1} and which selects x_{i+1}, y_{arg} is an argument selected by x_i, and z_{mod} is a modifier of x_i. As indicated in the diagram, the only possible order in which these relations may be formed is as follows: 1 $<x_{i-1},x_i>$; 2 $<z_{mod},x_i>$; 3 $<x_i,y_{arg}>$; 4 $<x_i,x_{i+1}>$.

3.1.2   Modifiers of v_{pred}

Having established some of the fundamental properties of modifiers, I consider next three classes of adverbs all of which are modifiers of v_{pred}. The well-known case of subject-oriented adverbs is discussed first, followed by a consideration of two other classes of adverbs that arguably also modify v_{pred}. A problem much discussed in the recent literature (cf. Ernst 2001) is posed by the fact that these modifiers can co-occur with one another in different orders with concomitant differences of scope. It is shown that this problem can be solved by permitting v_{pred} to project another instance of v_{pred}, thereby making it recursive.[10] I conclude by showing that frequentative adverbs such as *twice, often*, etc. are ambiguous depending on whether they modify v_{pred} or v_{tr}.

3.1.2.1   Subject-oriented Adverbs   Consider first the class of subject-oriented adverbs, which includes *inadvertently, intentionally, eagerly, willingly, unintentionally, accidentally*, etc. These adverbs occur most felicitously either immediately preceding the main verb or at the right edge of the clause:

(9)   He (??inadvertently) might (inadvertently) offend (*inadvertently) Mary (inadvertently).

As has frequently been observed, these adverbs are predicated of the subject, independent of its argument relation to the verb, as is shown by the difference in meaning between pairs such as the following:

(10)   a. The doctor unwillingly examined Mary.
      b. Mary was unwillingly examined by the doctor.

---

[10] The only alternative to the approach explored here is to permit more than one type of adverb to modify the same head. This entails either that semantic scope is free and determines linear order or that linear ordering is free and determines semantic scope. The first approach is inconsistent with the mainstream generative assumption of the autonomy of syntax, while the second (somewhat reminiscent of the approach taken by Jackendoff 1972) requires that the semantics be sensitive to representations at PHON, as well as to those of NS. In my view it is preferable to maintain the stronger assumption that semantic scope is determined by NS, only to be abandoned in the face of compelling evidence to the contrary.

The property of doing something against one's will is predicated of *the doctor* in (10a), whereas it is predicated of *Mary* in (10b).[11] This observation is explained under the assumptions outlined earlier if adverbs of this class are modifiers of the v_pred projection, since the meaning of the adverbial modifier must be composed with the meaning of the verb prior to selection by v_pred of whatever argument is the subject. Hence (9) is derived as follows:

(11)   inadvertent+ly$_\text{mod}$

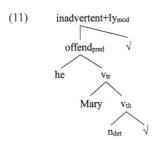

Obviously, if the phonetic form of *inadvertently* is ordered to the left of the phonetic form of *offend*$_\text{pred}$ before the latter selects the subject argument *him*, then (the phonetic form of) *inadvertently* will be placed immediately to the left of *offend*, producing the sentence *He might inadvertently offend Mary*. If, on the other hand, PF(inadvertently) is ordered after PF(offend$_\text{pred}$), then the phonetic form of the adverb will be linearized at the right edge of the clause, as in *He might offend Mary inadvertently*. Note that there is no possible way of linearizing these relations that can result in a v_pred adverb being ordered between the verb and the object. It was shown earlier that there is no way for manner adverbs to be linearized between a verb and its object either. Hence there is no type of adverb that may be ordered between a verb and its object, deriving the well-known generalization of English syntax that adverbs are prohibited between the verb and the direct object.

There is independent evidence in support of this analysis. Recalling the discussion of the minimal v_pred complement in English (i.e. the so-called "bare infinitive" complement) in Chapter 2, it is predicted, first, that agent-oriented adverbs should be able to occur in such complements, second, that they should only be able to follow the subject, not precede it, and third, that they

---

[11] I ignore here the interesting complications that arise in passive sentences when the adverb occurs further to the right, e.g. the fact that *unwillingly* may be predicated of either the theme or the agent in sentences such as *Mary was examined unwillingly by the doctor*. For an interesting recent approach to these issues, see Matsuoka (2013).

should also be able to occur at the right edge of the complement. All three predictions are correct, as the following examples show:

(12)   a. I saw (*inadvertently) him (inadvertently) score an own goal (inadvertently).

        b. The coach had (*deliberately) him (deliberately) foul the goalkeeper (deliberately).

This data argues strongly against Cinque's (1999) view that each adverb class is generated in the specifier of a dedicated head. The nearest equivalent of Cinque's theory in the relational framework would be to posit a special v-projection for each adverb class which would then select the adverb itself. Suppose, for example, we assume a projection v_{int} for subject-oriented adverbs such as *intentionally, deliberately*, etc. If v_{int} is projected above v_{tr} but below v_{pred}, then the adverb will incorrectly be linearized between the phonetic form of the verb and the object:

(13)

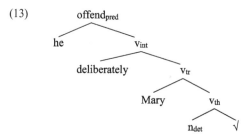

If, on the other hand, v_{int} is projected above v_{pred}, then the adverb will be correctly linearized after the subject in finite clauses and infinitival complements, but only by virtue of the fact that the subject is subsequently selected by v_{inf} or v_{tns}, causing its pronunciation to be displaced leftward. In bare infinitival complements such as those in (12), however, it will be impossible for the adverb to be correctly placed between the subject and the verb:

(14)

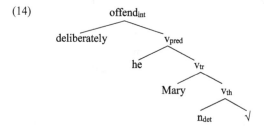

Depending on whether pronunciation of the root *offend* is or is not displaced to v_{int}, either *I saw deliberately offend him Mary* or *I saw deliberately him offend*

Mary will be produced, both of which are totally unacceptable. In short, positing a separate v_{int} head makes it impossible to place the adverb in the correct position between the agent of a minimal v_{pred} head and the verb. In contrast, if agent-oriented adverbs modify v_{pred}, then exactly the right results are predicted.[12]

This analysis makes another prediction. Consider a sentence containing both a manner adverb and an agent-oriented adverb. If both adverbs are linearized to the right, then the manner adverb is correctly predicted to precede the agent-oriented adverb at the right edge, since the former modifies a head lower in the v-projection than that of the latter:

(15)   a. John might kick the ball into the net perfectly (quite) inadvertently.
        b. *John might kick the ball into the net inadvertently perfectly.

Furthermore, it should be infelicitous to exchange the positions of a manner adverb and an agent-oriented adverb in a sentence containing both:

(16)   a. John might inadvertently kick the ball into the net perfectly.
        b. *John might perfectly kick the ball into the net inadvertently.
        c. John might inadvertently kick the ball perfectly into the net.
        d. *John might perfectly kick the ball inadvertently into the net.

This prediction also appears to be correct, lending further support to the hypothesis that pure manner adverbs such as *perfectly* select v_{tr}, whereas agent-oriented adverbs such as *inadvertently* select v_{pred}.

3.1.2.2   Prospective Aspectual Adverbs   Consider next the class of aspectual adverbs containing *almost, nearly, practically, just about*, etc. These adverbs are very similar to subject-oriented adverbs in that they may occur either immediately before the main verb or at the end of the clause:

(17)   John almost/nearly/just about hit him(, almost/nearly/just about).

---

[12] Another possible approach, in the relational framework, is to posit an adverbial projection v_{int} which is *modified* by an adverb such as *deliberately*. For this to work it would have to be assumed that v_{int} has an athematic selection feature, in order to ensure that the subject is linearized to the left of the adverb. Other adverb classes could be treated in similar fashion. A disadvantage of this approach is that in order to account for the scope alternations discussed in the next section, it would have to be assumed that adverbial projections can be selected in different orders. My working hypothesis for the moment is that there are enough independently motivated v-projections to support the different types of adverbial modifiers that exist in natural language. If, however, it turns out that this hypothesis is too strong, then the possibility of projecting further v-heads, motivated primarily (perhaps entirely) by the existence of particular adverb classes, is open for exploration. See §4.5.1 for some discussion of certain types of adverbs for which such an approach may be warranted.

A problem is posed by the fact that they may co-occur with subject-oriented adverbs in either order with a concomitant difference in scope:[13]

(18)   a. John nearly/almost deliberately hit him.= 'John came close to deliberately hitting him.'
       b. John deliberately nearly/almost hit him.= 'John deliberately came close to hitting him.'

Data of this sort is clearly incompatible with Cinque's (1999) theory that adverb classes are introduced in strict hierarchical order, but the question remains how these different possible orders can be produced.

The simplest solution to this problem is to assume that certain heads such as v_{pred} may project another head of the same category, thereby making them recursive.[14] If both subject-oriented adverbs and prospective aspectual adverbs modify v_{pred}, this will immediately permit derivations such as (19) and (20):

(19)

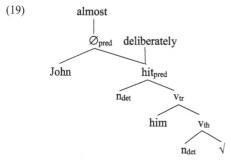

(20)

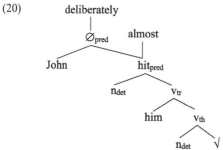

[13] Still a third interpretation (roughly 'John's hitting him was almost/nearly deliberate'), not relevant here, is accounted for by the fact that the adverbs *almost, nearly*, etc. can be modifiers of the following adjective: cf. §3.2.3 for discussion.
[14] Later on I discuss independent evidence of a very different kind in support of the claim that v_{pred} is recursive: cf. §6.2.1.

Given the principles governing linearization of modifiers proposed earlier, derivation (19) will produce examples such as (18a), while derivation (20) will produce examples such as (18b). In addition, examples such as the following will be produced, along with the correct interpretations:

(21)   a. John hit him deliberately, almost.= 'John came close to deliberately hitting him.'

        b. John hit him almost, deliberately.= 'John deliberately came close to hitting him.'

Notice that in order to produce the correct word order in English, it must be assumed that the higher v_{pred} head projects a null $\varnothing_{pred}$ head and that both heads have an athematic argument selection feature. Evidence in support of both assumptions comes from bare infinitival complements such as the following:

(22)   a. I saw (*almost) John (*hit) (almost) deliberately *(hit) him.

        b. I saw (*deliberately) John (*hit) (deliberately) almost *(hit) him.

It is predicted, however, that languages in which the main verb and/or the subject has greater freedom of occurrence will exhibit a wider range of variation than is found in English.

So far it has been assumed that the two adverb classes under discussion only modify v_{pred}, but the following data suggests that they may have other selection possibilities:

(23)   a. John might deliberately have (nearly) hit him.

        b. John might nearly have (deliberately) hit him.

        c. ??John might deliberately nearly have hit him.

        d. ??John might nearly deliberately have hit him.

Though it seems quite awkward to order both types of adverb (in either order) before the perfect auxiliary *have*, either one can appear by itself in that position with or without an adverb of the other type ordered after the perfect auxiliary. This pattern of data can be accounted for under the following assumptions: (i) both subject-oriented adverbs and prospective aspectual adverbs have the option of modifying either v_{perf} or v_{pred}; (ii) v_{perf}, in contrast to v_{pred}, is not recursive. Clearly, assumption (ii) is correct, since there can be no more than one perfect auxiliary per clause in English. Hence we may conclude that it is possible for a given type of adverb to select more than one projection in a clause.

3.1.2.3   Frequentative Adverbs   Still another class of adverbs that behave like typical modifiers of v_{pred} are frequentative adverbs such as *twice, many/few*/etc. *times, often, rarely, frequently*, etc.:

(24)   John (twice/many times/often) fouled the keeper (twice/many times/often).

Moreover, these adverbs can be ordered differently with respect to subject-oriented adverbs with accompanying differences in scope:

(25)   a. John twice intentionally fouled the keeper.
         b. John intentionally twice fouled the keeper.
         c. John fouled the keeper intentionally twice.
         d. John fouled the keeper twice, intentionally.

Examples (25a) and (25c) refer to two different occasions on which John intentionally fouled the keeper, whereas (25b) and (25d) refer to John's intentionally engineering two events of fouling the keeper. Such data is easily accounted for under the assumption that both frequentative adverbs and subject-oriented adverbs are v_{pred} modifiers and that v_{pred}, as proposed in the preceding section, §3.1.2.2, is recursive. Furthermore, frequentative, subject-oriented, and prospective aspectual adverbs can all be combined in varying orders (with varying degrees of naturalness) with concomitant differences of interpretation:

(26)   a. John almost twice intentionally fouled the keeper.
         b. John twice almost intentionally fouled the keeper.
         c. John intentionally twice almost fouled the keeper.
            etc.

Thus (26a) means that John came close on two occasions to intentionally fouling the keeper, (26b) means that John on two occasions came close to intentionally fouling the keeper, (26c) means that John intentionally engineered two occasions on which he came close to fouling the keeper, and so forth.

Further complications ensue from the fact (cf. Cinque 1999: 25–27, following Andrews 1982), that frequentative adverbs such as *twice, three times*, etc. may have either a "high" or a "low" interpretation, as shown by the fact that the two may co-occur:

(27)   John twice (often/rarely/ . . .) knocked twice (three times/ . . .) on the door twice (three times/ . . .).

The frequentative adverbs on the left quantify unambiguously over events, whereas those on the right refer to repetitive action, but there is no contradiction between having, for example, two separate events of repeating a knock three times. On the other hand, if a frequentative adverb occurs alone on the right edge it is ambiguous between the two interpretations:

(28)   John knocked on the door twice (three times/often/rarely/ . . .).

All of these facts fall into place if it is assumed that adverbs such as *twice, three times*, etc. may modify either v_{pred} or v_{tr}. In the first case, they are interpreted as quantifying over events, in the second as referring to repetitive action. Assuming that v_{tr}, in contrast to v_{pred}, is not recursive, then we predict correctly that it should be degraded to combine adverbs such as *well* and *hard*, which are unambiguously manner adverbs, with low frequentative adverbs, producing contrasts such as the following:

(29)   a. John hit the ball well twice. (=John twice hit the ball well.)
        b. ??John three times hit the ball twice well.

(30)   a. John knocked (hard) on the door (hard) twice. (=John twice knocked hard on the door.)
        b. ??John three times knocked twice (hard) on the door (hard).
        c. ??John knocked hard twice on the door.

Though judgments are necessarily delicate, given the possibility of parenthetical interpolation, it seems clear that (29a) is most naturally interpreted as referring to two occasions on which John hit the ball well, rather than a single occasion on which John performed an action both repetitively and hard. This is reinforced by the fact that examples such as (29b) with frequentative adverbs both to the left and to the right of the main verb, plus a manner adverb, seem quite degraded.

3.1.3   Epistemic Adverbs and the v_{Σ}-projection

Consider next the class of epistemic adverbs that includes *probably, certainly, possibly*, etc. Note first that these adverbs occur most felicitously between a modal verb and the main verb, or at the right edge of the clause, making them look superficially just like agent-oriented adverbs:

(31)   a. John will probably kick (*probably) the ball (*probably) into the net (probably).

They cannot, however, be v_{pred} modifiers because they cannot be felicitously interchanged with any of the v_{pred} modifying adverbs just discussed:

(32)   a. He will probably inadvertently/almost/twice foul the keeper.
        b. *He will inadvertently/almost/twice probably offend Mary.

Further evidence that these adverbs modify some projection higher than v_{pred} derives from the fact they are excluded from bare infinitive complements:

(33)   a. *I will see him probably/certainly/possibly score a goal.
        b. *The coach will make/have him probably/certainly/possibly score a goal.

The following data suggests that the head modified by epistemic adverbs must be at least as high as v_{perf}:

(34)   a. He might possibly have (??possibly) offended Mary.
       b. He might possibly have inadvertently offended Mary.
       c. *He might inadvertently have possibly offended Mary.

(35)   a. He will probably have (??probably) left by now.
       b. He will probably have deliberately snubbed Mary by now.
       c. *He will deliberately have probably snubbed Mary by now.

But since the v_{perf} head is optional, there must be some other head that epistemic adverbs can select. One obvious possibility is v_{tns}. However, that would predict the adverb to occur to the left of an auxiliary element in v_{tns}:

(36)   a. John probably will have left by now.
       b. John possibly could inadvertently have offended Mary(, though I doubt it).

In fact, this does seem to be a possible position for epistemic adverbs (cf. §3.1.6 for further discussion), but the optimal position of these adverbs after an auxiliary in v_{tns} is still not accounted for.

A clue to the correct analysis is provided by the fact that epistemic adverbs are robustly confined to a position to the left of negation:

(37)   a. John will (probably) not (*probably) have left yet.
       b. John has (certainly) not (*certainly) left yet.

To account for this data, as well as for the fact that epistemic adverbs optimally follow an auxiliary element, I propose to adapt Laka's (1990) analysis of polarity to the relational framework by assuming an obligatory projection v_Σ below v_{tns} but above v_{perf}. The projection v_Σ has a polarity feature with two values [pos] and [neg]. In English, if v_Σ has the value [neg], it is realized phonetically as the overt negative element *not*, whereas if it is [pos], it is null.[15] Examples (36a) and (37a) can then be derived as follows:

(38)

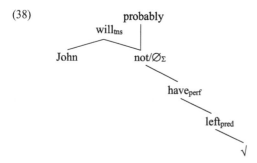

[15] It is possible that the elements *so* and *too* in sentences such as *John will so/too leave* are optionally selected by v_Σ[pos], but only in emphatic or contrastive contexts, since they are obligatorily stressed.

3.1.4   Structure of Infinitive Complements

To round out this discussion of *v*-projections in the middle field of English, it is necessary to consider the position of the infinitival marker *to*. The standard analysis is that infinitival *to* is generated in T along with modal auxiliaries and present or past tense features, thereby explaining the complementary distribution between these elements. This account is incorrect, however, for a number of reasons.

First, the unmarked position of negation (and certain adverbs) in infinitive complements shows that *to* is not in T but in some head position below T:

(39)   a. John (*not) will/did (not) leave (*not).
　　　　b. John left (*not).

(40)   a. I persuaded John (not) to (?not) leave.
　　　　b. For (*not) John (not) to (?not) leave would upset Mary.

The obvious suggestion is that there must be another head position between T and v/Pr containing *to*, which I shall label "Inf(initive)":

(41)

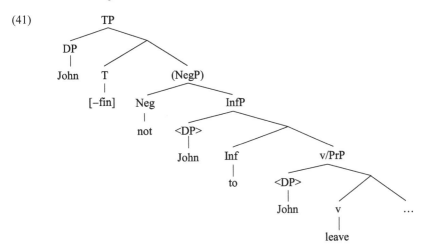

Importantly, this structure still leaves room for "focus" or "constituent" negation between Inf and v/Pr in "split" infinitives:

(42)   a. I persuaded John to NOT be polite.
　　　　b. For John to NOT be polite would upset Mary.

That both kinds of negation are necessary is demonstrated by the existence of "double negatives" in both finite and non-finite clauses:

(43)   a. John can't NOT be polite. (= 'John is incapable of not being polite.')
        b. I persuaded John not to NOT be polite. (= 'I persuaded John that he should
           not fail to be polite.')

Second, there are at least two modal elements in English that obligatorily co-
occur with the infinitival marker *to*:

(44)   a. He ought to eat.
        b. He is/was to leave tomorrow.

The nominative Case-marking of the subject shows that these clauses are finite,
while the position of negation after *ought* and *be* shows that the modal elements
ought and *be* are in T:

(45)   a. He (*not) ought (not) to leave.
        b. He (*not) is (not) to leave tomorrow.

As we would predict, double negatives are also perfectly possible in these
constructions:

(46)   a. He oughtn't/ought not to NOT be polite.
        b. He is not/isn't to NOT leave.

Third, neither *ought* nor modal *be* can be main verbs, because they cannot co-
occur with other T elements such as the regular modal auxiliaries:

(47)   a. *He can/will/didn't ought to leave.
        b. *He can/must/didn't be to leave.

On the other hand, auxiliary elements such as perfect *have* are free to occur
with these modals:

(48)   a. You ought to have been there.
        b. He was to have been there by now.

Most modal auxiliaries in T in English require that Inf have the null phonetic
realization $\emptyset$, but *ought* and modal *be* require that Inf must be lexically realized
as *to*, showing that both T and Inf are necessary.

   Finally, note that in many languages infinitival forms are marked with a
morphological suffix, e.g. Fr. *all-er* 'to go,' Ger. *geh-en* 'to go,' etc. I will
assume that in such languages the verbal root raises to Inf. That this is correct is
shown by the position of negative element *pas*, which, as is well known, must
precede the infinitive (cf. Pollock 1989):

(49)   Ne pas manger (*pas) le diner, c'est criminale.
        'Not to eat dinner, that's criminal.'

Incorporating this analysis of infinitive complements into the relational theory proposed here is straightforward. We may simply assume that there is another category v_{inf} in v-projections which is above v_{pred} but below v_{tns} and v_Σ. An example such as *he ought (not) to eat* will then be derived as follows:[16]

(50)

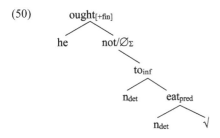

In contrast, if $v_{[+fin]}$ is realized as *must*, then v_{inf} must be realized phonetically as $\varnothing$:

(51)

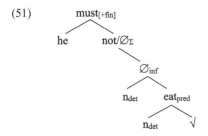

Similarly, $v_{[-fin]}$ in standard English is obligatorily realized as $\varnothing$, as in *I want him $\varnothing$ (not) to leave.*[17]

This analysis predicts correctly that subject-oriented adverbs optimally appear to the right of infinitival *to*, whereas epistemic adverbs appear to its left:

(52)   a. I wouldn't want (??inadvertently) to (inadvertently) offend Mary.
       b. I can't persuade John (??intentionally) to (intentionally) insult his best friend.
       c. For him (possibly) to (??possibly) unintentionally insult Bill would be unthinkable.
       d. *For him unintentionally to possibly insult Bill is unthinkable.

---

[16] I assume without argument that v_{inf} has an athematic [_n_{det}] selection feature.

[17] Perhaps in dialects that permit sentences of the form *I want him for to leave, for* is a lexical realization of $v_{[-fin]}$.

Furthermore, it seems that the preferred position for the adverbs *yet* and *ever* is either immediately to the left of *to* or in clause-final position:

(53)   a. He (*yet) will (*yet) not (yet) have (??yet) left (yet).
       b. He (*ever) will (*ever) not (ever) leave the house (ever).
       c. For him (*yet) not (yet) to (??yet) have (??yet) left the house (yet) is crazy.
       d. For him (*ever) not (ever) to (??ever) leave the house (ever) would be absurd.

Hence it may be concluded that these adverbs are modifiers of v_{inf}, providing evidence for yet another adverb class.

3.1.5   Evaluative Adverbs

Consider next adverbs such as *(un)fortunately, (un)luckily, (un)happily*, etc. If these adverbs are treated as modifiers of v_{tns}, we predict correctly that they can appear either to the left of a modal or auxiliary verb or at the right edge of a root clause and that they can co-occur with epistemic adverbs, which are modifiers of v_Σ:

(54)   a. United (unfortunately) will not win the Manchester derby (unfortunately).
       b. United unfortunately will probably not win the Manchester derby.

However, when used alone both epistemic and evaluative adverbs can appear either to the left or to the right of an element in v_{tns}, indicating that both can select either v_{tns} or v_Σ:

(55)   a. United (unfortunately) will (unfortunately) lose the Manchester derby.
       b. United (probably) will (probably) lose the Manchester derby.

This in turn predicts that exchanging the positions of the evaluative and epistemic adverbs in (54b) should be possible, though in fact such examples seem somewhat degraded:

(56)   ?United probably will unfortunately not win the Manchester derby.

This may be a purely semantic scope effect, however, as suggested by the fact that a similar contrast can be produced by embedding the corresponding adjectives in opposite orders:

(57)   a. It is unfortunate that it is probable that United will not win the Manchester derby.
       b. ?It is probable that it is unfortunate that United will not win the Manchester derby.

Finally, if it is assumed, as seems reasonable, that neither v_{tns} nor v_Σ are recursive nodes, then sentences with both types of adverb in either pre- or post-v_{tns} position are correctly predicted to be degraded:[18]

(58) a. ??United unfortunately probably will not win the Manchester derby.
 b. ??United will unfortunately probably not win the Manchester derby.

3.1.6 Pragmatic Adverbs

The last class of adverbs that will be considered here is that of pragmatic adverbs such as *frankly, sincerely, honestly,* etc., which normally (i.e. except when parenthetical) occur either at the beginning or the end of a root clause:

(59) a. Frankly, I don't like him(, frankly).
 b. Quite honestly, he is nothing but a windbag(, quite honestly).

This distribution is nicely accounted for under the assumption that pragmatic adverbs are modifiers of $\varnothing_{comp}[D]$:

(60)   frank+ly$_{mod}$

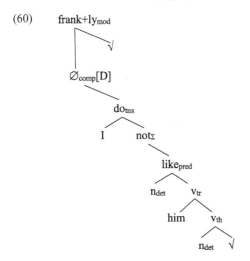

Support for this analysis is provided by the fact, noted by Cinque (1999: 12), that pragmatic adverbs cannot change positions with evaluative adverbs:

(61) a. Frankly, I unfortunately don't like him much.
 b. *Unfortunately, I frankly don't like him much.

---

[18] Note, however, that examples such as *United (probably unfortunately) will (probably unfortunately) lose the Manchester derby* have another interpretation under which *probably* is itself a modifier of the adverb *unfortunately*. See §3.2.3 for further discussion of adverbial modifiers of adverbs.

The same is true of epistemic adverbs:

(62)   a. Honestly, I will probably not see him again.
        b. *Probably, I honestly will not see him again.

3.1.7   Conclusion: Modification is Neither Adjunction Nor v-projection

At this point, it is useful to summarize and draw some preliminary conclusions. Let us start by comparing modification, as defined here, with adjunction, as defined in X-bar theory. Adjunction structures are recursive, since any adjunct can always project another adjunct with no upper bound: [$_{XP}$ YP$_n$ [$_{XP}$ YP$_{n-1}$ ... [$_{XP}$ YP$_1$ XP] ...]]. Modifiers, in contrast, have only a single selection feature, hence are not inherently recursive. In the case of adverbs, the empirical facts clearly support a theory of modification rather than a theory of adjunction, because in general there can only be one adverb of a given type (e.g. manner adverbs) per clause. The problem with adjunction is that it wildly over-generates, incorrectly predicting that there can be any number of adjuncts of a given type, arranged in any possible order.

Based on this observation, it might be proposed instead, following Cinque (1999), that each type of adverb is restricted to one and only one specifier position in a fixed hierarchy of adverbial heads in the extended projection of the verb. The problem with this theory is that it is too rigid, failing to account for a certain degree of variability in the ordering of adverb types that is empirically observable in natural language. There are at least three sources of variability identified earlier.

First, it has been shown that some adverb classes may select more than one v-projection, permitting them to occur in more than one position in PHON. In some cases, this arises from the fact that the same root may project adverbs of different types. Thus the adverb *honestly* is a pragmatic adverb in (62a), but a manner adverb in a sentence such *He deals with people honestly*. The adverb *honestly* is thus simply lexically ambiguous, since it may either select $\varnothing_{comp}$[D] or v_{tr}, with accompanying differences of interpretation. This type of variation is common to both Cinque (1999) and the theory proposed here. However, we have seen that there are also cases where an adverb of a given type is simply able to select more than one head in the v-projection with no discernible difference in interpretation, thereby enabling it to appear in more than one position at PHON. Variation of this type can only be dealt with in Cinque's theory by insisting that there is nevertheless some subtle difference of inter-pretation associated with the two positions. However, it is very difficult to discern any significant differences of interpretation between pairs such as *John probably will win/John will probably win, he could unintentionally have offended Mary/he could have unintentionally offended Mary*, etc.

Second, we have seen that adverbs quite generally can occur either in some clause internal position or at the right edge of a clause. The only way to account for this type of variation in a Cinque-style theory is to assume a fairly elaborate set of displacement operations, for which there is little, if any, independent motivation. In the relational theory proposed here, in contrast, variation of this kind arises simply from the fact that Spell-out (in the unmarked case) does not assign a fixed linear order to adverbs. This in turn is a consequence of the fundamental formal properties that distinguish modifiers from arguments and lexical projections.

Third, it was shown in §3.1.3 that certain v-projections such as v_{pred} are, for independent reasons, recursive, thereby permitting a potentially indefinite number of different kinds of v_{pred}-selecting modifiers to co-occur in different orders with concomitant differences in scope. Of the three types of variation, this is the most devastating for a theory such as Cinque's, as has been pointed out by critics such as Ernst (2001), who argue that adverb order must be semantically determined, at least in part. In the relation-based theory proposed here, however, there is a well-motivated syntactic explanation for such cases, making it unnecessary to abandon the autonomy of syntax.

In conclusion, a relational theory of syntax along the lines proposed here provides just the right degree of freedom needed to account for the empirically observed range of variation found in natural language systems of modification without massively over-generating, on the one hand, or being forced to resort to semantic explanations, on the other.

3.1.8   Degree Projections of Adverbs

To complete this discussion of adverbial modification, it is necessary to consider whether adverbs can have lexical projections of their own. In fact, it is widely assumed (cf. Abney 1987, Bowers 1987, 2001a, Corver 1990, 1991, 1997) that the degree words that typically occur with adverbs and adjectives are lexical projections of the category a in much the same way that determiners are lexical projections of the category n. Examples of degree constructions are the following:

(63)   a. John walked so slowly (that we got impatient with him).
       b. John walked too quickly (for us to keep up with him).
       c. John walked slowly enough (for us to keep up with him).
       d. John walked more slowly (than he needed to).
       e. John walked as slowly (as he could).

Ignoring for the moment the fact that degree modifiers may have an associated clause, let us see how they can be integrated into the structures proposed so far by adding the degree projection *too* to the derivation in (64):

(64)

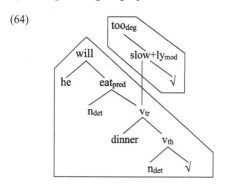

Assuming that a_{deg} is a lexical projection of a_{mod}, the adverbial projection in (64) will be linearized as <u>too-slowly-~~slow~~</u>. Note, however, that it is still the adverb *slowly* that selects v_{tr} to modify, even though it projects a further category v_{deg}, because modifier selection is, by hypothesis, a property of particular lexical roots.

One might wonder how such a derivation is possible. It was shown in Chapter 2 that an argument may only be integrated with a *v*-projection when it has no lexical projection features left to satisfy, but in this case the process of integrating the modifier projection with the *v*-projection it modifies, effected when *slow*$_{mod}$ satisfies its modifier feature by selecting *eat*$_{tr}$, evidently must take place right in the middle of both an *a*-projection and a *v*-projection. These requirements are not contradictory, however, for the simple reason that *slowly*-$_{mod}$ has two different *types* of selection feature, a projection feature [_a_{deg}] and a modifier selection feature [_v_{tr}]. Because they are different types of selection feature, they satisfy IG separately. The first satisfies IG within the subarray that produces the projection of the modifier *slowly*; the second satisfies IG at the point where the modifier projection is integrated into the *v*-projection of √eat. In fact, given these assumptions, IG dictates that this is the only derivation possible. With respect to linearization, no adverse consequences result, as the following derivation demonstrates:

(65)

a. 1   <√eat,eat$_{th}$>   eat-√eat

   2   <eat$_{th}$,dinner>   dinner- eat-√eat

   3   <eat$_{th}$,eat$_{tr}$>   eat-dinner-~~eat~~-√eat

   4   <slowly$_{mod}$,eat$_{tr}$>   too-slowly-√~~slow~~-eat-dinner-~~eat~~-√eat

   6   <eat$_{tr}$,dinner>   dinner-too-slowly-√~~slow~~-eat-~~dinner-eat~~-√eat

7 <eat$_{tr}$,eat$_{pred}$>   eat-dinner-too-slowly-√~~slow-eat-dinner-eat~~-√eat
8 <eat$_{pred}$,he>   he-eat-dinner-too-slowly-√~~slow-eat-dinner-eat~~-√eat
9 <eat$_{pred}$,will>   will-he-eat-dinner-too-slowly-√~~slow-eat-dinner-eat~~-√eat
10 <will,he>   he-will-~~he~~-eat-dinner-too-slowly-√~~slow-eat-dinner-eat~~-√eat
b. 1′ <√slow,slowly$_{mod}$>   slowly-√~~slow~~
   2′ <slowly$_{mod}$,too$_{deg}$>   too-slowly-√~~slow~~

Within the modifier subarray, which gives rise to the derivation shown in (65b), IG is satisfied by projecting first *slowly*$_{mod}$ and then *too*$_{deg}$. Within the main clause subarray, which produces the derivation in (65a), the selection feature of the modifier *slowly*$_{mod}$ is satisfied by forming a relation with *eat*$_{tr}$, after which the remaining selection properties of v_{tr} are satisfied. Thus a degree word will always be linearized immediately to the left of an adverbial modifier that projects it, despite the fact that the latter is required to integrate with the head it modifies as part of the derivation of a projection within another subdomain.

Consider finally the clauses that may optionally be associated with degree words. It is generally assumed that there is a close dependency between the degree word and the associated clause, as evidenced by the fact that the form of the clause is determined by the degree word. Thus *so* requires an associated finite *that*-clause, *too* requires a non-finite infinitive, *-er/more* requires a finite clause headed by *than*, etc. However, it has always been somewhat of a puzzle why degree clauses obligatorily appear to the right of the adverbs they modify while the degree word must appear to its left. In a theory based on constituent structure there is no way to express the dependency between degree heads and their associated sentences without assuming an extra unmotivated movement operation that moves the sentence into its correct position in PHON after the adverb:

(66)

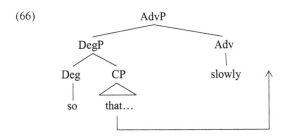

To solve this problem, we need to think a bit more about the nature of degree words and their associated clauses.

It has been assumed so far that degree words are simply lexical realizations of the category a_{deg}. There are, however, two reasons for thinking that this might be incorrect. First, there are two cases in English in which the degree element is not a word but a morpheme:

(67)   a. John ran fast+er than Bill did.
         b. John ran fast enough to catch Bill.

In (67a) the comparative is realized as a morpheme *-er* attached to the adverb root, while in (67b) the degree word *enough* is apparently cliticized to the right of the adverb root rather than appearing to its left. In order to account for these cases, it must be assumed that the phonetic form of the adverb root is pronounced at the position of the degree head in order to avoid morphological ill-formedness at PHON. Supposing, then, that a_{deg} in English is an illegible category, it follows that the adverb root must be pronounced there in order for a_{deg} to be interpretable at PHON. This in turn entails that morphologically simplex degree words such as *so, too, as, more*, etc. must actually be arguments of a special sort selected by a_{deg}, in which case they must themselves be projections of some category. What category could that be? An indication is provided by the fact that at least two degree words in English, namely, *too* and *more*, can themselves be modified by number expressions such as *much, a bit, a lot, a good deal*, etc.:

(68)   a. John ran much/a bit/a good deal too fast for me to catch him.
         b. John ran much/a bit/a lot more slowly than Bill did.

These quantifiers are associated with the $n_\#$-projection and modify mass nouns such as *milk, water, discussion*, etc., e.g. *much milk, a lot of water, a bit of cash, a good deal of discussion*, etc., suggesting that degree words are highly specialized "small nominal" projections selected by a_{deg}. Which degree word is selected, we may assume, is determined by features such as [comp(arative)], [equ(ative)], etc. in the degree head.

Returning now to the clauses associated with degree words, it is generally assumed, for the reasons noted earlier, that there is a close dependency between the degree word and the associated clause. Let us assume that degree clauses are in fact modifiers of the v_{deg} head, as is suggested by the fact that they are always optional:

(69)

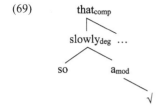

It is immediately apparent that the linearization principles for modification correctly predict the following possible order of elements:

(70)   so-slowly-~~slow~~-√~~slow~~-that . . .

The degree word *so* precedes *slowly* because it is selected by *slowly*$_{deg}$, whereas the phonetic form of the degree clause may follow the sequence of elements so-slowly-~~slow~~-√~~slow~~ because it is a modifier of *slowly*$_{deg}$. The correct ordering thus follows automatically from general principles in the relational theory proposed here without having to posit an additional unmotivated displacement operation.

There is, however, one problem. If, as I have argued, the linear ordering of modifiers is generally free in English, that would seem to predict, contrary to fact, that the degree clause should also be able to appear to the left of the degree word:

(71)   *that . . . -so-slowly

As it happens, this is just the order that tends to occur in postpositional languages (Greenberg 1963: 89). Clearly, what we are dealing with here is just a case of language-specific parameterization. In English, sentential modifiers of a degree head may only be linearized rightward, whereas in other languages it is the reverse. As noted earlier, this is part of the much larger problem of explaining syntactic variation, which will be addressed in Chapter 4.

3.2   Adjectival Modification

Perhaps the most immediately striking property of adjectival modification of nominals is the often noted difference between prenominal and postnominal adjectives. While the latter can be full APs with degree heads and complements, the former are sharply restricted, being unable to occur with either. However, prenominal adjectives, though unable to occur with degree words, may nevertheless be modified by certain -*ly* adverbial modifiers. These general-izations are illustrated as follows:[19]

(72)   a. that student so smart (that everybody is jealous of him)
        b. *that so smart student (that everybody is jealous of him)
        c. *that so smart that everybody is jealous of him student
        d. that (remarkably) smart student

To these observations we may add the fact that in many languages (e.g. Dutch and German), prenominal modifiers agree in number, gender, and Case with the head noun, whereas postnominal AP modifiers do not. If AP modifiers were simply NP-adjuncts that could occur on either a left branch or a right branch, as is often assumed in the literature, none of these differences could be explained systematically.

3.2.1   *Postnominal Adjectival Modifiers*

To account for the fact that full AP modifiers of nominals occur on the right edge of the nominal expression, let us assume that a_{prop} may be a modifier of n_{nom}. Thus a phrase such as *a student of physics so proud of his theory* would be derived as follows:

(73)

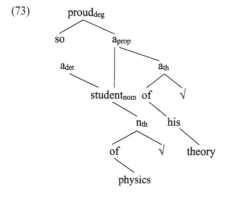

Since the entire phrase *so proud of his theory* is a modifier of n_{nom}, it must follow the phonetic form of *student*$_{nom}$, producing the correct linear order a-student-of-physics-so-proud-of-his-theory. Notice, however, that because modifiers in general either proceed or follow the head they modify, we should

---

[19] Note, however, that if the article is indefinite, it is possible to have both *a student so smart that everybody is jealous of him* and *so smart a student that everybody is jealous of him*, an observation I will not try to explain here.

also be able to produce the incorrect order: <u>a</u>-<u>so</u>-<u>proud</u>-<u>of</u>-<u>his</u>-<u>theory</u>-<u>student</u>-<u>of</u>-<u>physics</u>. Once again, we are up against the brute fact of syntactic variation: in some languages complex adjectival modifiers must appear to the right of the noun they modify and may not appear to the left, whereas in other languages it is just the opposite. Exactly the same problem arises with relative clauses, which may also be analyzed as modifiers of n_{nom}. In some languages, such as English, relative clauses must follow the phonetic form of n_{nom}, e.g. *the student of physics that I know*, and may not precede it: **the that I know student of physics*. In other languages it is the opposite. I put aside for the time being the problem of accounting for syntactic variation of this sort, returning to it in Chapter 4.

3.2.2   Prenominal Adjectival Modifiers

Turning now to prenominal adjectives, let us consider whether a relational theory can shed light on their special properties. An important insight is provided by Emonds (2012), who argues that prenominal adjectives are actually derived nominals formed by combining an adjective with the φ-features of gender and number (and in some languages Case as well). Thus he proposes the following structure for a phrase such as *a smart student*:

(74)

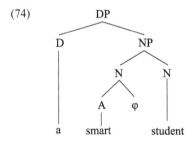

Emonds argues persuasively that this analysis explains a whole series of differences between prenominal and postnominal adjectives that correlate with agreement on the former and lack of agreement on the latter. What is distinctive about English, he claims, is that despite the fact that prenominal adjectives have lost all overt agreement morphology, they nevertheless behave exactly like the inflected prenominal adjectives of languages such as Dutch and German.

There is, however, one difficulty with Emonds' proposal, namely, the fact mentioned earlier that prenominal adjectives, though they cannot project degree heads or select arguments, *can* be modified by *-ly* adverbs:

(75)   an extremely smart, surprisingly nice student

This is a problem for Emonds' analysis because prenominal adjectives are *nouns* and nouns can never be modified by *-ly* adverbs:

(76)　　*a surprisingly house

I therefore propose to modify Emonds' theory, at the same time recasting it in relational terms, in the following way. Let us assume, first, that n_{nom} may optionally project a nominal head with φ-features that I will designate $n_φ$. Now let us assume that $n_φ$ may either project n_{det} or another $n_φ$, making it possible to project an unbounded number of $n_φ$ heads, ordered to the left of the nominal root pronounced in n_{nom}. The category $n_φ$ is thus recursive in much the same way as v_{pred}. Second, let us assume that each $n_φ$ projection, though itself phonetically null, selects as an argument a "small adjective" argument a_{prop} whose φ-features match those of $n_φ$. Given these assumptions, a phrase such as *the nice little old house* can then be derived as follows:[20]

(77)

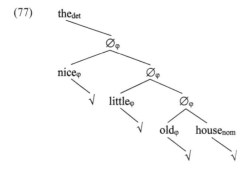

Assuming that the entire *n*-projection, including n_{nom} and n_{det}, has nominal φ-features and that the values of these features must be uniform for any given projection, this will ensure that prenominal adjectives agree in number and gender (and in some languages in Case as well). As far as I can see, this relational version of Emonds' hypothesis has all the desirable features he adduces in its favor with the added attraction of allowing prenominal adjectives to be modified by adverbs, since they are adjectives rather than nouns.

　　This analysis, if correct, makes the claim that prenominal adjectives bear quite a different syntactic relation to the noun they modify than do postnominal adjectives, providing support for the view first expressed by Abney (1987) that prenominal and

---

[20] As is well known, there is a surprisingly stable cross-linguistic unmarked ordering of prenominal adjectives in terms of semantic categories such as size, shape, color, etc. (e.g. *the nice, little house* is less marked than *the little, nice house*). Whether this reflects a universal unmarked hierarchy of concepts that is actually built into the syntax of natural language is a question I will not address here.

postnominal adjectives are not mere positional variants of one another. Specifically, whereas postnominal adjectives are modifiers, prenominal adjectives are *n*-projections of a special sort that select a restricted kind of adjectival argument. This analysis explains the fact that prenominal adjectives in English differ markedly from adverbs in that the direction of selection can only be uniformly leftward.[21]

Notice also that the constraints on the form of prenominal adjectives that are particular to English, i.e. lack of degree elements and complements, can easily be built into the selection conditions of nominal projections. Thus n_φ in English may only select a minimal a_{prop} projection, ruling out examples such as **a so tall student* and **a proud of his work student*, whereas in a language such as German prenominal adjectives are not so restricted.

Finally, it is worth considering briefly how the semantics of predication is derivable from structures in which prenominal adjectives do not modify nouns directly, but rather are selected by a nominal head which is itself a projection of the noun in question. Let us assume that the denotation of *man*$_{\mathrm{nom}}$ is a property, hence $[\![\mathrm{man_{nom}}]\!] = \lambda x\ \mathrm{man}(x)$, of type $<e,t>$. Assume now that selecting a new n_φ projection simply adds a new property whose denotation is associated with the *a*-projection selected by n_φ. To be more specific, suppose that the denotation of $[\![n_\varphi]\!] = \lambda f\lambda g\lambda x[f(x) \wedge g(x)]$, of type $<<e,t>,<e,t>>$. Applied first to the property $\lambda x\ \mathrm{man}(x)$, then to the property $\lambda x[\mathrm{tall}(x)]$, this reduces, by λ-conversion, to the expression $\lambda x[\mathrm{man}(x) \wedge \mathrm{tall}(x)]$. Thus each new n_φ-projection combines a new property with the property of the noun itself to form, in effect, a compound permanent property, whose individual variable x will eventually be bound by an operator such as ι, ∃, or the generic operator Gen.

3.2.3 Adverbial Modifiers of Prenominal Adjectives

Turning now to *-ly* modifiers of adjectives and adverbs, let us try to determine precisely what their nature is. One thought is that they are simply a kind of degree word that happens to lack an associated sentence. This cannot be correct, however, since they may co-occur with degree words:

(78) a. John ran so incredibly fast that nobody could keep up with him.
      b. Mary is even more amazingly generous than Sue is.
      c. Bill is too annoyingly condescending to put up with.

---

[21] As will be shown in Chapter 4, however, this is clearly a language-specific parameter as there are many languages in which adjectival modifiers line up in mirror-image order to the right of the head noun, exactly what is predicted if the direction of selection in *n*-projections in such languages is uniformly rightward.

Another important property of these adverbs is that, unlike the sentence adverbs discussed earlier, they only occur to the left of the adjective or adverb they modify, never to the right:

(79)   a. John ran (incredibly) fast (*incredibly).
         b. Mary is (amazingly) generous (*amazingly).
         c. Bill is an (annoyingly) condescending (*annoyingly) person.

These two properties of these adverbs, combined with the fact discussed in §3.2.2 that they can modify both prenominal and postnominal adjectives, suggest that rather than being modifiers of the adjectives and adverbs they are associated with, they must be projected by them. Under this view the relation between a -*ly* adverb and the adjective or adverb it modifies is very similar to the relation between a prenominal adjective and the noun it modifies. In support of this idea, notice that there are different types of adverbial modifiers, as is revealed by the appropriate paraphrases:

(80)   a. Extent: extremely condescending = 'condescending to an extreme extent'
         b. Psychological: annoyingly condescending = 'condescending in a way that is annoying (to someone)'
         c. Intentional: deliberately condescending = 'condescending in a deliberate manner'
         d. Possibility: improbably condescending = 'condescending in a way that seems improbable'
         e. Evaluative: absurdly condescending = 'condescending to the point of absurdity'

Furthermore, more than one type of adverb can modify the same adjective or adverb:

(81)   a. He is extremely, annoyingly condescending.
         b. He was deliberately, annoyingly condescending.
         c. He was extremely, improbably condescending.
         d. He was improbably, deliberately, annoyingly condescending.

Thus pre-adjectival and pre-adverbial -*ly* modifiers can be iterated in much the same way as prenominal adjectives.

To be more concrete, let us assume that a_{prop} can project a null head that I shall call a_{qual} with some feature such as [psych]. This a_{qual} can in turn select another null a_{qual} with a different feature such as [int], thereby permitting an indefinite number of -*ly* qualifiers to be projected, exactly parallel to the case of prenominal adjectives. Each of these a_{qual} heads is itself required to select an a_{mod} head projected from a root with the appropriate feature, thereby generating a projection such as the following:

(82) an_{det}

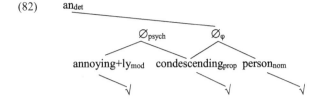

In short, the relation between -*ly* adverbial qualifiers of adjectives and adverbs is quite different from the relation between sentential -*ly* adverbs and the heads they modify, in a way that parallels the difference between prenominal and postnominal adjectives.

3.3   *Conclusion*

It was shown in the first two chapters that the two most fundamental relations between words in natural language syntax are argument selection and lexical projection. If the speculations advanced in this chapter are anywhere near the mark, there is one additional fundamental relation between words found in natural language, to which I have given the traditional name modification. Modification is quite different from selection and projection in a number of ways, all of which stem ultimately from the fact that a modifier is never, by definition, selected as an argument, hence operates orthogonally to the selection/projection plane of the head it modifies. First, modifiers only select unsaturated heads, hence do not interact in any way with the selection and projection properties of the modified head. Second, the Spell-out algorithm does not specify, in the unmarked case, the direction of selection of modification. Hence they are free to be linearized either to the right or to the left of the heads they modify unless restricted by a language-specific parameter. Third, modifiers are always optional because they are unselected. Despite these special properties of the modification relation, its existence is entirely predictable, given the primitives that underpin the relational theory proposed here. Finally, we have seen that not all elements traditionally described as modifiers, in a broad sense, are necessarily instances of the modification relation. In particular, prenominal adjectival modifiers, as well as adverbial qualifiers of both adjectives and adverbs, arise through an entirely different mechanism which is basically an extension of projection and selection, as is evidenced by the fact that their empirical properties are distinct in many ways from those of free modifiers.

4 Variation in Word Order

So far it has been assumed, in line with much current thinking, that the linearization algorithm is universal and that word order variation between languages is solely the result of differences in the points in a derivation at which heads and phrases are pronounced at PHON. In the highly restricted theory proposed here, however, there is scant motivation for the relational equivalent of many of the movement rules that would be required to account for the observed range of cross-linguistic variation in word order. At the same time, given the fact that linearization is a function of the fundamental relations of projection, selection, and modification, there is a rather natural way of loosening the linearization algorithm that will reduce to a bare minimum the degree to which the equivalent of movement must be appealed to. Accordingly, I argue in this chapter that word order variation is a function of just two factors: (i) language-specific parameterization of the Spell-out algorithm; (ii) language-specific variation in the points in a derivation at which heads (and to a very limited degree phrases) are pronounced. In addition, it will be shown that this system makes it possible to construct a complexity metric for word order variation that reflects fairly well the relative frequency with which specific word order variants occur in the world's languages.

4.1 Word Order Variation in n-projections: Cinque's Derivation of Greenberg's Universal 20 and its Exceptions

I start by examining Cinque's (2005) derivation of word order variation in nominal structures and proposing an alternative account within the relational framework that only relies to a very limited extent on the equivalent of movement. Cinque observes that of the 24 mathematically possible orders of the nominal elements demonstrative (Dem), numeral (Num), adjective (A), and noun (N), only 14 are attested in the world's languages. He argues that all and only the attested orders are derivable from a single, universal order of Merge, namely, Dem > Num > A > N, plus independent conditions on phrasal movement. I agree completely with Cinque that an essential component of any explanation for the attested orders is that the basic nominal elements in question are introduced in a fixed universal order. However, there is little independent motivation either for the phrasal movements required to generate the correct orders or for the AgrP projections between each of the nominal elements Det, Num, A, and N that are needed in order to provide landing sites for his proposed "roll-up" derivations. In addition, these extra AgrP projections seem quite inconsistent with the spirit of Minimalism. (See Abels and Necleman (2008) and Pereltsvaig (2006), among others, regarding these points.) I will show that in the relational theory proposed here eight of the 14 attested orders can be derived by simple language-specific parameters specifying the direction of selection, two can be derived by variations in the head position at which the nominal root is pronounced, and two by a combination of these two parameters. That leaves only two attested orders that cannot be derived by any combination of parameters. Of these, one is somewhat dubious, for reasons I will discuss, while the other can be derived by a type of head displacement for which there is independent evidence from an additional type of language, not discussed by Cinque, whose basic order is identical to one of the two most common orders but which arguably must be derived in a different way. There is one last type of language, also not discussed by Cinque, whose basic order is identical to the other most common order, but which can only be derived by invoking one further parameter. Finally, none of Cinque's 12 unattested orders can be derived by any combination of the permitted parameters.

4.1.1   The Two Most Basic Orders

Let us start by considering the two orders that are by far the most common in the world's languages:

(1)   a. Dem Num A N (=Cinque's (6a))
         b. N A Num Dem (=Cinque's (6x))

Following Cinque's terminology, I use the terms "Dem," "Num," and "A" as cover symbols for the set of elements selected by the lexical projections n_{det}, $n_{\#}$, and n_φ, respectively. Likewise, I label a lexical root pronounced at the minimal projection n_{nom} simply as "N." Assuming that in this case each of the heads of the *n*-projection above n_{nom} is occupied by the null LI $\varnothing$, it is easy to see that the order (1a) follows immediately from the Spell-out algorithm stated in Chapter 2, given the order of projection proposed there:[1]

(2)

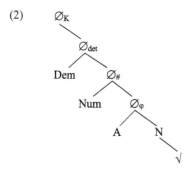

Suppose now that Spell-out can be set to order the PF of the dependent β in an argument selection relation <α,β> either to the left or to the right of the PF of the head α. If the order of selection is uniformly set as PF(β)-PF(α), then the linear order (1a) results. If, on the other hand, the order of selection is uniformly set at PF(α)-PF(β), then the mirror-image order (1b) results:

(3)

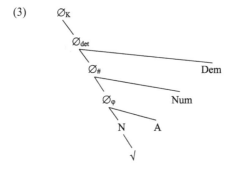

It seems intuitively clear that the reason these are by far the two most common orders is that in both cases the linear ordering of the elements Dem, Num, A, and N transparently reflects the order of projection of nominal heads, despite the fact that they are mirror images of one another. Also, in both cases the nominal root is pronounced in the minimal nominal projection n_{nom}, due to the fact that none of the higher n-projections is illegible at PHON. In other words, there is no displacement of the pronunciation of the root to disrupt the transparency of the relation between word order and order of projection.

---

[1] I also abstract away from the fact, discussed in Chapter 3, that n_φ is recursive, permitting an unbounded sequence of prenominal adjectives.

The fact that these two orders are almost equally common poses a serious problem for a theory of word order variation based entirely on movement operations, because (1a) is derivable without any movement operations at all, while (1b) requires a complex sequence of "roll-up" operations. Cinque claims that none of the operations required to generate (1b) are "marked options." Nevertheless the derivation of (1b) is massively more complex than that of (1a), predicting incorrectly that languages of type (1b) should be considerably less common than languages of type (1a). In contrast, the selection parameter proposed here predicts that both types should be almost equally common, since they are the result of a simple binary choice. We may assume that languages of type (1a) are slightly more common than those of type (1b) because in structures such as (2) the same direction between heads and dependents is chosen for both arguments and projections, whereas in structures such as (3) the head-dependent relation is mapped onto opposing directions for arguments and projections. It is interesting to note, incidentally, that it actually makes no difference in either of these cases whether projection relations are mapped to the left or to the right: the linear ordering that results will be the same, regardless. The same is true for the six attested orders produced by assuming non-uniform orders of selection, to be discussed in §4.1.2. However, when non-uniform orders of selection are combined with displacement, it becomes possible to detect whether projection is leftward or rightward, as will be discussed more fully in §4.1.4.

4.1.2 Basic Orders with Non-uniform Direction of Selection

Consider next the following six orders:

(4)   a. Dem Num N A   (=Cinque's (6b))
           b. A N Num Dem   (=Cinque's (6w))
           c. Dem A N Num   (=Cinque's (6n))
           d. Num N A Dem   (=Cinque's (6s))
           e. Dem N A Num   (=Cinque's (6o))
           f. Num A N Dem   (=Cinque's (6r))

As is immediately apparent, the successive pairs in this list are mirror images of one another. Let us consider first orders (4a) and (4b). The order (4a) will be derived automatically under the assumption that the order of selection for n_{det} and $n_{\#}$ is left, while the order of selection of n_{φ} is right:

(5)

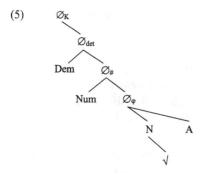

Conversely, the order (4b), the mirror image of (4a), is automatically produced under the opposite assumption, namely, that the order of selection of n_{det} and $n_\#$ is right, while the order of selection of n_φ is left:

(6)

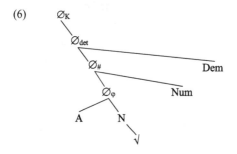

It is interesting to note that the number of languages of type (4a), according to Cinque, is "many," while the number of languages of type (4b) is "very few." I discuss this asymmetry in §4.1.8.

Consider next the orders (4c) and (4d). The first can be generated under the assumption that the order of selection of n_{det} and n_φ is left, while the order of selection of $n_\#$ is right:

(7)

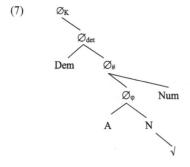

Conversely, if the order of selection of n_{det} and n_φ is right and that of $n_\#$ is left, (4d) results:

(8)

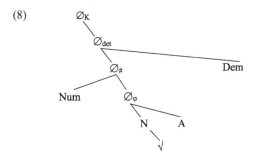

Again, there is a slight asymmetry in the relative frequency with which languages of these two types occur, the former being "very few," according to Cinque, and the latter "few," a difference I will try to explain in §4.1.8.

The final pair of orders (4e) and (4f) is accounted for by the last remaining set of non-uniform selection possibilities and its opposite. If the order of selection of n_{dem} is left and that of $n_\#$ and n_φ is right, (4e) results:

(9)

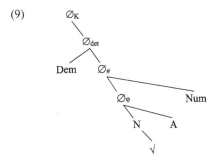

The order (4f) arises from choosing right as the order of selection for n_{det} and left for both $n_\#$ and n_φ:

(10)

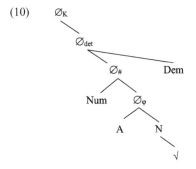

Languages of type (4e) are "many" in number, according to Cinque, while those of type (4f) are "very few." This is a fairly large asymmetry that I will attempt to explain in §4.1.8. As noted earlier, it makes no difference in these cases whether the order of projection is leftward or rightward: the resulting order of elements is the same regardless.

4.1.3   *Basic Orders with Uniform Direction of Selection and Head Displacement*

Let's consider next the following two orders:

(11)   a. Dem N Num A   (=Cinque's (6c))
        b. N Dem Num A   (=Cinque's (6d))

In both of these, the order of elements is as transparent as it is in the least marked order (1a), except for the position of N, which appears initially in (11b) and in second position following Dem in (11a). Assuming that selection is uniformly to the left in both cases, these orders can be derived under the assumption that pronunciation of the nominal root is displaced to n_{det} in (11a) and to n_K in (11b):

(12) $\emptyset_K$

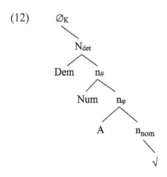

(13) N_K

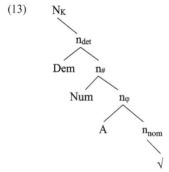

Neither of these orders is very common. Cinque states that the number of languages with (12) is "very few" and the number with (13) is "few," reflecting the fact that derivations containing illegible projections that require pronunciation of the nominal root to be displaced to the left are more complex than those that do not, as well as rendering these orders less transparent than either of the least marked orders (1a) and (1b). Why languages of type (13) should be somewhat more common than those of type (12) is a question I return to in §4.1.8.

4.1.4   Non-uniform Orders of Selection Combined with Head Displacement

The following two orders can be derived by combining a non-uniform order of selection, or its opposite, with head displacement:

(14)   a. N Dem A Num   (Cinque's (6p))
        b. N Num A Dem   (Cinque's (6t))

Type (14a) is generated by left selection of n_{det} and n_φ and right selection of $n_\#$, combined with head displacement to n_K:

(15)

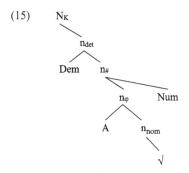

Notice that if N were pronounced at one of the lower heads $n_\#$ or n_φ, this would provide an alternative way of producing the orders (4e) and (4c), respectively, but would not change the set of possible orders. Type (14b) is generated by combining selection orders the opposite of those in (15) with head displacement to either n_K or n_{det}:

(16)

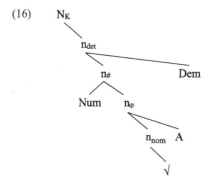

Note that in both (15) and (16) the order of selection of n_φ is actually irrelevant due to the fact that the pronunciation of the root has been displaced above it. Also, it should be pointed out that displacing the pronunciation of the root to either of the lower positions $n_\#$ or n_φ in (16) provides two alternative ways of generating the order (4d). Finally, if the order of selection of n_φ is leftward in (16) and pronunciation of the root is displaced to the same projection, an alternative way of generating the order (4f) results without producing any change in the set of possible orders at PHON.

The derivations discussed so far have the striking property of generating all the possible linear orderings of selected items that preserve the order of projection of the basic nominal categories n_{nom}, n_φ, $n_\#$, n_{det}, and n_K under Spell-out, albeit with differing degrees of transparency. The fact that all 12 of these orders are actually attested in the world's languages shows that order of selection is basically free and that the only cross-linguistic invariant of importance is the order of projection. It appears that languages are free to choose any basic word order they like as long as the order of projection can be recovered, given the general constraints imposed by the Spell-out algorithm. The word order parameters permitted in a relation-based theory of the sort proposed here are thus quite different from the head direction parameters assumed in constituent-based approaches such as X-bar theory. The problem with theories of the latter sort is that they vastly over-generate, producing numerous orders not attested in the world's languages, unless purely *ad hoc* restrictions such as permitting only leftward ordered specifiers are stipulated. The reason for their failure lies ultimately in the fact that they are based on constituent structure, which does not necessarily match up with basic relations between words such as selection and projection that constitute the fundamental building blocks of natural language syntax. In the theory proposed here, in contrast, it is entirely natural for selection relations to be parameterized in terms of linear ordering because the linearization algorithm itself operates directly on the fundamental relations of syntax.

There remain two of Cinque's attested word orders that do not appear to preserve the order of projection. Also, there are at least two possible types of system not discussed by Cinque that cannot be generated under the assumptions adopted thus far. I discuss the latter cases first, after which I will deal with the former.

4.1.5   The Order of Projection

It has been assumed thus far that the only relation parameterized for linear order is selection. I have simply taken it for granted that projection is uniformly leftward since the default case seems to be that dependents precede heads. Let us consider now whether projection can ever have the option of being linearized rightward. Notice first that if it were possible for projection to be uniformly rightward, derivations (12) and (13), which involve head displacement to n_{det} and n_K, respectively, would simply yield an order identical to the most basic unmarked order Dem-Num-A-N:

(17)

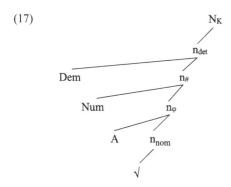

This might suggest that rightward projection is simply prohibited altogether in natural language. Such a conclusion would, however, be too strong, for there are at least two circumstances that make it possible to distinguish a language derived as in (17), with rightward projection plus head displacement, from one derived as in (2), with leftward projection and no head displacement. First, if the language has Case-markers in n_K, they are predicted to occur to the right of the displaced nominal root under a derivation such as (17), whereas no such result would be predicted under a derivation such as (2). Second, a nominal form containing one or more thematic arguments below n_{nom} is predicted to occur to the left of the nominal root in (17), but to the right of the nominal root in (2). Compare the following two partial trees:

(18)   a.

Are there languages with nominal forms having either or both of these properties? Arguably, there are. Languages such as Japanese and Turkish, as is well known, have N-final nominals with a rightward Case form and thematic arguments are uniformly prenominal.

We may tentatively conclude, then, that there are at least some languages in which projection is uniformly rightward. At the same time, it seems that there are heavy restrictions on when rightward projection is permitted. First, as the reader can verify for herself, rightward projection with displacement of the nominal root all the way to the top, combined with the non-uniform orders of selection discussed in §4.1.2, either yields one of the unattested orders (6m), (6q), or (6u) or, in one case (namely, (5)), simply provides yet another way of deriving the most unmarked order (1a). Second, a hypothetical language with both uniform rightward projection and uniform rightward selection, combined with head displacement, is impossible:

(19)

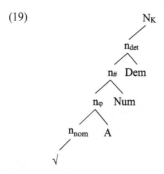

Such a derivation yields the order A-Num-Dem-N, which is unattested: cf. Cinque's (6u). Furthermore, if the nominal root is displaced only as far as n_{det}, the result is the unattested order A-Num-N-Dem: cf. Cinque's (6v). On the other hand, if N is only displaced as far as n_{φ} or not displaced at all beyond the minimal projection n_{nom}, the result is identical to the unmarked mirror-image order N-A-Num-Dem. Likewise, if N is pronounced at $n_{\#}$, the resulting order is identical to that of (4b). Theoretically, the latter two structures could be differentiated from their counterparts derived by leftward projection by the position of Case-markers and/or the position of thematic arguments. Thus if there were languages with unmarked mirror-image order or the order (4b) and some sort of free-standing Case-marker (perhaps analogous to the English genitive marker *'s*) on the right edge of the nominal, we might conclude that such languages were derived by rightward projection combined with no displacement of N or displacement only as far as n_φ, in the first case, or by rightward projection combined with displacement of N to $n_\#$, in the second case. If such languages also had thematic arguments ordered to the left of N, that would strengthen the conclusion. Whether such languages are attested is presently unknown. If not, then it would appear that rightward projection is possible, but only if argument selection is uniformly leftward and the nominal root is displaced all the way to the top, i.e. either to n_{det} or n_K, depending on how Case-marking is handled.[2] In short, though it is possible for languages to be parameterized for uniform rightward projection, the conditions under which such systems are permitted are very narrowly circumscribed. This in turn suggests that rightward projection is possible but heavily marked, whereas the order of selection is basically free.

4.1.6 *Snowballing Head Displacement in Hebrew*

On the face of it, the order of basic elements in the Hebrew (and Arabic) nominal is simply the standard mirror-image order (1b) produced by uniform rightward selection. However, Pereltsvaig (2006) argues persuasively that this order must be derived by an extension of head movement that she calls "snowballing head movement," rather than by snowballing phrasal movement of the sort proposed by Shlonsky (2004). Her arguments, which I shall not reproduce in detail here, rest on three main observations: (1) the fact that noun complements do not take part in leftward movement at all, but invariably remain on the right edge of the nominal after Dem; (2) the fact that only "light" adjectives appear in mirror-image order, while "heavy" adjectives stay in the normal unmarked order; (3) the fact that agreement in definiteness only occurs with postnominal adjectives and numerals, not with prenominal ones. To account for these facts, Pereltsvaig argues that the elements Dem, Num, and light A must actually be heads in Hebrew, rather than being selected. The correct linear order is then derived as follows. First, the Noun raises and

---

[2] Exactly the same constraints also seem to hold in *v*-projections of verb-final languages such as Japanese and Turkish.

adjoins to the left of the light A. This is followed by raising and adjunction of that entire head to the left of Num. Finally, the entire Num head adjoins to the left of D. The result is a structure of the following form:

(20)

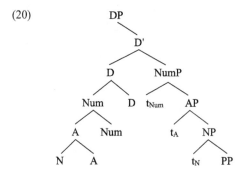

As can be seen, the result is the mirror-image order N-A-Num-Dem, produced in an entirely different way. Furthermore, the complement PP stays in rightward position and does not take part in head raising, since it is a complement of N, not a head. Likewise, if an A is "heavy," then it is generated in [Spec,A] rather than in head position and consequently does not enter into the snowballing head raising.

Pereltsvaig's analysis can be replicated in the relational framework by assuming that nominal elements such as Dem, Num, and A can either be selected by the appropriate head or be heads themselves. Thus if an A is light, it will be in n_φ, whereas if it is heavy, it will be selected by n_φ. Now let's assume that an element in head position such as a light A is, in effect, a morphological suffix that cannot exist in PHON unless it combines with the phonetic form of a nominal root. Similarly, a Num element in head position will have to be suffixed to the phonological form of the head it is a projection of; and so forth. The result will be complex words of the form [N-A-Num-Dem], whose phonological form is pronounced in the n_{det} (or perhaps n_K) position. In contrast, if an A is heavy, it will be selected by n_φ, leaving the phonological form of N alone to be pronounced in n_φ, and ultimately in some higher head position, leaving the heavy A in the position where it was originally selected.

Pereltsvaig's analysis, if correct, introduces another possible source of parameterization, namely, whether or not a nominal element such as A, Num, or Dem is itself a head, projected by the head below it, or an element selected by the head in question. In the case of prenominal adjectives, the latter possibility was proposed for English in Chapter 3 on independent grounds, claiming in effect that all prenominal adjectives in English are "heavy," whereas in Hebrew prenominal A can be either heavy or light. Obviously, more data is needed to determine whether the heavy/light distinction holds for A in other languages and whether it also holds for other nominal categories such as Num and Dem. One obvious possibility, for example, might be the distinction between pre-nominal and postnominal articles in many Scandinavian languages, where the latter, as is well known, seem to behave more like morphological suffixes, while the former function as independent words.

4.1.7   Two Problem Orders

Of the 14 attested orders listed by Cinque (2005), the only two that remain to be discussed are the following:

(21)   a. A N Dem Num   (=Cinque's (6k))
        b. N A Dem Num   (=Cinque's (6l))

Neither order can be derived by any combination of order of selection, whether uniform or non-uniform, and head displacement. I discuss them in turn.

First of all, I am somewhat doubtful whether (21a) is a genuine instance of a basic word order. In his footnote on this order Cinque states that Koiari also has the order (21b) "with most adjectives." He also notes that Bai has the alternative order N-Dem-Num-A, which I have argued is produced by uniform leftward selection combined with head displacement at n_K. Furthermore, the order (21a) is cited as an alternative to "the unmarked Dem Num A N order of Icelandic" when the Dem element is [−def]. The fact that all the languages claimed to have this order have one or another type of alternative order strongly suggests that it might well be a secondary order, produced, for example, by an operation focusing A, a phenomenon by no means unheard of. In short, the evidence that this is a genuine basic order seems quite weak and is certainly in need of further investigation before any firm conclusion can be drawn.

As for (21b), the languages cited in Cinque's footnote appear to be more numerous and on firmer ground, so I will assume that this is indeed a genuine basic word order. There are a number of possible ways of generating this order, but the one that seems most promising to me is to treat it as an instance of partial snowballing of the type found in Hebrew. Suppose that in some languages all prenominal adjectives are "light," as in Hebrew, hence generated as heads in n_φ. The nominal root would then have to be pronounced at n_φ, where it would combine with A to produce the compound word [N A]. Assuming that the remaining nominal heads $n_\#$, n_{det}, and n_K in these languages are illegible, as in languages of type (4b), the compound head [N A] would then be displaced to the left and ultimately end up being pronounced at n_K, thereby producing the attested order. Again, more research into the languages claimed to have this as a basic word order is clearly called for.

4.1.8   *Toward a Metric of Transparency for Word Order Types*

I conclude this discussion of word order variation in nominals by trying to account in a rough way for the relative frequency of occurrence of the basic word orders discussed in §§4.1.1–4.1.4. It seems reasonable to assume that the major determinant of the frequency of occurrence of a basic word order is the degree of transparency between it and the invariant order of projection of the basic nominal categories. There are some fairly obvious ways that one might measure degree of transparency. First, it is very clear from the data that the two word orders Dem-Num-A-N and its mirror image N-A-Num-Dem, produced by the two uniform orders of selection, are by far the most frequent among the world's languages. The reason is obvious: in both cases the linear order of elements corresponds directly to the order of projection. Hence these orders should certainly score highest on any proposed measure of transparency. In particular, an order of selection should be "rewarded" if it is uniformly leftward or uniformly rightward. Second, even if an order is not produced by one of the two uniform orders of selection, it seems reasonable to suppose that the more pairwise subsequences it contains that are the same as those found in one of the two uniform orders, the more transparent it is. Third, if an order begins with Dem or N, that should increase its transparency, since these are the leftmost elements of the two most frequent orders. Fourth, it is clear from the data that displacement of the pronunciation of the head detracts from the relative transparency of a given ordering. Hence it is reasonable to assume that this is a negative factor, tending to reduce the transparency of a given order.

I propose therefore to construct a measure of transparency based on these factors. There are four measures of transparency, three positive and one negative. Each of the positive measures adds a single point to the "transparency score" of a given word order, while the negative one subtracts a point. The higher the score a given word order receives, the more transparent it is. The four measures are as follows:

(22)   Measures of transparency:
1. Uniform versus non-uniform order of selection: a uniform order of selection adds 1 point.
2. Number of pairwise sequences that are transparent: each one adds 1 point.
3. Whether an order begins with Dem or N: adds 1 point.
4. Whether the derivation of an order involves head displacement: subtracts 1 point.

In addition to these measures of transparency, I will assume that there is one other factor that plays a role in determining relative frequency of occurrence, namely, whether there is more than one way of deriving a given order. If there is, I will assume that each extra derivation adds a point to its measure of transparency.

Given these measures, the two most common orders (1a) and (1b) each receive a total score of 5, because the order of selection is uniform for both (1 point), both have three pairwise subsequences that are transparent (Dem-Num, Num-A, and A-N, in the case of (1a)) (3 points), and both start with Dem or N (1 point). I assume that a score of 5 or more corresponds to Cinque's ranking "very many" and that the possible lower scores correspond to his rough rankings as follows:

(23)   *Score   Frequency*
      5   very many
      4   many
      3   few
    1–2   very few

With these principles in hand, let us see how they apply to the major word order types discussed.

Consider first the word orders (4a), i.e. Dem-Num-N-A, and (4b), i.e. A-N-Num-Dem. Recall that these are mirror images of one another, yet the number of languages with the order (4a) is "many," whereas the number with (4b) is "very few." Applying the proposed principles to (4a), we see that it has two pairwise orders that are transparent (namely, Dem-Num and N-A) and that it begins with Dem, making a total of 3. However, there is also an alternative way of deriving this order, namely, by pronouncing the nominal root at $n_\#$, in which case it is irrelevant whether the order of selection of n_φ is right or left. That adds another point for a total of 4, predicting correctly that the number of languages with this order should be "many." In contrast, the order (4b) only manages a score of 2 by virtue of the fact that its only points come from having two pairwise orders that are transparent (A-N and Num-Dem). Hence the number of languages with this order is predicted correctly to be "very few."

The next pair of non-uniform mirror-image orders is (4c) (Dem-A-N-Num) and (4d) (Num-N-A-Dem). The number of languages with the former order is, unsurprisingly, "very few," since there is only one transparent pair A-N, though it does begin with Dem. More surprising is the fact that the number of languages with (4d) is "few," despite the fact that this order has only one transparent pair and does not begin with either Dem or N, hence should have a score of only 1. Note, however, that there are *two* additional ways of deriving this order. If N is pronounced at n_φ, rather than n_{nom} and the order of selection of n_φ is rightward, the same order is generated, as is the case if N is pronounced at $n_\#$, in which case the order of selection of n_φ can be either right or left. Adding 2 points for these two alternative derivations raises the total to 3, predicting correctly that the number of languages with this order should be "few."

The final pair of mirror-image orders, (4e) and (4f) is similar to the first pair in that the number of languages with the former is "many," whereas the number with the latter is "very few." The score of the latter (Num-A-N-Dem) is 2, as expected, since there are two pairwise orders that are transparent, but no other source of points. In contrast, (4e) (Dem-N-A-Num) has a total of 4 points, since it has two pairwise transparent orders (N-A and A-Num), begins with Dem, and has another possible derivation in which the nominal root is pronounced at $n_\#$ and the order of selection of n_φ is left.

We see, then, that the proposed metric of frequency correctly predicts that of the six non-uniform derivations, the first and third pairs differ significantly in frequency of occurrence, despite the fact that these pairs are mirror images of one another. The reason, as has been shown, is that mirror-image pairs produced by a non-uniform order of selection, unlike those produced by a uniform order of selection, can result in orders that differ significantly in transparency.

Consider next orders (11a) and (11b), discussed in §4.1.3, which combine uniform order of selection with head displacement. The first of these receives a score of 2, correctly predicting that languages with this order should be "very few" in number. The reason is that even though this order (Dem-N-Num-A) has one transparent pairwise subsequence Num-A, starts with Dem, and has uniform order of selection, it must be demoted a point because its derivation requires head displacement. In contrast, the second order (N-Dem-Num-A) gets a score of 3, correctly predicting a higher frequency of occurrence "few," because even though it has two pairwise transparent subsequences Dem-Num and Num-A, starts with N, and has uniform direction of projection, yielding a total of 4, this amount must be reduced by 1 since its derivation requires head displacement.

Now let's look at the two orders (14a) and (14b), discussed in §4.1.4, that are produced by a combination of non-uniform order of selection and head displacement. The first of these (N-Dem-A-Num), according to the proposed metric, only manages to achieve a score of 1. The reason is that even though there is one pairwise transparent subsequence A-Num and this order begins with N, the score of 2 must be reduced by 1 because its derivation requires head displacement. Interestingly, this order can only be derived in Cinque's system by an extremely marked sequence of movement operations, leading him to suggest in footnote 27 that it might actually be a "spurious" order. Cinque bases this conclusion on the fact that there are only three languages reported to have this order and that two of these have the alternative order N-Dem-Num-A. However, Abels and Neeleman (2008) take issue with his argument, concluding after a closer consideration of the available literature that the basic order in two of these languages (namely, Pitjantjtjara and Nokore-Kiga) is clearly N-Dem-A-Num, hence the order cannot be spurious. Notice, however, that the extreme rarity of this order accords well with the fact that it only achieves a score of 1—the lowest of any of the attested orders—according to the metric proposed here. The second order (14b) (N-Num-A-Dem) should also be quite rare by my metric, also apparently managing only a score of 1, since the existence of one pairwise transparent subsequence Num-A, together with the fact that it begins with N, is offset by the fact that its derivation involves head displacement. Cinque claims that the number of languages with this order is "few." However, looking at his footnote 17, we find that it is in fact firmly reported to occur in only six languages, whereas the order Num-N-A-Dem (my (4d), Cinque's (6s)), also claimed to be "few" in number, is reported to occur in approximately 15 or so languages. I must therefore conclude that the data in these cases is simply too sketchy to permit any definite conclusion at this point as to the relative rarity of this order.

There are only three more cases to be discussed. Languages of the Japanese/Turkish type have three pairwise transparent subsequences and begin with Dem, as well as having a uniform direction of selection, but should be penalized a point because they require head displacement. They would thus have a score of 4, predicting them to belong to the "many" category. As for languages such as Hebrew and Arabic, I have no idea at this point how prevalent languages with snowballing head displacement are, nor do I have a clue whether languages should be rewarded, penalized, or neither for making use of such derivations. Similarly, the status of the problematic order (21b) discussed in §4.1.6 is fraught with too much uncertainty to make any confident prediction as to its relative frequency of occurrence. Cinque (cf. footnote 12) cites only eight clear attestations of this order in the literature, yet states that the number of languages with this order is "few," which seems perhaps a bit high, given that the number of attested languages at this level of frequency in other cases such as (4d) is double that number.

4.1.9   Summary and Discussion

If, as I claim in this work, the primitives of syntactic theory are relations between words rather than constituents, then linearization is necessarily a function of the basic relations of projection, selection, and modification. It makes sense, then, that the major source of variation in word order should be simple directionality parameters associated not only with each type of relation but with specific instances of each relation, though other factors such as head displacement play a role as well. I have shown in this analysis of nominal structures that each of the attested orders of the basic nominal elements Dem, Num, A, and N can be accounted for by some logically possible combination of values of directionality parameters associated with the selection features of lexical heads, together with parametric variation in the height at which the nominal root is pronounced. Choice of linear order is thus basically free for the selection relation. Linear ordering of the projection relation may also be either uniformly leftward or uniformly rightward, though the latter is only possible as long as selection is uniformly leftward.[3] Another possible source of variation, about which much less is known, arises from the possibility that nominal elements such as Dem, Num, and A may be heads in some languages rather than selected items. In such languages there may exist the possibility of snowballing head displacement. Finally, I have tried to show that the relative frequency of occurrence of the attested word order variants is at least roughly predictable as a function of four measures of the transparency of the relation between linear ordering and the universal order of projection of nominal categories. Frequency of occurrence is also increased if a given word order can be derived in more than one way. It emerges very clearly from this account of word order variation that the only cross-linguistic invariant of importance is the (bottom-up) order in which projection relations between nominal heads are formed. This appears to be a core universal property of the syntax of nominals and, by extension, of other syntactic projections, as well.

This raises an important conceptual issue that is in need of clarification. Proponents of the antisymmetric approach to word order often argue that languages with different word orders should be derived by movement from a single universal order because their syntactic structures are basically identical. This, however, is a non-sequitur. The *reason* languages exhibit variation in word order is precisely *because* linear order is structurally irrelevant. As I have tried to show throughout this work, it is the *relations* of selection and projection that are syntactically important, irrespective of how they are mapped onto linear order at PHON. As long as the order in which the fundamental relations of projection and selection are constructed remains invariant, we should expect the linear order of selection (and also modification) to show any and all possible

---

[3] But see the discussion of Malayalam in §6.2.6.1.

variants consistent with the incremental nature of the Spell-out algorithm. From this viewpoint, the additional assumption that there is a single underlying linear order from which all the other linear orders are derived is not only completely redundant but somewhat perverse, since it appears to be asserting, contrary to its own assumptions, that linear order *does* have syntactic significance. Those who believe that there is a single linear order of elements from which all other variants are derived have been misled, I believe, by the fact that some orders are more transparent than others. As I have tried to show, however, it is possible to construct measures of transparency that are sufficient to explain why some orders are more commonly found in the world's languages than others that do not depend on the extra, and completely unnecessary, assumption that all of the attested orders must be derived from one single privileged order by complex and often unmotivated movement operations.

Why has the idea that there is a single universal underlying linear order, from which all others must be derived, exerted such a tenacious hold on the imagination of theoretical linguists? The reason, ultimately, lies in the fact that the primitives of mainstream syntactic theory are constituents rather than relations. The problem is that there is no inherent directionality between the terms of a constituent, hence no way to represent the fact, using only the primitives of the theory, that relations between words are fundamentally asymmetrical. To make up for this deficiency, antisymmetric analyses introduce asymmetry through the back door in the guise of linear order. In effect, the rightward head–complement relation and the leftward head–specifier relation required in the underlying universal linear order become roundabout ways of representing the asymmetric relations of projection and selection, respectively. Ironically, far from banishing linear order from the fundamental representations of narrow syntax, antisymmetry has unwittingly reintroduced it as a primitive! Because this method of representing the fundamental asymmetry of syntactic relations fails to tackle the problem directly, using instead the inappropriate primitive of linear order, the inevitable result is a proliferation of redundant and unnecessary projections and movement operations. Though the pronunciation of a head or a phrase is sometimes "displaced" on account of the legibility requirements of PHON and SEM, the conditions under which such displacement may occur are highly constrained, and displacement itself is not part of narrow syntax *per se*. Still another problem with antisymmetry, as shown in earlier chapters, is that it makes it impossible for lexical projection to be fully bottom-up. If argument selection is represented by the leftward head–specifier relation, then the only way to represent projection is indirectly by means of the rightward head–complement relation, which is inherently top-down. In addition, because the head–complement relation is a relation between a head and a maximal projection, the notion of an "extended projection" can only be incorporated into syntactic theory by fiat. In a theory based on relations, in contrast, "extended" projections are produced directly by successive instances of projection.

4.2   Word Order Variation in v-projections

Because there are more heads of various kinds in *v*-projections than there are in *n*-projections, the number of possible word order variations is much greater. Hence it will only be possible to scratch the surface of the possible word order variations found in clausal structures. Rather than attempting a broad survey, I shall instead focus on a few selected problems, some of which have been discussed quite intensively in the recent literature. In particular, I shall devote some attention to word order phenomena uncovered recently in verb-initial (VSO and VOS) and verb-final (SOV) languages. Another difference between *v*-projections and *n*-projections is that argument structure generally plays a much more important role in the former than in the latter, further increasing the combinatorial possibilities. Perhaps for that reason, much more attention has been focused in the literature on the order of the verb and the most basic subject (S) and object (O) arguments than on the order of the higher functional categories. There are, however, some quite exotic variations attested in the latter area that deserve notice. A third difference between *v*-projections and *n*-projections is that displacement, both of heads and of projections, plays a much larger role in the former than in the latter, which often obscures the basic structure of a language. Hence care must be taken to ensure that any given sentence type is not the result of one or more displacements in trying to determine how the word order parameters of a language are set.

4.2.1   The Most Basic Word Orders: SVO, VSO, and SOV

It has been a standard observation in the typological literature since Greenberg (1963) that the most common basic word orders in sentences are those in which subject (S) precedes object (O). Accordingly, I start by showing that, just as is the case for nominal projections, the most common orders are just those in which the relation between linear order and the order of projection is the most transparent. In particular, languages with uniform leftward selection and uniform leftward projection are predicted to occur most frequently. A good example of this type is English, whose word order properties have been argued at length in the preceding chapters to be predicted, in a theory whose primitives are relations rather than constituents, by setting the parameter for selection as uniformly leftward. The basic SVO word order of such languages is thus derived as follows:

(24)

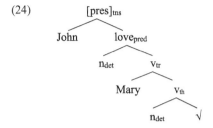

Furthermore, as has been argued extensively in the literature, the basic word order VSO is simply a special case of SVO produced by displacement of the lexical head of the *v*-projection to a higher position, combined with the absence of an athematic argument selection feature in the head v_{tns}. Thus, for example, the same sentence in a typical VSO language might be derived as follows:[4]

(25)

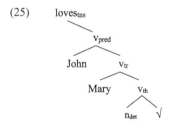

Since the basic word orders SVO and VSO are both cases of the most basic word order type produced by selecting uniform leftward projection and uniform leftward selection, I will henceforth group them together as a single class typologically. Hence I will not spend more time here on languages with uniform leftward selection, focusing instead on less familiar language types that have only begun to attract attention more recently.

Consider next the class of SOV languages. It was pointed out earlier that N-final nominals with rightward projection can be distinguished from N-final nominals with leftward selection by examining (a) the position of arguments relative to the head, and (b) the presence of rightward Case-marking particles. In the case of *v*-projections, it is even more straightforward to determine rightward projection combined with leftward argument selection, since the position of arguments relative to the head is immediately obvious, as is the

---

[4] Obviously, other, more articulated analyses are possible, the details of which will not be of concern here.

presence of tense and aspect morphology, complementizer elements, etc. located to the right of the verbal root. The same basic sentence type in an SOV language would thus be derived as follows:[5]

(26)

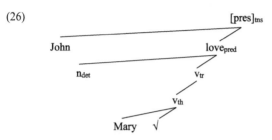

Based on these criteria, all SOV languages with which I am familiar are of this type. They also occur at least as frequently as SVO and VSO languages combined, and by some estimates more frequently. A somewhat more articulated structure for a typical SOV language would look as follows (with the root potentially pronounced at v_{pred}, v_{tns}, or v_{comp}, depending on the language):

(27)

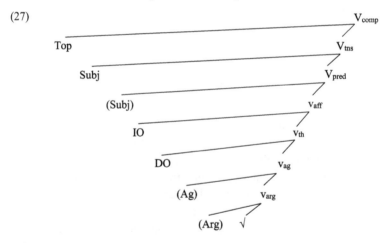

Setting aside some issues regarding the position of non-core quasi-argumental elements such as instrumentals, source and goal phrases, comitatives, low benefactives, etc., this is more or less the structure found in classic SOV languages such as Japanese, Turkish, and many others. Such languages

---

[5] There is evidence that v_{tr} in Japanese neither assigns structural accusative Case nor has an athematic selection feature (Bowers 2010: 92–94). Whether this is true generally of verb-final languages I shall not try to decide here. Likewise, I put aside here many other contentious issues in the syntax of SOV languages that have been discussed in the recent literature.

typically have agglutinative-type tense, agreement, and aspect morphology after the verb on the right edge, followed by complementizers, clause-typing elements, etc., combined with left-periphery elements such as topic and focus on the left, followed by core arguments ordered more or less the same as in SVO and VSO languages.

4.2.2 VOS Languages

One question of particular concern here is whether there are languages (and language families) in which the direction of projection is uniformly leftward and the direction of selection uniformly rightward. I shall argue that VOS languages such as Malagasy, Tzotzil, Q. Zapotec, Palauan, etc. (and perhaps some VSO languages as well) are of precisely this type. Let us start by considering the following Malagasy examples from Travis (2005):

(28) a. [Mansa   ny   lamba   ho an'ny   ankizy]   ny   lehilahy
         PRES-AT.wash   DET   clothes for-DET   children   DET   man
         'The man washes clothes for the children.'

      b. [Sasan'ny   lehilahy ho an'ny   ankizy]   ny   lamba
         TT.wash-DET   man   for-DET   children   DET   clothes
         'The clothes are washed for the children by the man.'

      c. [Anasan'ny   lehilahy ny   lamba]   ny   ankizy
         CT.wash. DET   man   DET   clothes DET   children
         'The children are washed the clothes by the man.'

These examples illustrate the well-known fact that a wide range of elements can appear in a sentence-final subject/topic position. The function of this element is morphologically marked on the verb: actor topic morphology (AT) in the first example, theme topic morphology (TT) in the second, and circumstantial topic morphology (CT) in the third. As is by now well known, the position of argument expressions can vary quite widely in languages such as English with uniform leftward selection. Exactly the same is true of languages with uniform rightward selection. I propose to explain the essential properties of Malagasy and similar languages by means of four assumptions. First, I assume that selection is uniformly rightward. Second, I assume, following Bowers (2010), that the order of projection of the argument categories that introduce agents, themes, and affectees is, starting from the bottom, $v_{ag} < v_{th} < v_{aff} < v_{pred}$. Third, I assume that the minimal verbal projection category v_{pred} has an athematic selection feature that must be satisfied by forming a relation with one of the arguments previously selected. Fourth, I assume that the morphology of the verb marks which argument is selected by v_{pred}.[6] Thus AT morphology on the verb accompanies selection of the agent argument, TT morphology accompanies selection of the theme argument, and CT morphology accompanies selection of the affectee argument (among others). The derivation of the examples in (28) will then proceed as shown schematically as follows:

(29)

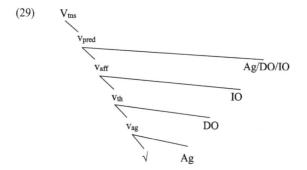

If the Ag argument is selected as subject by v_{pred}, the resulting order is: AT +V - ~~Ag~~ - DO - IO - Ag. If the Th argument is selected, the order is: TT+V - Ag - ~~DO~~ - IO - DO. Finally, if the IO is selected, the order is: CT+V - Ag - DO - ~~IO~~ - IO. Basically, then, the word order of Malagasy is the mirror image of English, though there are a few language-specific differences between them that somewhat obscure this fact. In particular, v_{ag} arguments in English can only be realized in low (hence rightmost) position in sentences with passive morphology, whereas in Malagasy the v_{ag} argument appears in lowest position (hence closest to the verbal root) unless it is selected by v_{pred}.[7]

Another apparent difference between English and Malagasy is that the DO and the IO in English can appear in either the order IO-DO or DO-IO, though in the latter case the IO must be marked with a preposition:

(30)   a. John gave Mary the book.
        b. John gave the book to Mary.

---

[6] I will not spell out here the exact mechanism required to ensure that the morphology of the verb is correctly matched with the argument selected by v_{pred}. Basically, what is needed is an extension of the mechanisms at work in systems with agreement and structural Case assignment. For further discussion, see Chapter 5.

[7] In fact, Malagasy and related VOS languages provide crucial support for the claim of Bowers (2010) that the v_{ag} argument is projected before any other thematic arguments, because it is extremely difficult to account for the appearance of the agent immediately adjacent to the verb in TT and CT constructions without positing massive reordering operations.

As was argued in §2.4.2.2, following Bowers (2002, 2010), this alternation is best explained by assuming a category v_{tr} below v_{pred} that has an athematic selection feature that also requires its argument to have so-called "structural" ACC Case. If the DO is Case-marked, then it appears adjacent to the verb and the IO must be marked with a preposition, whereas if the IO is marked with Case, it appears adjacent to the verb and the DO is marked with inherent ACC Case:

(31)

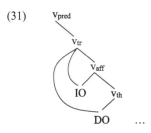

Interestingly, however, it seems that how far to the right a v_{th} argument occurs in Malagasy depends on whether it is definite or indefinite. This is shown by the fact (cf. Rackowski 1998) that indefinite v_{th} arguments occur to the left of all adverbs, including manner adverbs, whereas definite v_{th} arguments occur to the right of manner adverbs and to the left of other adverbs:

(32)   a. Manasa   tsara   ny   lambany   foana   i   Ketaka
            PRES.wash well   DET   clothes   always   DEF Ketaka
            'Ketaka always washes his clothes well.'
    b. Nijinja   vary   haingana   ny   mpamboly
            PAST.cut rice   quickly   DET   farmer
            'The farmer harvested rice quickly.'
    c. Nijinja   haingana   ny   vary   ny   mpamboly
            PAST.cut quickly   DET   rice   DET   farmer
            'The farmer harvested the rice quickly.'

To account for these observations, let us assume that the category v_{tr} is projected in Malagasy below v_{pred} with an athematic selection feature, just as it is in English, but that v_{tr} in Malagasy selects an n-projection with the feature [+def] rather than an n-projection with a particular Case feature. Now observe that if, as argued in Chapter 3, adverbs such as *foana* 'always' (Adv$_1$) are modifiers of v_{pred}, whereas manner adverbs such as *tsara* 'well' (Adv$_2$) are modifiers of v_{tr}, then under the linearization principles outlined there,[8] the

---

[8] I assume that the direction of selection of adverbial modifiers is uniformly rightward in Malagasy, consistent with the direction of selection of arguments and contrasting with English, which allows either direction. See §4.3 for further discussion.

former will be linearized to the left of the subject Ag and to the right of DO [+def], while the latter will be linearized to the left of DO[+def]:

(33)

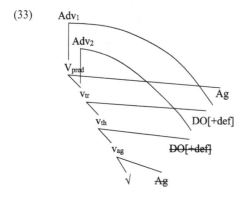

If, on the other hand, DO is [−def], hence not selected by v_{tr}, it will occur to the left of Adv$_2$. We have thus succeeded in predicting correctly the linear order of elements V-DO[−def]-Adv$_2$-DO[+def]-Adv$_1$-Ag simply by assuming that Malagasy has uniform rightward selection of both arguments and modifiers, making it unnecessary to resort to the complex series of "intraposition" movements of predicates posited by Rackowski (1998), Rackowski and Travis (2000), and Travis (2005).

Let us consider next the placement of the interrogative particle in Malagasy, comparing it with the related Austronesian languages Seediq and Atayal, both spoken in the northern part of northern Taiwan. Holmer (2005) provides the following data:

(34)   a. **ye=su**   m-n-ekan   hlama   kiya?   Seediq
            INTERR-2SG.NOM   ACT-PST-eat   steamed.rice   that
            'Did you eat that steamed rice snack?'

       b. kia'   'i'   ma-qilaap   'i'   yaya'   **quw?**   Atayal
            ASP   LINK   ACT-sleep   NOM   mother   INTERR
            'Is mother sleeping?'

       c. Nanome   vola   an-dRobe   **ve**   ianao?   Malagasy
            gave   money   ACC-Rabe   INTERR   you
            'Did you give Rabe money?'

As can be seen, the interrogative particle is initial in Seediq, final in Atayal, and occurs before the subject in Malagasy. The first two cases are straightforward. We may assume that in Seediq, the interrogative particle *ye* is located in the head v_{comp}, while in Atayal the equivalent particle *quw* is selected by $\varnothing_{comp}$:

(35)

(36)

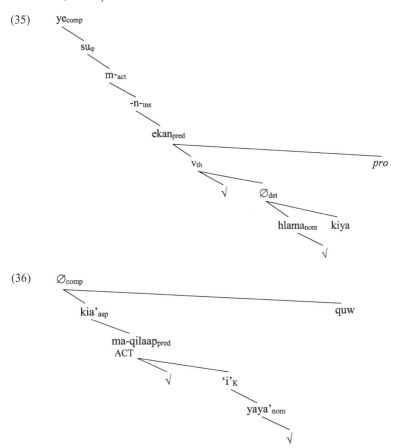

As for Malagasy, it is interesting to note that there has been quite a bit of discussion in the literature as to whether the rightmost argument is a subject or a topic. Since substantive arguments in support of both views can be found in the literature, I will assume it is both. We can then account for the position of the interrogative particle *ve* as shown in the following derivation:

(37)

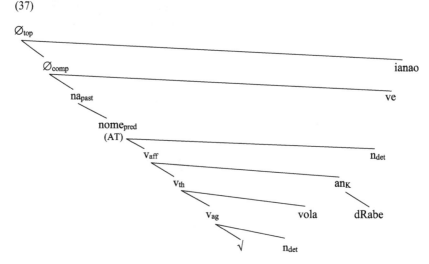

All three positions of the interrogative particle in the linear ordering of these related languages can thus be accounted for under the assumption that they have essentially identical syntactic structures, as well as uniform rightward selection. In contrast, the analysis proposed by Holmer (2005) requires head movement, predicate movement of different size constituents, as well as positing that the interrogative particle is in a different head in Malagasy than it is in Seediq and Atayal.

Seediq is particularly interesting because though its interrogative particle is on the left, due to the fact that it functions as a head rather than being selected, it has many other particles that occur on the right. These include the aspectual particles *di* and *na*, the evidential particle *si* (quotative), and the subordinators/discourse connectors *do* and *peni*. (See Holmer 2005 for the data and discussion.) Since these particles can also co-occur with one another, it is possible to determine the order of projection under the assumption that they are selected by their appropriate heads roughly as follows:

(38)

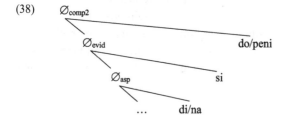

Finally, Tagalog differs from Seediq in that the corresponding particles occur as enclitics to the highest head$_{comp1}$, which is projected from v_{comp2} in (38). This is easily accounted for if (a) the particles in question are enclitics contained in heads in

Tagalog, and (b) the element that is displaced to the highest head v_{compl} has to move through these head positions before reaching its ultimate position of pronunciation.

In summary, the two most transparent ordering parameters in v-projections, namely, uniform leftward selection and uniform rightward selection, are both well represented in the world's languages, with the most common, predictably, being the former. An interesting question is why there seem to be so many more languages that exhibit uniform rightward selection in nominals than in sentences. While I do not have a fully satisfactory explanation to propose here, it is worth considering the possibility that there is a universal tendency to place more prominent elements such as subjects before less prominent elements, which would obviously conflict with the basic word order produced by uniform rightward selection. In contrast to sentences, relative prominence is rarely formally marked in nominals, making it possible for rightward selection to be utilized without coming into conflict with this principle.

4.2.3   OVS and OSV Languages?

For many years it was believed, following Greenberg (1963), that languages with the basic word orders OVS and OSV were not attested. Since it was known that there were a non-trivial number of languages (and language families) of the sort just discussed with the order VOS, this made it difficult to explain the absence of OVS and OSV languages solely on the grounds that subjects universally precede objects. However, in recent years researchers have uncovered at least a few possible languages of these very rare types (cf. particularly Derbyshire and Pullum 1981), though more work needs to be done before it can be concluded with any degree of certainty that the languages in question are genuine examples of these basic word orders.

Regardless of whether these word orders are attested or not, the theory proposed here predicts that they should be either impossible or extremely rare, because the only way they can be produced is by combining uniform rightward projection with uniform rightward selection, as shown in the following derivation of OVS order:

(39)

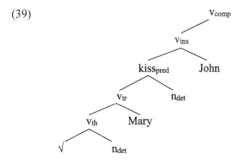

As we saw in the case of *n*-projections, the orders produced by uniform rightward projection combined with uniform rightward selection are unattested, strongly suggesting that the same is true of *v*-projections. It would be even more difficult to produce OSV order, requiring either displacement of the verbal root to v_{tns} combined with absence of an athematic selection feature in v_{tns} (i.e. the mirror image of VSO languages) or displacement of the verbal root all the way to v_{comp}. These orders thus not only violate the general condition that places prominent elements such as subjects in leftward position, but also can only be produced in the framework proposed here by a combination of rightward projection and rightward selection, the only combination of parameter settings completely disallowed in *n*-projections. It is therefore not surprising that such orders are also extremely rare, if not non-existent, in *v*-projections.

4.2.4   Direction of Negation

I have not so far found any convincing cases of non-uniform argument selection, including both thematic and athematic argument selection, which suggests that maintaining a transparent relation between linear ordering and the direction of projection of arguments is virtually obligatory in natural language.[9] In contrast, as was shown earlier in this chapter, the direction of selection in the case of functional elements such as Dem, Num, and non-argumental elements such as prenominal modifiers is basically free. Hence the same might be expected to be true of *v*-projections. As a test case, I next examine the data usefully assembled in Dryer (1988) concerning the order of negation relative to the other basic elements of the clause.

There are 16 logically possible orders that negation (Neg) can have relative to the basic clause elements V, S, and O. Of these, ten orders are well attested with differing degrees of frequency of occurrence, one is only attested in one of the languages in his sample of 354 languages, and five are unattested. In (40) I present the 16 orders arranged in groups of four corresponding to the four main types of clause discussed in §§4.2.1–4.2.2, namely, SVO, SOV, VSO, and VOS. Within each group the orders are arranged from most to least common, unattested orders are starred, and the one order of which there is only one example is indicated with a question mark:

---

[9] Some apparent cases, such as the fact that v_{aff} and v_{th} arguments are ordered v_{aff}-v_{th} in some languages but the opposite in other languages, can be shown to arise as the result of displacement caused by an athematic selection feature associated with v_{tr} in some languages (cf. Bowers 2010, Chapter 3, for discussion). See also the discussion of indefinite versus definite v_{th} arguments in Malagasy in §4.2.2 above.

(40)   a. SVO   b. SOV   c. VSO   d. VOS
         1. S Neg V O   1. S O V Neg   1. Neg V S O   1. Neg V O S
         2. S V O Neg   2. S O Neg V   2. ?V Neg S O   2. *V Neg O S
         3. Neg S V O   3. Neg S O V   3. *V S Neg O   3. *V O Neg S
         4. S V Neg O   4. S Neg O V   4. *V S O Neg   4. *V O S Neg

I assume, following the discussion of negation in §3.1.3 (see also §6.1), that there is a projection v_Σ above v_{pred} and below v_{tns} which is responsible for negative and positive polarity in clauses. Let's assume in addition that v_Σ[neg] may either left-select or right-select an element represented abstractly as "Neg." Given a language (such as English, for example) in which S is displaced leftward due to an athematic argument selection feature in v_{tns}, this will immediately produce the two most commonly found orders in SVO languages listed in (40a):

(41)

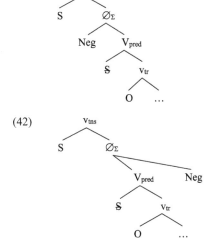

(42)

In a language lacking an athematic argument selection feature in v_{tns}, however, leftward selection of Neg will produce the third order Neg-S-V-O in group (40a):[10]

---

[10] Note that rightward selection of Neg in this configuration provides an alternative way of deriving order 2, presumably helping to explain why it is one of the two commonest orders of Neg in SVO languages. Whether there are languages of this type is unknown.

(43)

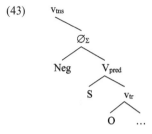

Finally, the least common order of the four can only be derived if pronunciation of the verbal root is displaced to v_{tns} and v_{tns} has an athematic argument selection feature:[11]

(44)

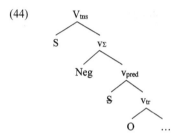

As was shown earlier, displacement of the pronunciation of the verbal root contributes to lack of transparency, explaining in part why this is the least common of the four orders.

Consider next the possible orders in verb-final languages. Interestingly, the most common word order in SOV languages is immediately generated by right-selection of Neg combined with the canonical structure for such languages suggested in (40b):

(45)

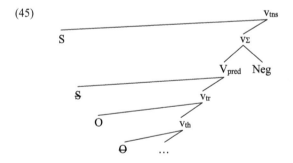

---

[11] Again, rightward selection of Neg in this configuration will produce order 2. Whether there are languages in which order 2 can be shown to be derived in this way, I do not at present know.

This analysis, however, may not be correct in all cases. For the Lakota example Dryer (1988: 97) cites as an example of this type of language, this might well be the right derivation:

(46) Lakota kiŋ k'aŋgí s'e iynuŋka-pi kiŋ he iyókip'i-pi śni.
      Lakota the crow like lie.down-3PL the that like-PL NEG
      'The Lakotas don't like lying down like crows.'

But in languages like Japanese and Korean, the negative element that appears in examples with this word order is an inflected morpheme, suggesting, as proposed by Whitman (2005), that it is in the head of v_Σ rather than selected by it:

(47) Mica ka hakkyo ey ka-ci **anh**-ass-ta. (Korean)
      Mica NOM school to go-SUSP NEG-PAST-INDIC
      'Mica didn't go to school.'

There are thus two possible ways of producing Neg-final order in SOV languages. If the Neg element is a free-standing uninflected word, then it is selected by v_Σ, as shown in (45). If, however, it is in the head of v_Σ, then it blocks displacement of the verbal root and acts in effect like an inflected verbal element, being displaced first into v_{tns} and finally into v_{comp}:

(48)

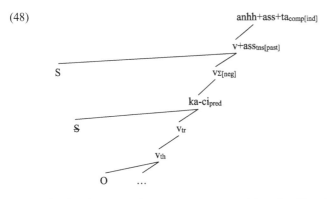

Interestingly, the second most common position for Neg in verb-final languages is immediately preceding the inflected verb. Again, it is instructive to look at a Korean example such as the following (Whitman 2005: 880):

(49) Mica ka hakkyo ey **an** ka-ss-ta. (Korean)
      Mica NOM school to NEG go-PAST-INDIC
      'Mica didn't go to school.'

Here the verbal root is inflected, while the Neg element *an* is a free-standing uninflected element. To derive these examples, let us assume that *an* is right-selected by v_Σ, thereby permitting the verbal root to be displaced through it on its way to v_{comp}:

(50)

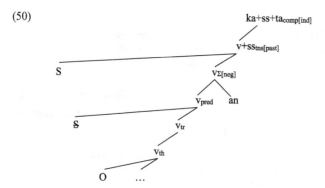

As Whitman (2005: 881) notes, uninflected *an* in Korean is parallel to *pas* in French, while the inflected negator *anh-* is parallel to French *ne*. In fact, French negation can be regarded as precisely the mirror image of Japanese, except that both Neg elements appear simultaneously in French, as shown in the following derivation of the sentence *Vous n'allez pas*:

(51)

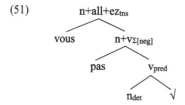

The remaining two orders in SOV languages are straightforwardly derived by leftward selection of the Neg element, with or without leftward displacement of the subject:

(52)

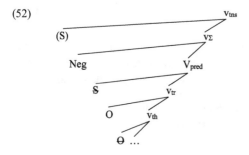

All the attested orders of Neg in both SVO and SOV languages are thus derived simply by specifying right or left selection of the Neg element or by placing it in the v_Σ head, while maintaining uniform right or left selection of arguments, both thematic and athematic.

To conclude, let us look briefly at the possible word orders in verb-initial languages. For VSO languages the overwhelmingly most common pattern is Neg-V-S-O. This order is derived straightforwardly in a language with the following properties: (i) v_{tns} lacks an athematic selection feature, (ii) v_Σ left-selects Neg, and (iii) v_Σ is phonetically illegible, forcing displacement of the verbal root:

(53)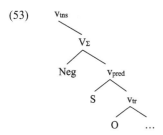

The same result could be achieved if there were a negative prefix in the v_Σ head, requiring the verbal root to be displaced and combined with it. Whether such a language is attested I do not at present know.

Suppose next that there existed a language exactly like the one just discussed except that pronunciation of the verbal root had to be displaced to v_{tns} for morphological reasons. The result would be the order V-Neg-S-O, of which there is only one attested example in Dryer's sample:

(54)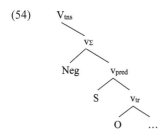

This order could also be derived if the negative element were a suffix in the v_Σ head which was required to combine with the displaced verbal root. The one attested example of this order cited by Dryer from Cariri (an extinct language once spoken in Equatorial Brazil) could in fact be of precisely this type:[12]

---

[12] I do not at present know whether there are languages in which v-projections require the kind of "snowballing" head displacement apparently found in n-projections in languages such as Hebrew (cf. §4.1.6 for discussion). However, Cariri is the type of language that would be a possible candidate.

(55)   netso-kié   di-dè   i-ña
        be.seen-NEG   his mother   him-by
        'His mother has not been seen by him.'   (Adam 1897: 29)

Further investigation is obviously needed in order to decide which type of language this is and whether or not the paucity of examples of this type of word order is an accidental gap.

The remaining two orders are both unattested in Dryer's sample. The order V-S-O-Neg is predicted to be possible by the theory proposed here, by specifying rightward selection of Neg in a derivation such as that in (54), while the order V-S-Neg-O could also be derived, but only if there were a type of VSO language produced by displacement of the verbal root all the way to v_{comp}, combined with selection of the subject by v_{tns}. Whether the absence of these two possible orders is an accidental gap is a question that can only be decided by further investigation.

The situation with VOS languages is similar in that of the four possible orders only one, namely, Neg-V-O-S, is attested in Dryer's sample. This order is straightforwardly derivable by leftward selection of Neg in a VOS structure such as (25), or by assuming that the Neg element is present in v_Σ:

(56)

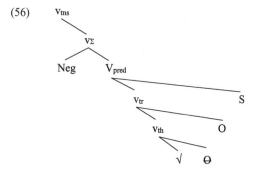

The order V-Neg-O-S could also be derived if there were a VOS language in which the verbal root was displaced to v_{tns}. Likewise the orders V-O-Neg-S and V-O-S-Neg could be derived by rightward selection of Neg with or without displacement of S further to the right in order to satisfy an athematic argument selection feature in v_{tns}. Given the fact that the least common basic word order is VOS, it does not seem unreasonable to suppose that these gaps are simply accidental. Dryer's solution is to state the following universal:

(57)   If a language is verb-initial, then the negative will precede the verb.

However, this merely summarizes the data without explaining it and is not, in any case, exceptionless, since the language Cariri is, as was mentioned above, a counterexample, having the order V-Neg-S-O.

In summary, then, apart from a few unattested orders in the least common word order types, it appears that negation can either be in the head of v_Σ or selected by it, and that the direction of selection in the latter case is free. This lends further support to the general conclusion of §4.1.8 that the linear order of elements in PHON is basically free, as long as the fundamental order of projection is preserved and the constraints imposed by the incremental nature of the Spell-out algorithm are respected. At the same time, some evidence has emerged that while this conclusion may hold for functional elements, the order of projection of true arguments is uniform in any given language, a possibility that will be investigated further in §4.3. Broadly speaking, the word order data in *v*-projections also supports the idea advanced earlier that the frequency of occurrence of a given type of word order reflects the degree to which the fundamental order of projection is transparently preserved in linear order. In the case of *v*-projections, however, there are many more independent factors that affect word order than there are in nominals, making the measures of transparency proposed earlier harder to apply. There are also more projections that have to be taken into consideration, further complicating the task. The observations set forth here are therefore only a beginning.

4.2.5   *Non-uniform Direction of* v-*projection*

So far I have focused exclusively on orders produced by non-uniform direction of selection, but orders produced by non-uniform direction of projection are to be found as well, though they appear to be far less common. Also, since there does not exist in the literature a survey of the range of variation in clauses as systematic as that provided by Cinque (2005) for nominals, my discussion of this topic will necessarily be confined to a few preliminary observations, leaving much room for future research.

One well-known example of non-uniform projection is provided by German and Dutch, in which *v*-projection is rightward up to the v_{tns} level, but leftward above that. Let us assume that the directionality parameter for projection is generally rightward in German. Obviously, then, it must be stipulated as a special property of German that the projection feature for v_{tns} is (uniformly) leftward: $[\_v_{comp}]_L$. The parameter for argument selection, in contrast, is uniformly leftward. Another well-known and much analyzed property of German is that the verb is final if the v_{comp} head is occupied by a complementizer such as *daß, weil*, etc., If not, the topmost auxiliary must be displaced to

v_{comp}, accompanied by displacement of some projection to its left. This is the famous V2 phenomenon, which reduces in this framework to the stipulation that v_{comp} may either contain an illegible head v with an obligatory athematic argument selection feature underspecified as to the category of the selected argument, or an overt complementizer with no athematic argument selection.[13] With these assumptions in place, the clauses *Heute wird Johann das Buch lesen* and *daß Johann das Buch lesen wird* may be derived as follows:[14]

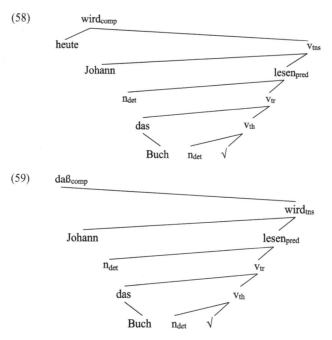

Similar word order variations dependent on clause type are found in a variety of different languages and can be accounted for in much the same way (see Siewierska 1988: 89–93), for a useful survey).

As one further example of non-uniform direction of projection, let us consider briefly an interesting variation found in the Niger-Congo language Kru

---

[13] The facts are more complicated in other Germanic languages such as Icelandic, Yiddish, Danish, Faroese, Norwegian, Swedish, etc., in which complementizers co-occur with V2, suggesting either that v_{comp} is recursive (Vikner 1995: 65–57) or that more than one head above v_{tns} is required.

[14] I omit from these derivations many details not relevant to the discussion such as the initial position of the time adverbial *heute*, about which I will have more to say in §4.2.6.1, as well as the final position of definite objects such as *das Buch*.

(Siewierska 1988: 92, citing Givón 1979: 124), in which the usual SVO order becomes SOV in negative clauses:

(60)   a. Nyeyu-na   bia   nyino-na.
          man-the   beat   woman-the
          'The man beat the woman.'
       b. Nyeyu-na   si   nyino-na   bia
          man-the   neg   woman-the   beat
          'The man didn't beat the woman.'

Assuming the projection parameter for Kru is set leftwards, the language-specific variation in word order in (60b) can be accounted for by specifying a rightward projection feature $[\_v_{tns}]_R$ for the head v_Σ, just in case it has the value [neg], leaving it to project v_{tns} leftwards if it has the value [pos].[15] Examples (60a,b) can then be derived as follows:

(61)

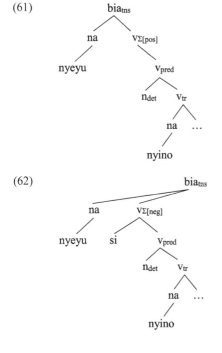

(62)

Crucially, the direction of argument selection is uniformly leftwards, as was also the case in German.

4.2.6   *Word Order Variation of Modifiers*

It is tempting to imagine that there is a relationship between direction of argument selection and direction of modification. Specifically, it was proposed by Greenberg (1963) and others that OV languages tend to be AN, while VO languages tend to be NA. This hypothesis, however, has been comprehensively refuted by Dryer (1992, 2007), who shows that there is simply no correlation at all, even a weak one, between the order of A and N and the order of V and O. From the point of view adopted here, that is exactly the result that would be expected. Not only is the basic principle that governs the linearization of the modification relation fundamentally different from that which governs projection and argument selection, but, as was argued extensively in Chapter 3, there is simply no dependency between the two, since modification is orthogonal to the projection/selection plane.

To be more specific, modification differs from projection and argument selection in that the phonetic form of a modifier, in the unmarked case, may occur freely either to the right or to the left of the phonetic form of the head that it modifies, whereas uniform directionality is the unmarked case for projection and argument selection. Variation from the norm in modification relations thus occurs when the position of a given type of modifier in some language is fixed on either the right-hand or the left-hand side of the head it modifies rather than being freely ordered. For example, though the vast majority of adverbial modifiers of v-projections in English are linearized either to the right or to the left of the head they modify, as was shown in Chapter 3, there are a few, such as "retrospective" *just*[16] (yet another modifier of v_{pred}), that may only occur in leftward position:

(63)   He has (just) arrived (*just).

To account for this very language-particular fact, the selection feature of the modifier *just*$_{mod}$[retro] must simply be specified as follows, indicating that it can only be linearized leftwards:

(64) $\lfloor v_{pred} \rfloor_L$

A more general property of English is that postnominal adjectival modifiers of n_{nom} can only, as the name suggests, be linearized to the right:

---

[16]   See Cinque (1999: 96–98) for discussion.

(65)   the (*most interested in linguistics) students (most interested in linguistics)

The modifier selection feature for a_{rel} can thus be stated quite generally as follows:

(66) a_{rel}: $[\_n_{nom}]_R$

Modifiers of nouns in a language such as Chinese, in contrast, are obligatorily linearized leftwards, hence the selection feature of a_{rel} in that language would have the subscript "L."

Rather than piling up more examples of word order variation of this kind, I will finish this section by discussing another type of modifier that may require a somewhat different syntactic analysis. Interestingly, the variations in word order exhibited by modifiers of this kind also seem to interact more systematically with the word order parameters of argument selection.

4.2.6.1   Circumstantial Modifiers   It was shown in Chapter 3 that the position of many types of adverbial modifiers, including most -*ly* adverbs derived from adjectives, can be accounted for under the assumption that they are modifiers of one or more independently motivated v-projections. There remain, however, other types of modifiers for which such an analysis is problematic. These modifiers, which I shall term "circumstantial" modifiers, fall into two classes. The first class includes expressions of time, place, and reason, which modify the event as a whole. The second includes a variety of quasi-argumental expressions such as source, goal, instrument, benefactive, comitative, etc., as well as modifiers of duration, which further articulate the internal structure of an event. For convenience, I refer to modifiers of the first type as C_{event} modifiers and those of the second type as C_{arg} modifiers. In English all circumstantial modifiers, with only a few exceptions, are expressed as prepositional phrases and must occur to the right, rather than being freely ordered. The problem posed by these modifiers is that there are no obvious heads in the v-projection for them to modify, despite which they seem to occur in a characteristic unmarked linear order. Consider, for example, an English sentence such as the following:

(67)   John put books on the shelves for Mary for three hours in the library on Friday.

As the reader can easily determine for herself any other order of the various post-object elements in (67) is to one degree or another marked.[17] To account

---

[17] A useful test for unmarked (i.e. unscrambled) order of postverbal constituents based on the displacement of *wh*-expressions out of PPs is proposed by Goodall (1997); cf. Bowers (2010: 37–38) for discussion.

for such observations, I will make use of a possibility alluded to briefly in note 4 in Chapter 3, namely, positing specific heads in the *v*-projection that must be selected by a circumstantial modifier of the appropriate type. Such heads differ from argument heads in lacking a thematic selection feature, but must nevertheless be projected in a fixed universal order. Circumstantial modifiers thus share properties of both arguments and modifiers. They are like arguments in that they are tied to a head that is part of the projection system, but they are like modifiers in that they select the relevant head rather than being selected by it, hence are always optional. It is useful to distinguish modifiers of this kind from the modifiers discussed in Chapter 3 that select some independently motivated projection. I will therefore refer to the former from now on as *modifiers* and the latter as *adverbs* or *adjectives*. I will also make the assumption, for which some empirical evidence is supplied at the end of this section, that C_{arg} modifiers are projected above v_{tr} but below v_{pred}, whereas C_{event} modifiers are projected above v_{pred} but below v_{tns}. Finally, I will assume that the selection feature for circumstantial modifiers is uniformly rightward in English. Given these assumptions, example (67) can be derived as follows:

(68)

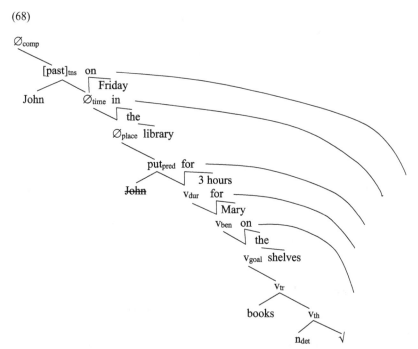

As shown in (68), both the C_{event} and C_{arg} modifiers will line up in the correct order on the right edge of the clause. The unmarked order of elements in SVO languages is thus as follows:

(69)   S V $(DO/IO)^{18}$ IO DO (Ag) C_{arg} C_{event}

I assume without further argument here that VSO languages are basically the same apart from the fact that the lexical root is displaced to some head position higher than that which selects the subject.

Consider next a VOS language such as Malagasy. In this language the C_{arg} modifiers line up on the right after the arguments Ag, O, and IO but before the subject S, while the C_{event} modifiers may appear quite naturally either before or after S (Keenan 1976: 250):

(70)   V (Ag) DO IO C_{arg} (C_{event}) S (C_{event})

Though the linear order of the core arguments in a VOS language is, as was shown earlier, the mirror image of that in an SVO language, the circumstantial modifiers nevertheless occur in the same order in both. All of this follows from the same basic structure proposed in (68) under the assumption that selection of both arguments and circumstantial modifiers in Malagasy is uniformly rightward, whereas in English selection of arguments is leftwards, while selection of circumstantial modifiers is, as just shown, rightwards. I will assume that the reason C_{event} modifiers in Malagasy can appear either to the left or to the right of the subject is that the subject may either be selected by the athematic selection feature of v_{pred} and remain there, or be further displaced to the right to satisfy an optional athematic selection feature of v_{tns}.

Consider next SOV languages. The data available in the literature suggests that in these languages the direction of selection of both circumstantial modifiers and arguments is uniformly leftward,[19] resulting in the following ordering:

(71)   S C_{event} C_{arg} IO DO (Ag) V

Thus in these languages the order of core arguments is the same as in SVO languages, while the order of circumstantial modifiers is the mirror image of that which is required in SVO and VOS languages.

---

[18] The extra position here is to allow for languages such as English in which v_{tr} has an athematic argument selection feature.

[19] See Boisson (1981: 80), who reports that the order Tmp-Loc-Man-Vrb is found in Mandarin Chinese, Gujarati, Lamani, Punjabi, and Zuni. Cinque (2006: 162, n. 19) also reports that the following SOV languages have this same order: German (Haider 2000, Hinterhölzl 2001, 2002), Turkish (Jaklin Kornfilt, p.c.), Nenets (Vilkuna 1998: 203), and Konda (Krishnamurti and Benham 1998: 266).

I discuss next a few pieces of empirical evidence culled from the literature in support of the syntactic ordering claims made earlier in this subsection. Consider first the claim that v_{place} modifiers are projected before v_{time} modifiers. Some supporting evidence is provided by the fact that when both are pronominal the order is rigidly fixed:[20]

(72)   a. I ate lunch there then.
        b. *I ate lunch then there.

Exactly the same is true of a language such as Norwegian (Nilsen 2000: 72f., cited in Cinque 2006: 151):

(73)   a. Jeg møtte ham   der   da
           I   met   him   there then
        b. *Jeg møtte ham da der.

In German, however, the order is exactly the opposite (Frey 2000: 113):

(74)   a. Hans sollte wann   wo   darüber   vortragen.
           Hans should sometimes somewhere   about that   talk
           'Hans should talk about it somewhere sometimes.'

        b. *Hans sollte wo wann darüber vortragen.

This of course is exactly what we would predict if the selection feature of circumstantial modifiers in German is leftwards, as is the case in other SOV languages.

Consider next the claim that C_{arg} modifiers are projected below v_{pred} whereas C_{event} modifiers are projected above v_{pred}. Supporting evidence comes from Mandarin Chinese, in which the direction of selection for C_{event} adverbs is leftwards while the direction of selection for core arguments and C_{arg} adverbs is rightwards. For example, an expression of location in preverbal position is interpreted as the location of the event as a whole, whereas the same expression in postverbal position is interpreted as a v_{goal} expression (Li and Thompson 1978: 229):

(75)   a. Tā zài   zhuōzi-shang   tiào.
           he at   table-on   jump
           'He jumped (up and down) on the table.'

        b. Tā tiào   zài   zhuōzi-shang.
           he jump   at   table-on
           'He jumped onto the table.'

---

[20] Cinque (2006: 162, n. 14) credits David Perlmutter with a similar observation (in conversation with Richard Kayne), albeit with a directional adverb rather than a place adverb: *He went there then* versus *He went then there.*

Examples (75a) and (75b) are thus derived as shown in (76a) and (76b), respectively:

(76) a.

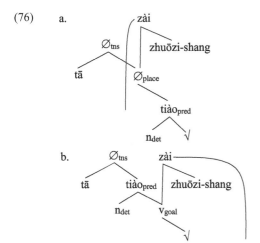

b.

Similarly, preverbal time phrases are interpreted as v_{time} modifiers, whereas postverbal time expressions are interpreted as v_{dur} modifiers:

(77) a. Wǒ sān-diǎn-zhōng kāi-huì.
      I   3:00   hold-meeting.
      'I have a meeting at 3:00.'

   b. * Wǒ kāi-huì sān-diǎn-zhōng.

(78) a. Wǒ shùi le sānge zhōngtou.
      I   sleep ASP 3   hours
      'I slept for three hours.'

   b. * Wǒ sānge zhōngtou shùi le.

For Chinese, then, the order of elements is as follows:

(79)   S C$_{event}$ V IO O C$_{arg}$

This data shows, then, that there are at least some languages in which the order of selection of circumstantial adverbs is non-uniform, varying according to the type of modifier. To what extent such non-uniform directions of modifier selection are found in other languages is a question I shall have to leave for future research.

4.3   Universals of Word Order

I conclude by taking a broader view of the word order facts discussed in this chapter and attempting to distil from them some universal principles. Let us start by summarizing the predominant word orders discussed in this chapter and the parameters that produce them in the form of a chart:

(80)

	attested			very rare/unattested
	SVO/VSO	VOS	SOV	OSV/OVS
Projection	L	L	R	R
Selection	L	R	L	R
Modification	R	R	L	?

One solid conclusion that can be drawn from examining the attested word orders in both nominals and sentences is that word orders that would be produced by setting the parameters for both projection and argument selection rightwards are extremely rare, if not impossible. This suggests a universal principle of parameter setting along the following lines:

(81)   The parameter for direction of selection must be L for at least one of the two most basic relations of projection and argument selection.

This entails that if the parameter for projection is L, then the parameter for argument selection can be either L or R, whereas if the parameter for projection is R, then the parameter for argument selection can only be L. However, given the fact that VOS languages are far less common than SVO and SOV languages, a better way of formulating the principle might be as follows:

(82)   The universally preferred parameter setting for argument selection is L, but if it is set at R, then the parameter setting for projection must be L.

Why the most fundamental relations of natural language syntax should display such a strong bias in favor of leftward parameter settings I can only speculate about here. Given that linear ordering ultimately translates into temporal order in actual performance, the inference seems virtually inescapable that it has to do with the fact that the human processing system is constrained to operate in real time. The fact that by far the two most common basic word orders in sentences are SVO and SOV, both produced by leftward argument selection, suggests two conclusions. The first is that the identification of thematic arguments is the most fundamental step in sentence processing. The second is that the optimal system for parsing is one in which the linear ordering of constituents directly reflects the order in which arguments are selected. The actual position of the verb, in contrast, seems less crucial. In any case, attempting to answer these questions by arbitrarily decreeing that the structure of one type of language (say, SVO) is primary and that all the others are derived from it by movement rules, themselves stipulated to be only leftward, is not adequate, because it incorrectly predicts that SVO orders are massively simpler than other orders and should therefore be much more common.

A second solid conclusion that can be drawn, as already indicated in §4.1.8, is that the more transparent the relation between the linear ordering of elements and the order in which relations are formed in the syntax, the better. It follows, as emerged most clearly in the discussion of nominals in the first part of this chapter, that uniform orders of selection are optimal. In particular, it seems that the most common word orders in sentences are produced by uniform selection, whether leftward or rightward, of the core arguments of the verb. In fact, it is doubtful whether there is any language in which the selection of core arguments is non-uniform. I therefore propose as a second universal the following:

(83)   The direction of selection of core arguments is uniform.

In contrast, non-uniform direction of projection is certainly attested, as was shown in §4.2.5, though fairly rare, while non-uniform direction of selection in the case of non-thematic functional elements is so common as to render the choice of direction virtually free, though the frequency of occurrence of languages with non-uniform direction of selection does vary, as was argued earlier, according to the degree of transparency between the order of elements and the order of selection. Finally, for adverbial and adjectival modifiers, free choice of direction is simply the unmarked case, as was argued in Chapter 3. Clearly, then, maintaining a maximally transparent relation between the linear order of the core arguments of the verb and the order in which they are projected is a universal, perhaps invariant, property of natural language.

The principles proposed so far seem fairly clear and predict correctly the attested types of languages presented in chart (80). However, as soon as modifiers are thrown into the mix, matters become murkier. Another generalization that can be gleaned from (80) is that the predominant direction of selection for circumstantial modifiers is just the opposite of the direction of projection. Why should this be the case? We could of course formulate a principle stating just that, but such an approach hardly seems explanatory. To obtain a better understanding of what is really going on here, let us compare the basic word orders produced by the parameter settings for modifiers in (80) with those that would result from setting the parameters in the opposite way:

(84)   a. SVO (Mod_R): S V IO O (Ag) C_{arg} C_{event}
        b. SVO (Mod_L): ?S (V) C_{event} (V) C_{arg} IO O (Ag)[21]

(85)   a. VOS (Mod_R): V (Ag) O IO C_{arg} (S) C_{event} (S)
        b. VOS (Mod_L): ?V C_{event} C_{arg} (Ag) O IO S

(86)   a. SOV (Mod_L): S C_{event} C_{arg} IO O (Ag) V
        b. SOV (Mod_R): ?S IO O (Ag) C_{arg} C_{event} V

The first question is whether the b.-orders in (84)–(86) are actually attested. Dryer (2007: 40) states that no language with the order VXO is known to him. Presumably, that covers both SVO and VOS languages, in which case neither (84b) nor (85b) is attested. As for SOV languages, Cinque (2006: 152), citing data from Boisson (1981), states that languages with the order *Manner-Loc-Temp-V are unattested. Though the data available is a bit skimpy in this case, I will assume that languages with the pattern (86b) are also unattested.

Suppose that all of the b.-patterns in (84)–(86) are in fact ruled out. Then an interesting generalization emerges. In all the attested a.-patterns in (84)–(86) the phonetic form of the verb is immediately adjacent to the phonetic form of one of its core thematic arguments, while in the unattested b.-patterns the phonetic form of the verb is separated from the phonetic form of its core thematic arguments by one or more modifiers. Let us therefore formulate a further universal of linearization along the following lines:

(87)   The phonetic form of a verb must be immediately adjacent in its minimal
        projection (v_{pred})[22] to the phonetic form of a core thematic argument.

This approach, if correct, provides a principled explanation for the pattern of parameterization of modifiers in chart (80), namely, that the direction of selection of modifiers must be set in such a way that it will not violate the adjacency condition (87). A crucial piece of evidence in support of this proposal is provided by the order of elements in Chinese (cf. (79)). Despite the fact that the direction

---

[21] I place V either before or after C_{event} to allow for the possibility that in some SVO languages (e.g. English) the verb is pronounced in v_{pred}, while in others it may be displaced to v_{tns} (e.g. French).

[22] This stipulation is necessary in order to account for the fact that the adjacency condition no longer applies when pronunciation of the verb is displaced to a higher position, as shown by the well-known contrast between English *John kisses often Mary* and French *Jean embrasse souvent Marie*. It is interesting to note that principle (87) thus applies, in effect, only within the first v_{pred} phase projected by the verb.

of selection for modifiers is non-uniform, the word order in Chinese nevertheless conforms to principle (87), showing that it applies quite independently of the parameter settings in any particular language.

Principle (87) is somewhat reminiscent of the so-called "adjacency condition on Case assignment" that was frequently invoked in the Government–Binding framework to explain why languages like English resist putting anything between the verb and the object. It seems, however, that the data that motivated this condition may reflect a much wider cross-linguistic phenomenon. Thus it has often been noted that in SOV languages the preferred position of the object is immediately adjacent to the verb unless it is definite, in which case it must move to a leftward position, as happens in many languages. Similarly, Keenan (1976) and others have observed that in Malagasy, whatever argument is immediately adjacent to the verb is closely bound to it. In "active" constructions the v_{th} argument is immediately adjacent to the verb, while in a variety of "passive" and circumstantial constructions characteristic of this family of VOS languages, it is the v_{ag} argument that is immediately adjacent to the verb and therefore most closely bound to it. The Malagasy data is in fact crucial, because it shows that the phenomenon cannot be explained simply by positing the existence of a VP constituent that universally combines the verb and the thematic object, as Keenan (1976) insightfully noted. Rather, there is a far more general principle at work, along the lines proposed here, which ensures that immediate adjacency is maintained at PHON between the phonetic form of a verb and at least one of its core thematic arguments.

Putting all this together, notice that the combined effect of principles (82), (83), and (87) is to guarantee that in the first instance (i.e. before displacement operations of various kinds take place) the phonetic form of a verb and its core thematic arguments are arranged in a strict linear order that preserves in maximally transparent fashion the universal order of projection and selection. It is not too difficult to imagine how a procedure of this sort might play a crucial role in facilitating real-time production and perception of natural language. This in turn suggests that at least some of the general constraints on word order variation discussed in the latter part of this chapter, together with the range of cross-linguistic variation observed, are ultimately to be explained as the optimal solution to the problem of instantiating a fixed universal set of syntactic relations, together with a formally determined set of word order possibilities, in a realistic model of actual linguistic performance.

5 *The Role of Morphology*

The three fundamental syntactic relations, as has been shown in the preceding chapters, are projection, selection, and modification. These are the absolute minimum required to mediate between the semantic representations of SEM and the most basic property of representations at PHON, namely, linear ordering. In the unmarked case, an ordered pair, or dependency relation, $<\alpha,\beta>$ between two lexical items α and β, produced by FR to satisfy a selection or projection feature, is systematically mapped onto the linearly ordered string PF (β)-PF(α), where PF(α) and PF(β) are the phonetic representations of α and β, respectively, while at the same time mapping $<\alpha,\beta>$ onto a semantic representation of the appropriate kind. If the main problem of language design was simply to find the minimal means of mapping function–argument structures onto linear ordered sequences of phonetic forms, then it seems that it would be sufficient for each LI to be mapped onto a single invariant phonetic form at PHON. Surprisingly, such minimal systems are never found. Instead, natural languages, to one degree or another, map syntactic representations onto morphological alternations as well. A fundamental question, then, is whether the existence of such morphological alternations requires positing any new primitives of the theory, or whether they can be accounted for with the theoretical apparatus already at our disposal, together with the legibility conditions imposed by CI and SM. I will argue in this chapter that the latter view is correct. I start by considering in very general terms two questions: (a) What sort of morphological structures are available at PHON?; (b) What kinds of information contained in syntactic representations could naturally be conveyed by morphological alternations at PHON?

5.1 *Morphological Alternation*

Reduced to the simplest terms, a morphological alternation is nothing more than a set of two or more phonetically distinct forms of a given root, only one of which, setting aside free variation, may be realized in any given syntactic position. The ways in which morphological alternates can differ from one another seem to be limited only by the phonetic representations available at PHON. For example, morphologically distinct forms of a root may be produced by adding a fixed string of phones to the left, right, or interior of the phonetic form of a root, by varying the vowel(s) and/or consonants of a root, or by changing the tone associated with a root. Any systematic feature of phonetic representation has the potential to serve as a source of morphological alternation. To complicate matters further, morphological alternation may be regular or suppletive. In this work, however, I abstract away from the descriptive and theoretical problems involved in a universal characterization of the possible phonetic forms of morpheme alternates, assuming simply that for any given root there may be a set (often referred to as a *paradigm*) of such alternate forms available that can be associated with syntactic structure in systematic ways.

It seems intuitively obvious that the primary function of morphemic alternation is to make certain properties of the syntactic system visible at PHON. Let us therefore consider next what sort of information contained in syntactic derivations/representations might be naturally represented at PHON by means of morphological alternation. By hypothesis, the syntactic objects produced in NS are severely limited to: (i) LIs consisting of sets of features; (ii) ordered pairs of LIs produced by FR. Given (i), an obvious way of utilizing morphological alternation would be to make visible the different combinations of features (and different possible values of those features) that constitute the syntactic representation of an LI. For example, the morphological form of a verb frequently varies systematically depending on the value of the feature of *tense*. Likewise the form of a noun may vary depending on what value is chosen for the feature *number*. Similarly, the category n_{det} may take different morphological forms depending on whether it is definite or indefinite. Notice that while it is not *necessary* for any given language that some particular combination of features and/or feature values be mapped onto distinct morphological alternates at PHON, it is clearly always *possible*.

Consider next the relations between LIs produced by the application of FR. In fact there are just a few natural and simple ways of making a given syntactic relation visible at PHON by means of morphological alternation. Suppose we have an ordered pair $<\alpha,\beta>$, produced by the application of FR. There are in principle three ways that the relation between α and β might be represented morphologically. First, it might be required that a particular morpheme M always accompany the *first* coordinate α of the ordered pair (i.e. the head), yielding an ordered pair of the form $<\alpha+M,\beta>$.[1] Second, there might be some particular morpheme M that always accompanies the *second* coordinate β of the ordered pair $<\alpha,\beta>$ (i.e. the dependent), yielding an ordered pair of the form $<\alpha, \beta+M>$. Third, it might be required that α and β combine with *correlated* morphemes, M_1 and M_2, that regularly mark the phonetic form of *both* coordinates of the relation, so that $<\alpha,\beta>$ would have the form $<\alpha+M_1,\beta+M_2>$, where the morphemes M_1, M_2 are in turn systematically correlated with some intrinsic syntactic property of α or β. These three possible devices are exemplified in natural language by applicative morphology, Case-marking, and agreement morphology, respectively.

Many languages, for example, identify the thematic relation between a verb and one of its arguments by means of an *applicative* morpheme attached to the phonetic form of the root. Alternatively, verb-argument relations can be signaled by choosing a particular inherent Case form of the argument. Finally, the relation between a verb and a subject nominal, for example, is frequently marked by an agreement system in which specific morphological forms of the verb correlate with corresponding morphological forms of the nominal. The latter in turn are typically a function of certain intrinsic properties of the nominal, such as number, gender, noun class, etc. Many languages have similar agreement systems that mark the relation between a verb and its object nominal. However, an equally common way of morphologically marking the relation of a verb to a subject or object is to provide the phonetic form of the subject with a morpheme conventionally referred to as *nominative* (NOM) Case and the phonetic form of the object with a morpheme conventionally referred to as *accusative* (ACC) Case. It is also not uncommon for agreement morphology and case morphology to coexist in the same language. Finally, many languages, such as the VOS languages discussed in Chapter 4, combine marking of the subject with what might be thought of as a kind of applicative morphology added to the verbal root, signaling what type of argument the subject is.

Clearly, such morphological marking systems are just the simplest logically possible ways of rendering the fundamental syntactic relations of NS legible to SM, given the kinds of morphological paradigms available in natural language.

---

[1] I use M here as a cover symbol for any of the various ways mentioned in the text of producing morphemic alternates available at PHON and $\alpha+M$ as an abbreviation for the result of applying M to α.

In the following sections I consider in more detail the ways in which certain types of relations are morphologically marked. I will argue that in every case the required correlation between syntactic derivation and morphological alternation can be explained either by directly mapping different combinations of (values of) features onto distinct morphemic alternates or by incorporating such combinations of (values of) features into the selection properties of heads. In other words, no syntactic apparatus beyond that which we have assumed so far is needed to account for any known type of morphosyntactic alternation. I will argue, in particular, that there is no need to introduce a new primitive such as the Agree operation proposed in the minimalist framework (cf. Chomsky 2000, and subsequent publications). Rather, all the properties of φ-agreement and structural Case assignment can be accounted for in terms of the morphological realization of heads and dependents in some particular relation, plus selection properties of the head.

5.2   Thematic Argument Selection

I start by considering the most common ways that selection of thematic arguments is morphologically marked, in part because the relation between syntax and morphology in such cases is relatively transparent. I then turn to the kinds of morphological devices most often used to mark subjects and objects. These appear at first glance to be qualitatively more complex than those used to mark thematic arguments, but it will be shown that they are in fact not.

5.2.1   Applicative Morphology

In many languages, one or more of the core thematic arguments or quasi-arguments of a sentence may optionally be marked by adding a specified affix to the verbal root. The argument relation most commonly marked in this way is the dative or indirect object argument, which I have argued (Bowers 2010) is universally introduced by the lexical projection v_{aff}, where [aff] is a feature indicating that the relevant argument bears the "affectee" relation to the verb. Consider, for example, the following pair of sentences from Chichewa (Baker 1988):

(1)   a. Mbidzi   zi-na-perek-a   msampha   kwa   nkhandwe.
           Zebras   SP-PAST-hand-ASP   trap   to   fox
           'The zebras handed the trap to the fox.'

         b. Mbidzi   zi-na-perek-er-a   nkhandwe   msampha.
           Zebras   SP-PAST-APPL-ASP   fox   trap
           'The zebras handed the fox the trap.'

One way of making the affectee relation legible to the SM systems is, as shown in (1a), to combine the argument nominal with the preposition *kwa* 'to.' I return to this kind of marking shortly. However, an alternative is to leave the nominal argument itself morphologically unmarked and add the suffix *-er* to the verbal root, as shown in (1b).[2] To account for the morphological form of the verb in such cases, let us assume that the v_{aff} projection in Chichewa may optionally have the phonetic form /-er/. I also assume that /-er/ is specified as a bound morpheme suffix, which simply means that in order to be well-formed at PHON it must be added to the right of the phonological representation of a root such as /perek-/ 'hand.' In other words, a representation at PHON must not only have a phonetic representation legible to SM but must also be morphologically well-formed (cf. Chapter 1, note 10). It follows that when the relation $<\sqrt{perek}, -er_{aff}>$ is formed, a copy of the phonetic form of the root must be provided for the phonetic form of the suffix /-er/ to combine with, in order to conform to morphological well-formedness conditions at PHON. The result is the well-formed expression /perek+er/, which is then ordered by Spell-out to the left of the phonological form of the root itself:

(2) $<\sqrt{perek}, v_{aff}>$ perek+er-~~perek~~

Next, v_{aff} forms an argument relation with the nominal *nkhandwe* 'fox,' ordering the phonetic form of the latter to the left of the output of (2):

(3) $<v_{aff}, nkhandwe>$ nkhandwe-perek+er-$\sqrt{~~perek~~}$

Subsequent applications of FR, which I will not detail here, result in the pronunciation of the head /perek+er/ being displaced further to the left at PHON. The net result of these operations is to make the affectee relation between the argument head v_{aff} and its nominal argument legible to the SM systems in the form of the morphological suffix /-er/ added to the verbal root. Notice that in this case nothing is required in the syntax other than differential feature marking of argument projections, making it straightforward to ensure that only a head with the feature [aff] is associated with the bound verbal morpheme /-er/.

5.2.2   *Inherent Case*

Consider in contrast a language such as Russian in which affectee arguments are systematically made legible to the SM systems by assigning the value [DAT] to the Case feature of the affectee argument:

---

[2] The linear ordering of the two arguments also changes from theme-affectee to affectee-theme. See Bowers (2010) and §5.4.2 for an explanation.

(4)   Vanya   poslal   Maše   pis´mo.
           Vanya.NOM   sent   Masha.DAT   letter.ACC
           'John sent Mary a letter.'

Let's assume as a general syntactic property of Russian that the head v_{aff} is not merely required to select an argument head of category n_{det}, but one whose Case feature has the specified value [DAT]. This requirement can be incorporated directly into the selection feature of the v_{aff} head in Russian as follows:

(5)   [__ n_{det}]
            Case: DAT

Example (5) stipulates that in order for FR to form the relation $<v_{aff}, n_{det}>$ in Russian, the value of the Case feature of the selected n_{det} must be [DAT]. In the particular example at hand, this will ensure that the dative Case-marked form of the proper noun *Masha* is spelled out at PHON in the correct phonological form /maše/.

A selection feature such as (5) states that in order to form the relation $<v_{aff}, n_{det}>$, the value of the Case feature of the selected n_{det} head must match that specified to the right of the dash in (5). Let us assume that if the matching procedure is successful and the relation $<v_{aff}, n_{det}>$ is formed, the selection feature of v_{aff} is automatically deleted, as shown in (6) in the case of example (4):

(6)   <   posl-aff,   ,   maše   >   maše-posl-pis´mo-~~posl~~-√posl
                ~~n_{det}~~ n_{det}
                ~~Case: DAT~~   Case: DAT

I assume as a general constraint on derivations that a representation containing any undeleted selection features is rejected as ill-formed. In contrast, the dative Case feature of the n_{det} argument is not deleted, because it contains information that may be relevant at a later stage of the derivation. Adapting standard terminology, we may define a particular value of the Case feature required when a thematic argument projection such as v_{aff} forms a relation with an argument nominal selected by it as *inherent* Case. As we have just seen, there is no need to add any new primitives to the theory in order to ensure that inherent Case is assigned correctly, because the necessary condition can simply be built into the selection feature of the relevant *v*-projection.

5.2.3   Prepositional Marking

Another common way of making argument relations visible at PHON is to require that the argument be incorporated into a *p*-projection, headed by a specified preposition. This is illustrated by both Chichewa and English. In the former the v_{aff} argument may optionally be marked with the preposition *kwa* 'to,' while in the latter such arguments are regularly marked with the preposition *to*. Once again, the simplest assumption is that marking of this sort is carried out via selection. One of the selection features available to the v_{aff} projection in English, for example, will be of the form: [_to$_{rel}$], understood as an instruction to select a *p*-projection of the following form:[3]

(7)   to$_{rel}$

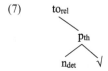

Similarly, in Chichewa the v_{aff} projection may have a selection feature of the form [_kwa$_{rel}$]. English and Chichewa differ only in that the morphological form of the v_{aff} head in English is the same (namely, [v:]) regardless of whether it selects a prepositional phrase or a nominal argument, whereas the morphological form of v_{aff} in Chichewa correlates with the form of the selection feature, so that [v:]$_{aff}$ selects a prepositional argument, whereas [v:-er]$_{aff}$ selects a nominal argument.[4]

5.3   Athematic Argument Selection (1): Structural Nominative Case and Subject–Verb Agreement

It has already been mentioned that the athematic subject relation can be made legible at PHON by morphologically marking it in one of two ways: (a) by providing the Case feature of the subject nominal with the value NOM; (b) by imposing a morphological agreement relation between a finite verb form and the subject nominal such that both have the same value for inherent nominal features such as [Person] and [Number]. In many languages *both* ways of morphologically marking the subject relation in finite clauses are required, as noted earlier. At first glance, this kind of morphological marking might seem

---

[3] Words commonly classified as "prepositions" may either be lexical roots of category *p*, as is the case in English, or they may be true Case-markers, in which case they are to be analyzed as n_K projections. In some cases, a particular LI may be ambiguous. See, for example, the discussion in Bowers (2010: 92–94) of Japanese *-ni*, which may be either a Case-marker of a v_{aff} argument or a preposition heading a v_{goal} argument.

[4] This leaves open the possibility of there being a language in which a v_{aff} head with an applicative affix selects a prepositionally marked argument. I do not at present know whether such cases are attested, but I will assume that they tend to be quite rare simply because it would be redundant to morphologically mark the affectee relation on both the verb and the selected argument.

radically different from that which was used to mark thematic arguments, leading to the idea that there is a fundamental difference between *inherent* Case, said to mark arguments to which a θ-role is assigned, and *structural* Case, said to mark arguments lacking a θ-role. I shall argue, however, that there is in fact no essential formal difference between inherent Case and structural Case.

Let's start by looking again at the way the subject relation is derived in the framework proposed here. Consider, for example, the following derivation of the sentence *She has kissed him*:[5]

(8)

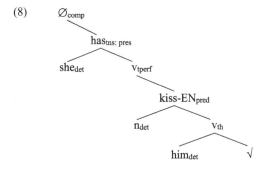

Recall that because the v_{tns} head in English has an athematic $[\_n_{det}]$ feature, it must form a relation with an accessible nominal projection headed by n_{det} that was interpreted at an earlier stage of the derivation as a thematic argument. In this case, the only such argument is *she*, the v_{pred} argument of *kiss*, because everything below the phase head *kiss*-EN$_{pred}$ becomes inaccessible as soon as it is saturated. Crucially, however, the athematic argument selection feature in v_{tns} that drives FR in this case *is formally identical to the argument selection feature that drives FR in the case of a thematic argument head*. Hence there is no reason not to expect the same range of morphological possibilities to obtain here as well. In particular, we would expect to find that either the dependent or the head of the relation $<v_{tns}, she_{det}>$ could be morphologically marked. The first possibility is realized in languages in which the Case feature of the n_{det} argument (the dependent) is marked with so-called "structural" NOM Case. In example (8) this would yield the correct pronominal form *she* at PHON. Clearly, the Case-marking requirement of v_{tns} may be built into its selection feature in exactly the same way it was for inherent Case:

---

[5] See Chapter 2 for arguments in support of this analysis. I use an example with perfect aspect in order to avoid the problems that arise in English in the case of simple present or past tense forms of main verbs (cf. §6.1 for discussion). I also simplify the derivation of the thematic arguments *she* and *him*.

(9)   [_____ n$_{det}$]
              Case: NOM

The second possibility is realized in languages in which the values of the φ-features of v_{tns} (the head) are required to agree with the inherent values of the φ-features of n_{det} (the dependent). In this particular example, the φ-features of v_{tns} are valued [Number: pl] and [Person: 3], agreeing with the inherent values of the φ-features of *she*. Assigning these feature values to the perfect aspect root *have* yields the correct morphological form *has*.

Structural NOM Case-marking is thus formally identical to assignment of inherent Case, in the sense that in both instances the Case feature of the dependent β in a relation $<\alpha,\beta>$ is required by the head α to have a certain value. Similarly, agreement between the φ-features of v_{tns} and those of its dependent is similar to applicative morphology in the sense that it is the head of the relation, rather than the dependent, that is required to have some particular morphological marking. The only significant difference between the two cases is that the selection feature that induces the subject relation is athematic. Why should morphological marking of the head in this case be accomplished by agreement in φ-features rather than by adding a fixed applicative morpheme to the head, as typically happens in the case of the thematic argument heads discussed earlier? Clearly, it must have something to do with the fact that the selection feature of v_{tns} is athematic. Notice, in particular, that in a situation where more than one argument nominal is potentially accessible to v_{tns}, there will be no way of telling at PHON which one is selected as the subject if it is only marked by a fixed morpheme in the v_{tns} head, similar to an applicative morpheme marking a thematic argument. If, however, the subject is identified by an agreement relation (or of course by NOM Case-marking of the nominal), then the chances of determining which nominal is the subject via inspection of the morphological form of the verb are significantly increased.

Deferring until later a deeper explanation of this systematic difference between thematic argument projections such as v_{aff} and athematic argument projections such as v_{tns}, let us assume for the moment that a v-projection has φ-features if and only if its selection feature is athematic. Because the φ-features of v_{tns} have no inherent value of their own, the only way their value can be determined is by establishing a relation with an n_{det} that does have inherently valued φ-features. This can be accomplished, as shown in (10a), by stipulating as part of the selection feature of v_{tns} that the value of the φ-features of the head v_{tns} must be the same as the (inherent) value of the φ-features of n_{det}, resulting in the ordered pair (10b) after the application of FR:

(10)   a. [__ n_{det}]
              φ:x   φ:x
                 Case: NOM

   b. < v_{tns}, n_{det} >
           φ:x   φ:x
                 Case: NOM

In this way, it is possible to build both subject–verb agreement and assignment of structural NOM Case into the selection features that drive FR in essentially the same way that morphological requirements were built into the selection feature in instances of thematic argument selection. Both NOM Case assignment and subject–verb agreement can thus be accounted for in parsimonious fashion in the relational theory without having to introduce a new primitive relation analogous to the Agree operation assumed in Minimalism.

5.3.1   A Potential Problem: Long-distance Agreement with Expletive there

There is, however, a potential difficulty with this approach that must be addressed. An important motivation in Chomsky (2000) for introducing a new primitive operation Agree into the minimalist framework lay in the fact that in sentences with expletive *there* agreement can apparently take place "long-distance" between the matrix verb and a nominal embedded indefinitely far away from it,

(11)   a. There seems/*seem to be a book on the table.
       b. There *seems/seem to be books on the table.

just as it does in both short-distance expletive constructions and non-expletive constructions:

(12)   a. There is/*are a book on the table.
       b. There *is/are books on the table.
       c. A book is/*are on the table.
       d. Books *is/are on the table.

Assuming the standard view that *there* is merged in the embedded infinitive complement and subsequently raised into the matrix clause, it appears that the matrix verb *seem* is required to agree with the theme-DP *a book/books* despite the fact that it does not even belong to the same clause as the matrix verb, and despite the fact that the expletive *there*, which is merged with T in the complement at the point where agreement takes place, intervenes between them. Chomsky's explanation for this long-distance agreement phenomenon is that expletive *there* is defective in not having a full complement of φ-features. Since the probe in T in the matrix clause is looking for the nearest DP with matching φ-features, it will not be able to form an Agree relation with *there*, forcing it to search further until it finds the theme-DP in the infinitive complement. Notice that such a non-local Agree operation is required even for simple expletive constructions such as (12a,b) under either the standard assumption that *there* is merged in Spec,T or Bowers' (2002, 2010) proposal that *there* is merged in a position below T. Rather than trying to reduce long-distance agreement to strictly local agreement of the sort required for non-expletive sentences, as was strenuously attempted in earlier work, Chomsky proposes to introduce a new primitive operation into syntactic theory, namely, the Agree relation, which is inherently long-distance.

If this analysis of expletive constructions were correct, then a new primitive operation analogous to Agree, not reducible in any way to FR, would also be necessitated in the relational framework proposed here. This would be an unfortunate innovation, increasing immeasurably the complexity of the theory and thereby undermining much of its appeal. There is, however, empirical evidence (not previously noticed, to the best of my knowledge) against the existence of any such long-distance agreement relation. Consider first the following paradigm:

(13)   a. Only I am/*is/*are on deck.
        b. Only you (sg.) *am/*is/are on deck.
        c. Only he *am/is/*are on deck.
        d. Only we *am/*is/are on deck.
        e. Only you (pl.) *am/*is/are on deck.
        f. Only they *am/*is/are on deck.

Pronouns in subject position in English show a full agreement paradigm with different morphological forms of the verb *be*, depending on the value of plurality and (in singular forms) person. In sharp contrast, consider the following paradigm in expletive sentences with *there*:

(14)   a. There is/*am/*are only ?I/me on deck.
        b. There is/*am/*are only you (sg.) on deck.
        c. There is/*am/*are only ??he/him/the sailor on deck.
        d. There ??are/*is only we on deck.
        e. There is/*are only us on deck.
        f. There is/?are only you (pl.) on deck.
        g. There are/*is only ??they/the sailors on deck.
        h. There is/??are only them on deck.

Though it is somewhat unclear to what extent number agreement is even possible in expletive constructions in which the associate has the form *only+pronoun*, and if so, whether the nominative form of the pronoun is or is not possible, what is absolutely clear is that the full range of agreement forms *required* in (13) is simply *impossible* in the existential construction. Particularly striking is the total absence of first person singular *am* and second person singular *are*.[6] Exactly the same is true in long-distance constructions:

(15)   a. There is/*am/*are believed to be only ?I/me on deck.
       b. There is/*am/*are believed to be only you (sg.) on deck.
       c. There is/*am/*are believed to be only ?he/him/the sailor on deck.
       d. There ?are/?is believed to be only we on deck.
       e. There is/??are believed to be only us on deck.
       f. There ?is/?are believed to be only you (pl.) on deck.
       g. There are/*is believed to be only ??they/the sailors on deck.
       h. There is/??are believed to be only them on deck.

What these paradigms show is that normal subject–verb agreement simply does not exist in existential sentences. It follows that whatever mechanism is assumed to account for normal (strictly local) subject–verb agreement *cannot* simply be extended to apply long-distance between matrix T and the associate of *there*. Note also that the fairly clear preference for ACC Case-marked pronouns in these existential sentences casts considerable doubt on the claim that structural NOM is assigned in conjunction with Agree in such constructions, as would be expected if normal subject–verb agreement were really operating there. This data, then, argues strongly against the idea of introducing a new primitive relation Agree that operates uniformly in both strictly local and long-distance agreement relations.

If normal subject–verb agreement is not operative in *there*-expletive sentences, then what does account for the number agreement required in (14) and (15)? Notice first that number agreement between a subject and predicate nominal is required in copular sentences such as the following:

(16)   a. He/the sailor is/*are my friend.
       b. They/the sailors *is/are my friends.

---

[6] The nearest equivalent to these sentences in Icelandic, however, do show full number and person agreement (Sigurðsson 1996: 5):

(i)   Það   erum/??er   bara **við**.
      it   are/??is   only we(N)
      'It's only us.'

This can be accounted for under the assumption, argued for in Bowers (2002), that the expletive *Það* in Icelandic is selected by v_{comp}.

Second, observe that a similar agreement pattern is found in pure existential sentences without a complement:

(17)   a. There is/*are no god.
        b. There *is/are no unicorns.

Putting these observations together, I suggest that expletive *there* is defective in having only a number feature and an (inherent) third person feature. Since the number feature of *there* is obviously not inherent, it must be valued via agreement with a predicate noun-phrase, utilizing the same mechanism that accounts for agreement in (16). In both existential constructions such as (14) and raising constructions such as (15), once the number feature of the expletive has been valued in the complement clause, it is available via multi-attachment to the $[\_n_{\text{det}}]$ selector in v_{tns} that imposes φ-feature agreement between head and dependent. The reason that only third person singular and plural agreement forms appear in existential constructions is that these are the only number and person features that *there* can provide to value the φ-features of v_{tns}. Crucially, the data in (10)–(12) can *only* be explained if agreement is restricted in such a way that it operates strictly locally between v_{tns} and the n_{det} it selects. In the relational framework proposed here, this constraint follows automatically from the fact that agreement can only take place in conjunction with FR. In other words, because agreement can only take place between a head and the nominal it selects, any form of long-distance agreement is prohibited in principle.[7]

5.3.2   *Nominative Case and φ-features of the Verb are Not Uninterpretable Features*

It was suggested earlier that a *v*-projection (such as v_{tns}) has φ-features and assigns structural NOM Case if and only if its argument selector is athematic. This, however, is mere stipulation and fails completely to explain why the lack of any thematic interpretation associated with the v_{tns} selector should be so heavily marked morphologically. Certainly, it is not normally the case in natural language that special morphology is used to signal the *absence* of semantic content, yet that is essentially what the standard theory of structural Case and agreement claims. The central idea behind the minimalist approach to

---

[7] A full discussion of other putative cases of long-distance agreement, such as the well-known case of Icelandic agreement with nominative "objects," is beyond the scope of this work. It is interesting to note, however, that LDA with nominative "objects" in Icelandic is similar to existential sentences in English, in that it only involves agreement in number, not in person (Sigurðsson 1996). See Kučerová (2016) for a recent critique of minimalist analyses based on a long-distance Agree operation and a defense of the locality of the agreement relation.

Case and agreement is that a structural Case such as NOM is an "uninterpretable" feature that must be eliminated in order for syntactic representations to be legible to the CI systems. Likewise, the φ-features of the T head are also said to be uninterpretable, hence must be eliminated for the same reason. It would be more explanatory, as well as more elegant, if the presence of φ-features on v_{tns} and/or structural Case on the nominal it selects actually signaled the *presence* of some interpretable syntactic property. If that were the case, then the φ-features of v_{tns} and the NOM Case feature of its dependent would not be fundamentally different from other cases we have looked at (e.g. inherent Case) in which morphological alternation functions to make some interpretable feature of the syntax visible at PHON. Since structural Case and subject–verb agreement are the paradigm cases (perhaps the only ones) where it has been argued that syntactic processes are driven by the need to value and eliminate uninterpretable features, that particular mechanism could be dispensed with entirely in syntactic theory.

Pursuing this line of thought further, I would like to argue that there is in fact an interpretable syntactic feature that triggers agreement and NOM Case assignment. That feature, I suggest, is the traditional notion of *finiteness*. What exactly is finiteness? Various ways of distinguishing finite from non-finite clauses are to be found in the traditional literature, none of them very satisfactory. For example, it is sometimes claimed that a finite clause is one that can stand alone as a *root*, whereas a non-finite clause is dependent and cannot stand alone. This cannot be correct, however, since finite clauses can perfectly well be dependent, e.g. *Mary believes that John left, That John left astounded Mary*, etc. Conversely, there are root clauses such as imperatives that are non-finite. Another traditional definition is that a finite clause is one that contains a *finite verb*, where a finite verb is one that is inflected for features such as tense, person, number, etc. Again, this cannot be correct since clauses with uninflected modal auxiliaries such as *will, can, may, might*, etc. are clearly finite. Conversely, there are languages such as Portuguese in which non-finite verbs are inflected. Finally, it is sometimes suggested that finite clauses have overt subjects whereas non-finite clauses do not, but that definition also fails miserably since there many non-finite clauses that clearly have overt subjects, e.g. *For John to leave would upset Mary, We want John to leave*, etc.

What does seem clear, however, is that there is some kind of semantic difference between finite and non-finite clauses. I will therefore assume that there is an interpretable syntactic feature [+/−fin] and I will assume, as a very rough approximation, that a finite clause refers to an actual event in some possible world, whereas a non-finite clause refers merely to a possible or potential event in some possible world.

5.3.3   *Syntax of Case in Finite and Non-finite Clauses*

Turning next to more detailed syntactic arguments in support of the claim that differential Case-marking of subjects conveys the value of the feature of finiteness, I start by taking a critical look at the classical Government–Binding theory of structural Case, the historical precursor of the current minimalist approach. I will argue that there is empirical evidence against the so-called "PRO theorem," one of the key features of classical Case theory, which has, as one of its consequences, the necessity of positing "exceptional" Case-marking across an IP boundary. Since such an operation cannot even be formulated in the relational framework proposed here, arguments against exceptional Case-marking are *ipso facto* arguments in favor of the relational approach. Note that I am assuming throughout this discussion the analysis of infinitive complements proposed in Chapter 3, according to which the infinitival marker *to* is located in a distinct projection v_{inf} which is selected by v_{pred} and which selects v_{tns}.

5.3.3.1   Critique of Classical Case Theory   Recall that the basic form of the Case Filter in Chomsky and Lasnik's (1977) paper "Filters and control" (henceforth referred to as "F&C") is as follows:

(18)   *[NP to VP], unless ..., NP lexical.

where the ellipsis specifies basically the ECM contexts. The Case Filter was incorporated into classical Case theory in an unpublished letter by Vergnaud (reprinted in Freidin et al. 2008: 3–15) in the following way. First, the Case Filter throws out any structure containing a lexical NP that fails to be assigned Case. Second, non-finite T is not a Case assigner, hence a lexical NP subject in a non-finite clause violates the Case Filter. Third, PRO, in contrast to lexical NP, is obligatorily Caseless and therefore can appear (only) in such positions. This accounts for the basic complementary distribution of lexical NP and PRO. Finally, apparent violations of the Case Filter are precisely the ECM cases covered by the "unless"-clause in (25), according to which Case is "exceptionally" assigned across an IP boundary.

I claim, however, that the supposed complementary distribution of lexical NP and PRO, on which the whole theory rests, is a false generalization. This is shown by examples such as the following, in which the subject of a non-finite complement can be *either* lexical NP *or* PRO:

(19)   a. I want/prefer him to leave.
          b. I want/prefer PRO to leave.
          c. *He is wanted/preferred to leave.

The lack of passive forms such as (19c) shows that the examples in (19a) are not instances of ECM, which are quite generally passivizable:

(20)   a. I expect/believe them to be on time.
        b. They are expected/believed to be on time.

Interestingly, in F&C examples like (19b) were *not* accounted for by assuming a PRO subject but by "reflexive deletion" (itself a later version of "Equi-NP Deletion") from underlying forms such as the following:

(21)   I want/prefer (myself) to leave.

Such an analysis has long since been abandoned, of course, because it produces the wrong interpretation in cases where the matrix subject is quantified, e.g. *All the men wanted themselves to leave ≠ All the men wanted PRO to leave*. Subsequently, it was suggested that these apparent counterexamples to the complementary distribution of lexical NP and PRO could be explained under the assumption that the complements in question were actually CP complements with a null complementizer rather than defective TP complements. However, no empirical arguments in support of this analysis have ever been produced, to the best of my knowledge, apart from the fact that some of these verbs may optionally occur with the overt complementizer *for* (see §5.3.4.1 for discussion). In any case, the end result of this sequence of developments was to obscure the fact that examples such as (19) are true counterexamples to the claim that lexical NP and PRO are in complete complementary distribution.

    Fortunately, it is not necessary to rely solely on infinitival complements to arrive at this conclusion, because there is another construction in English, the so-called "ACC-ing" construction, which supports the same conclusion even more clearly:

(22)   a. I dislike/prefer him doing that.
        b. I dislike/prefer PRO doing that.
        c. *He is disliked/preferred doing that.

As the position of negation in the following examples shows, the suffix *-ing* must be located in Inf, where it combines with the raised lexical root, much as in French and German:

(23)   I prefer/dislike him not being polite.

Hence there exists another type of non-finite clause whose subject can either be a lexical NP or PRO, but in this case trying to avoid the problem by claiming that the complement is a CP with a null complementizer has no plausibility at all. I conclude therefore that the supposed complementary distribution between lexical NP and PRO, on which the whole of classical Case theory rests, is simply a false generalization.

5.3.3.2   Case Assignment in Finite and Non-finite Clauses   Having cleared the ground, we are now in a position to propose an explicit alternative to the classical theory of structural Case, based on the idea that the function of structural Case is to make visible at PHON an interpretable syntactic feature, namely, finiteness. Specifically, I propose the following principles of Case valuation in finite and non-finite clauses:[8]

(24)   A. [+fin] T assigns NOM to the closest DP in its domain with an unvalued Case feature.
          B. [−fin] T assigns ACC to the closest DP in its domain with an unvalued Case feature.[9]

I assume the following standard definition of "domain" and "closest to" from Chomsky (2000):

(25)   Suppose K is a Case-assigner. Then the *domain* D(K) is the sister of K and G is *closest* to K if there is no G′ with an unvalued Case feature such that G is in D(G′).

Given these principles, NOM Case is assigned by condition A in finite clauses as follows:

(26)

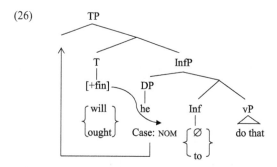

In non-finite clauses, in contrast, condition B assigns ACC Case as follows:

---

[8] I first develop my analysis of structural NOM Case in more familiar minimalist terms, and then show in §5.3.4 that such an approach is virtually required in the relational framework.

[9] In many languages subjects of non-finite clauses are marked with DAT Case. It may well be that this is a universal principle, but that in languages such as English, where there is no longer any overt morphological distinction between ACC and DAT Case, DAT is simply spelled out in the same way as ACC Case.

(27)

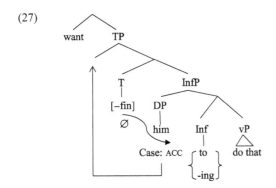

Under the standard view that PRO is obligatorily Caseless, it would necessarily be excluded from subject position in both finite and non-finite clauses, but, as was shown in §5.3.3.1, PRO is in fact possible as the subject of non-finite clauses, though not of course of finite clauses.

To account for the distribution of PRO, while maintaining the assumption that it is obligatorily Caseless, there are two possible ways to proceed: (i) assignment of NOM Case in finite clauses is *obligatory*, but assignment of ACC Case in non-finite clauses is *optional*; (ii) assignment of both NOM and ACC Case is *obligatory*. Under option (i), if ACC Case assignment applies, the subject must be lexical, whereas if it does not apply, the subject must be PRO. Under option (ii), the subject of non-finite TP is always lexical, and instances where the subject appears to be PRO must instead be cases of obligatory control:

(28)   a. John tried [PRO to leave].
         b. *John tried [(for) Bill leave].

How then is obligatory control to be treated? I propose that this comes down to a matter of selection: whereas verbs such as *want* select T[−fin]P, verbs such as *try* select InfP. Obligatory control sentences such as (28a) would then be derived as follows:

(29)

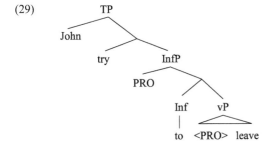

Since there is no Case-assigner in whose domain the subject of InfP appears,[10] it can only be PRO.[11] Under this scenario, then, the difference between *want* and *try* is that the former may select either Inf or T[−fin], whereas the latter only selects Inf.

Are there empirical arguments that could decide between (i) and (ii)? If (ii) is correct, then the infinitive complement in *I want him to leave* is TP, whereas it is InfP in both *I want to leave* and *I tried to leave*. If (i) is correct, on the other hand, then all these complements are TPs. One possible way to decide the issue rests on selection. If (i) is correct, then a verb such as *want* should uniformly take complements with both lexical and PRO subjects, unless we are willing to allow individual verbs the undesirable power to decide whether Case assignment is optional or obligatory. If, however, (ii) is correct, then we would expect to find a verb similar to *want* that can have a lexical subject but not a PRO subject. In fact, there appear to be verbs of just this kind:

(30) a. I fear him to be lost.
      b. *I fear PRO to be lost.
      c. *He is feared to be lost.

(31) a. I remembered him to be tall.
      b. *I remembered PRO to be tall.[12]
      c. *He was remembered to be tall.

Under (ii), the verbs *fear* and *remember* can be classified as selecting T[−fin]P but not InfP. The c.-examples are provided to show that they are not instances of ECM.

I conclude that (ii) is correct and that NOM and ACC Case are assigned obligatorily to subjects by T[+fin] and T[−fin], respectively. Assuming that the feature [+/−fin] is interpretable, this entails that the function of differential Case-marking of subjects is to signal at PHON whether the clause containing them is finite or non-finite.

This conclusion is further strengthened by the observation that Case-marking applies to lexical nouns regardless of whether they are referential or expletive:

(32) a. She left.
      b. It rained.
      c. There was rain.
      d. It appears that Mary is right.

---

[10] See the next paragraph for evidence that *try* in these contexts is not a Case-assigner.

[11] Alternatively, a lexical DP must raise to a θ-position, following Bowers (1973, 2008) and Hornstein (1999, 2001). See §5.4.4 for further discussion.

[12] *Note*. Example (31b) is ungrammatical with an interpretation equivalent to 'I remembered myself to be tall.' The sense of *remember* in an example such as *I remembered to take out the garbage* is quite different, suggesting that *remember* in this sense selects InfP rather than T[−fin]P.

(33)   a. I want *(her) to leave.
        b. I want *(it) to rain.
        c. I want *(there) to be rain.
        d. I want *(it) to appear that Mary is right.

PRO, in contrast, can only be referential:

(34)   a. He wants PRO to leave.
        b. ??It wants PRO to rain.[13]
        c. *There wants PRO to be rain.
        d. *It wants PRO to appear that Mary is right.

What this shows is that the semantically relevant information carried by structural NOM and ACC in subject position has nothing to do with inherent properties of DPs such as θ-role assignment and referentiality, but instead carries information about the finiteness of the TP containing the subject-DP. That in turn explains why it is not contradictory for so-called structural Case to mark an interpretable feature, while at the same time being assignable to DPs with different θ-roles, or with no θ-role at all.

5.3.4   *Relational Derivation of* NOM *Case and Subject–Verb Agreement*

Returning to the main theme, it is easy to see that a revised approach to structural NOM Case and subject–verb agreement along the lines sketched in §5.3.3.2 is exactly what is *required* by the relational theory proposed here. The only way morphological Case alternations can arise at PHON in this theory is by virtue of the fact that different heads may require their dependents to have different combinations of features and/or particular values of those features. As has just been shown, the value of the Case feature associated with subjects— and likewise the presence or absence of agreeing φ-features in v_{tns}—is determined by the value of an interpretable feature of v_{tns}, namely, the feature of finiteness. Not only can these dependencies be expressed directly in the selection features of v_{tns}, but that is in fact the *only* way that the theory permits such morphological variation in Case and agreement to arise. Principles A and B in (24) therefore reduce to simple selection features of v_{tns} of the following form:[14]

---

[13] Modulo Chomsky's (1981) suggestion that "weather *it*" might be "quasi-referential."

[14] Whether the Case properties expressed in (35) are universally present in all languages regardless of whether Case is morphologically realized at PHON or not, i.e. whether Case is abstract, is an issue I shall not try to decide here.

(35)   a. $v_{[+fin]}$:   [__ n_{det}]
            $\varphi{:}x$ $\varphi{:}x$
                              Case: NOM
        b. $v_{[-fin]}$:   [__ n_{det}]
                              Case: ACC

These features in turn produce derivations such as the following for examples like (26) and (27):[15]

(36)

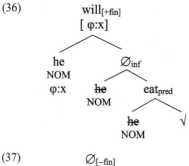

(37)

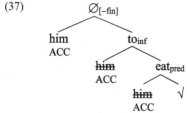

Since the selection of NOM and ACC Case by $v[+/-\text{fin}]$ is now formally identical to selection of inherent Case, it may be assumed that exactly the same mechanisms developed earlier apply here as well. In particular, a so-called structural Case feature satisfies the Case requirements of a selection feature such as (35a) or (35b), as shown in derivations (36) and (37), in exactly the same way that an inherent Case feature does. Similarly, the requirement that the φ-features of v_{tns} agree with those of the subject in finite clauses is analogous to the requirement that there be a morphological reflex in v_{aff} of the interpretable feature [aff].

Summarizing, in the relational theory proposed here, exceptional Case-marking across a defective TP category is not only unnecessary, but impossible. The fact that there are empirical grounds for eliminating it therefore provides

---

[15] In the interests of clarity, I retain the phonological forms of displaced arguments in their correct Case forms, marking them with a strike-through to indicate that they are unpronounced phonetically, in this and subsequent derivations in this chapter.

strong support for a more restrictive theory of syntax based on relations rather than constituent structure. Furthermore, once it becomes clear that assignment of NOM Case and subject–verb agreement is contingent on the feature of finiteness, the way is clear for a theory in which the function of all Case and agreement features, without exception, is to make visible at PHON certain interpretable syntactic features.

5.3.4.1   Non-finite CP: ECM with *for*   It still remains to be shown, however, how the ECM cases can be dealt with in a relational framework. I consider first the case of ECM within infinitive complements headed by *for*, deferring until §5.4 an account of ECM in infinitival complements. Let us assume first that both v_{tns} and v_{comp} have the feature [+/−fin]. We may also assume, as a general property of projection, that the value of any features shared by a head and a dependent must agree. Combining [+/−fin] with the feature [+/−wh] (cf. §6.2 for further discussion of this feature) in v_{comp} yields the following possible types of complementizers:

(38)   that   for   Ø   Ø

$$\begin{bmatrix} +\text{fin} \\ -\text{wh} \end{bmatrix} \quad \begin{bmatrix} -\text{fin} \\ -\text{wh} \end{bmatrix} \quad \begin{bmatrix} +\text{fin} \\ +\text{wh} \end{bmatrix} \quad \begin{bmatrix} -\text{fin} \\ +\text{wh} \end{bmatrix}$$

The fact that verbs such as *amuse, worry, bother, upset, annoy*, etc., whose subjects are marked with ACC Case, require the non-finite complementizer *for* is then simply a matter of selection of v_{comp} [−fin,−wh] rather than v_{tns} [−fin]:

(39)   a. It annoys Mary *(for) him/*he to lose.
          b. *(For) him/*he to lose that annoys Mary.

Conversely, the fact that these same verbs require the complementizer *that* when the subject is marked with NOM Case and v_{tns} is finite follows if they also have the option of selecting v_{comp}[+fin,−wh]:

(40)   a. It annoys Mary *(that) he/*him does that.
          b. *(That) he/*him does that annoys Mary.

There is thus no need to assume that *for* "exceptionally" assigns Case across a TP boundary. Rather, these are just ordinary non-finite clauses with a *for*-complementizer projected from *v*[−fin], which selects a subject with ACC Case for the reasons discussed in §5.3.4:

(41)   for$_{[-fin,-wh]}$

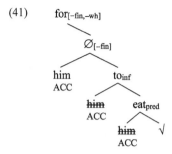

Further support for this conclusion comes from the fact that ACC-ing complements in subject position also require their subjects to have ACC Case despite
the fact that there is no complementizer at all:

(42)   a. Him/*he doing that annoys Mary.
          b. It annoys Mary him/*he doing that.

This demonstrates conclusively that ACC Case is not assigned to the subjects of
non-finite clauses by v_{comp} but by $v_{[-fin]}$.

Consider, in contrast, verbs such as *like, love, hate,* etc. These verbs may
select either $v_{comp}[-fin,-wh]$ or $v_{tns}[-fin]$, accounting for the fact that the
complementizer *for* appears to be optional for many of these verbs:

(43)   I would like (for) him to be there on time.

Notice, finally, that verbs such as *annoy, amuse,* etc. also permit complements
with a PRO subject:

(44)   a. (*For) PRO to be arrested would amuse Mary.
          b. It would amuse Mary (*for) PRO to be arrested.

The fact that *for* can never co-occur with PRO shows that these complements
are simply bare v_{inf} projections, as is the case for other control and PRO$_{arb}$
constructions we have looked at:

(45)   a. It would amuse Mary PRO to be arrested.
          b. PRO to be arrested would amuse Mary.
          c. PRO$_{arb}$ to swim would be fun.

Hence these verbs may select either $v_{comp}[-fin,-wh]$ or v_{inf}, but not $v_{tns}[-fin]$.
The fact that other varieties of English systematically allow *for* in these
constructions suggests that this is just an accidental gap in standard English,
as well as providing a further argument against the ECM analysis of *for–to*

complements, since *for* would uniformly disallow PRO in all dialects if it were really a Case-assigner.

5.3.4.2   Non-finite *wh*-complements   To complete this discussion of possible complement types, consider infinitival *wh*-complements such as the following:

(46)   a. I wonder what PRO/*for him to eat ~~what~~.
        b. What PRO/*for him to eat ~~what~~ is the question.

The fact that a *wh*-phrase cannot co-occur with *for* follows from the feature structure of v_{comp} proposed in §5.3.4, since *for* is always [−wh]. As has often been noted, however, *wh*-infinitive complements in English also uniformly disallow lexical subjects:

(47)   a. I wonder what PRO/*him to eat ~~what~~.
        b. What PRO/*him to eat ~~what~~ is the question.

It seems to be the case, then, that v_{tns}[−fin] uniformly selects v_{comp}[−fin,−wh] and that v_{inf} is able to select v_{comp}[−fin,+wh] directly:

(48)

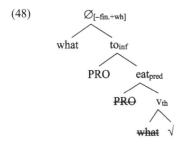

Whether this is an accidental gap in English or a more systematic one that requires deeper explanation is a question I will not try to decide here.

5.4   Athematic Argument Selection (2): Structural Accusative Case

To conclude this chapter, I propose a relational account of structural ACC Case assignment which, in contrast to the standard constituent-based approach, does not require exceptional Case-marking across a TP boundary. Modifying the split VP hypothesis of Koizumi (1993, 1995) along the lines suggested in Bowers (2002, 2010), I propose that there is a *v*-projection v_{tr} below v_{pred} which is similar to v_{tns} in two ways. First, it contains an athematic selection feature [_n$_{det}$]; second, it is responsible for selecting structural ACC Case. As was true of structural NOM Case, assignment of structural ACC is simply a grammatical requirement that a particular head—in this case v_{tr}—imposes on its dependent. It may therefore be incorporated directly in the selection feature of v_{tr} in the following way:

(49) v_{tr}: [___ n_{det}]
                Case: ACC

A transitive sentence such as *They will find him* can then be derived, with the correct morphology, as follows:

(50)

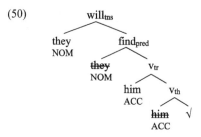

Assuming, along the lines proposed earlier, that the Case feature of a nominal projection is already valued when it is selected as an argument, all the selection feature of v_{tr} has to do is check that the n_{det} head it selects has the required value. If they match, the derivation continues; if not, it crashes.

Now consider an example of ECM such as the following:

(51)   We believe him to like her.

Let us assume that the matrix predicate *believe* selects a v_{inf} projection as its v_{th}-argument and is transitive, hence has the projection v_{tr}. Then the correct syntactic and morphological form of (51) can be derived straightforwardly as follows:

(52)

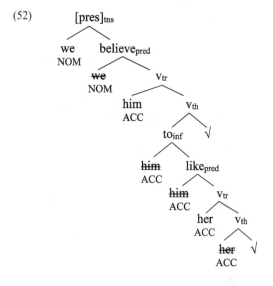

The only *n*-projection accessible to v_{tr} in the matrix clause is *him*, the subject of the infinitive argument. Since its Case feature is valued ACC, as required by the selection feature of v_{tr}, it is selected and pronounced to the left of *believe*$_{tr}$. As is evident, neither the Case Filter nor exceptional Case-marking are required, since the positive, strictly local Case requirement built into the selection feature (49) is sufficient to ensure that the Case feature of the nominal projection selected by v_{tr} in the root clause has the correct value. If the Case feature of *him* had been valued NOM, the requirements of (49) would not be met and the derivation would crash.

Consider next how an example of subject raising such as the following would be derived:

(53)   He seems to like Mary.

For reasons that will be explained shortly, it must be assumed that predicates such as *seem*, even though they are intransitive, nevertheless project v_{tr}, the difference being that the selection feature of v_{tr} in this instance does not impose a Case requirement on the argument it selects. Hence (53) is derived as follows:

(54)

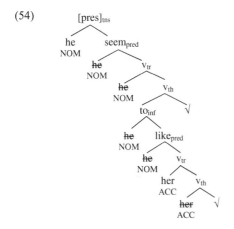

Because the selection feature of v_{tr} in the matrix projection does not, in this instance, impose a Case requirement on the argument that it selects, the Case feature of the infinitival subject must be valued NOM, in order to satisfy the selection requirement of v_{tns} at the point in the derivation where it is finally pronounced.

Consider finally the derivation of an obligatory control sentence such as *He tried to like her*. The only difference between this sentence and the raising sentence (53) just discussed is that the matrix subject bears a thematic relation to the verb *try*. The simplest way to derive such obligatory control structures in the relational framework is to permit displacement to a thematic argument position, along the lines suggested in Bowers (2008).[16] The derivation is then virtually identical to (54), the only difference being that the selection feature of v_{pred} is thematic rather than athematic:

(55)

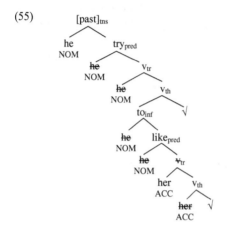

Note that it would be considerably more complicated in this framework to treat the subjects of control complements as PRO. First of all, a checking procedure would be required for Case-marked arguments, from which PRO would be uniquely exempt. Second, verbs would have to be able to select infinitival complements with either PRO or lexical subjects, in order to distinguish the complement of *try* from the complement of *seem*, an extension of the notion of selection for which there is no independent motivation.

5.4.1   *Obligatory Projection of* v_{tr}

It is necessary at this point to consider more carefully the status of the v_{tr} projection and its selection properties. *A priori*, it could be the case that v_{tr} is required in some projections but not in others.[17] Alternatively, it could be the case that it is obligatorily present in all *v*-projections, with different "flavors" of v_{tr} being distinguished by different possible selection properties. I will argue that the latter hypothesis is empirically correct.

---

[16]   See also Bowers (1973) and Hornstein (1999, 2001) for earlier versions of the movement theory of control.

[17]   This is the approach developed in Bowers (2002), which I propose to modify here.

It was shown in Chapter 3 that the distribution of manner adverbs in transitive sentences, shown in (56a), follows from the assumption that they are modifiers of v_{tr}. Consider in this light the examples in (56b–d):

(56)   a. John (*perfectly) threw (*perfectly) the ball (perfectly) to first base (perfectly).
        b. Smith (*uncontrollably) screamed (uncontrollably) at the umpire (uncontrollably).
        c. The ball (*perfectly) rolled (perfectly) into the hole (perfectly).
        d. It (*torrentially) rained (torrentially) on the spectators (torrentially).

This data shows that regardless of whether the verb is transitive, unergative, unaccusative, or even a 0-place predicate, pure manner adverbs have exactly the same distribution: they are barred from occurring to the left of the main verb or between the verb and the object, but may occur either before or after a prepositional phrase argument of the verb. Since manner adverbs are modifiers of v_{tr}, the only way this can be explained is to assume that the v_{tr} projection is available in all sentence types, regardless of argument structure.

Let us see, then, whether the possible combinations of selection properties of v_{tr} and a-selection properties of verbs provide a plausible typology of argument structures in natural language. I have already shown that assignment of structural ACC Case can be accounted for in relational terms by assuming that v_{tr} may have a selection feature of the form (49), requiring that the Case feature of the selected argument be valued ACC. There are only two other possible selection features that v_{tr} can have:

(57)   a. $[\_n_{det}]$
        b. $[\_]$ (i.e. no selection feature)

Example (57a) specifies selection of a nominal as argument by v_{tr} but does not require that its Case feature have any particular value, while (57b) simply states that v_{tr} does not select an argument at all. It was shown previously that (57a) suffices to account for the NOM Case-marking of subjects of raising verbs such as *seem*, but in fact it will also explain the properties of all unaccusative verbs, i.e. those that select a v_{th} argument but not a v_{pred} argument. Evidence in support of this analysis comes from two observations: (i) the thematic argument of unaccusatives is marked with structural NOM (except under one particular circumstance to be discussed shortly); (ii) the thematic argument may appear immediately to the right of the verb in existential constructions of the kind discussed earlier:

(58)   a. He/*him arrived at the party.
        b. There appeared a package at the door.

Since there is no v_{pred} argument with NOM Case that can be selected by v_{tns}, the v_{th} argument must be marked NOM instead. Obviously, that is only possible if the selection feature of v_{tr} does not require ACC Case in this instance. Example (58a) can thus be derived as follows:

(59)

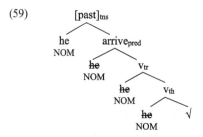

As discussed in Chapter 1 (cf. §1.1.4.3), v_{pred} also has the option of selecting expletive *there* under certain conditions, requiring the v_{th} argument to be pronounced to the right of the main verb:

(60)

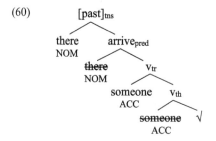

Following the discussion of expletive *there* in §5.3.1, let us assume that the athematic selection feature of v_{tr} requires an n_{det} with ACC Case. It follows, then, that v_{pred} has no option but to select the expletive *there*, whose Case feature must itself be valued NOM in order to satisfy the athematic selection feature of v_{tns}.

The single v_{pred} argument of an unergative verb, in contrast, can never appear to the right of the verb with expletive *there*, though it requires NOM Case just like the subject of an unaccusative:

(61)   a. *There screamed someone at the umpire.
        b. He/*him screamed at the umpire.

Both properties can be explained if v_{tr} has no selection feature at all in this instance, in accordance with option (57b). Since the v_{pred} argument of an unergative is not selected by v_{tr}, the value of its Case feature can only be NOM, as required by v_{tns}. Hence it is impossible for an unergative to appear in an expletive construction. At the same time, since it is the only argument available to be selected by v_{tns}, its Case feature must be valued NOM. The same is obviously true for 0-place predicates of the kind found in (56d), except that its subject must be the default expletive *it*, selected by v_{pred}.

There remain two further possibilities. First, is it possible for a predicate that a-selects both a v_{th} argument and a v_{pred} argument to select v_{tr} with the selection feature (57a)? Second, is it possible for a predicate with only a v_{th} argument to project v_{tr} with the selection feature (49) that requires ACC Case? The answer to both questions is in the affirmative. The first is simply the case of passive sentences. In such constructions the v_{pred} argument is either marked with an inherent Case such as INSTR or assigned Case by a preposition (depending on the language), leaving only the v_{th} argument to be marked NOM, as required by v_{tns}. The second is the case of existential sentences discussed earlier, to which we may add impersonal transitive constructions (or "adversity impersonal" sentences, as they are termed in the Slavic literature) found in Russian, German, and other languages, as well as impersonal passives with ACC Case-marked v_{th} arguments in languages such as Ukrainian. The latter two cases are discussed extensively in Bowers (2002), to which the reader is referred. The main point here, details aside, is that the typology of argument structures obtained by combining the selection possibilities of v_{tr} with the a-selection possibilities of verbal roots corresponds precisely to the range of argument structures attested in the world's languages.

5.4.2 Ditransitive Argument Structures

Further evidence that selection of structural ACC Case is built into the selection feature of v_{tr} is provided by the well-known alternation between prepositional dative and double object constructions in English, as shown in the following examples:

(62) a. I gave a book to her.
      b. I gave her a book.

Evidence that the v_{th} argument is assigned structural ACC in (62a) and the v_{aff} argument in (62b) comes from the well-known fact that both are passivizable:

(63) a. The book was given to her.
      b. She was given the book.

Following Bowers (2002), it was argued in Chapter 2 that all four variants in (62) and (63) derive from ditransitive structures projecting a v_{th} and a v_{aff} argument. Assume first that v_{tr} has a selection feature of the form (49). Then, if

v_{aff} selects a p-projection, v_{th} must have the ACC Case required by v_{tr}. If, on the other hand, v_{aff} selects an n-projection, then it must be marked with ACC Case and selected by v_{tr}. The v_{th} argument in the latter case is assigned inherent ACC Case by the v_{th} head, explaining why it cannot be passivized. To account for the passive forms in (63), we may assume that v_{tr} has the selection feature [_n$_{det}$]. Whichever argument is selected by v_{tr} will therefore have to be marked with NOM Case feature in order to satisfy the selections requirements of v_{tns} later in the derivation. The main point of relevance here is that the systematic alternation between double object and prepositional dative constructions observed in (62) is difficult to explain unless structural ACC Case is selected by a separate head such as v_{tr}.

5.4.3   Case in p-*projections*

Transitive prepositions in English systematically require that their objects be in ACC Case, suggesting that p-projections must also contain a head with an athematic selection feature that selects a nominal projection with ACC Case. Let us call this projection p_{tr}. Then a p-projection such as *to her* would be derived as follows:

(64)

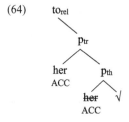

Evidence that Case assigned by propositions in English is structural comes from the existence of so-called pseudopassives of the following form (cf. §2.4.2.3 for discussion):

(65)   She will be talked about __.

To account for such constructions, let us assume that p_{tr}, like v_{tr}, may either select ACC Case or not. If it does not, then the object of the preposition may be marked with NOM Case, which will be selected later in the derivation by v_{tns}. Combining these assumptions with the analysis of passive proposed in Chapter 3 yields the following derivation for (65):

(66)

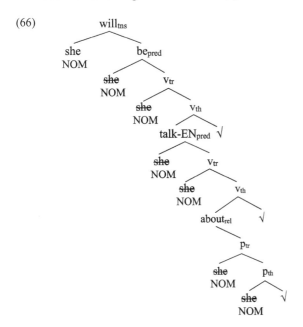

Pseudopassives of this kind are quite marked cross-linguistically, being completely impossible in most languages. This suggests that p_{rel} is a phase in those languages, but not in English. Since p_{rel} is saturated as soon as its selection feature, if it has one, is satisfied, all the material in p_{tr}—in particular the object of the preposition—is inaccessible in languages of the former type. Alternatively, if it is deemed desirable to avoid direct parameterization of the property of phase-hood, it might be conjectured instead that p_{rel} is universally a phase, but that in some languages such as English, p_{rel} may project another p_{rel} head with an athematic selection feature, along the lines suggested for v_{pred} in Chapter 2, thereby allowing the object of the preposition to escape:

(67)

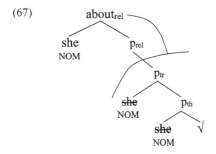

Confirmation of the correctness of this approach may be derived from the fact that pseudopassivization usually correlates with preposition stranding. The latter phenomenon can then be accounted for in a parallel fashion, by supposing that p_{rel} in such languages may also select a p_{rel} head with a *wh*-selection feature, along the lines to be developed in Chapter 6 (cf. §6.2.1 for details). In languages lacking both pseudopassivization and preposition stranding, in contrast, p_{rel} is simply unable to recursively select a p_{rel} head, thereby disallowing any displacement from inside a *p*-projection.

I have argued that ACC Case required on objects of prepositions in English is selected by p_{tr}. However, in many languages Case assigned to prepositional objects is clearly inherent, hence assigned by an argument head. In German, for example, prepositions may assign GEN, DAT, or ACC, all inherent cases, as shown by the fact that German allows neither pseudopassivization nor preposition stranding. For example, in *aus dem Hause* 'out of/from the house,' inherent DAT is assigned to the selected n_{det} by the p_{th} head:

(68)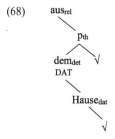

I leave open here a number of interesting questions that arise, such as whether or not *p*-projections have argument projections other than p_{th}, whether languages that do not have structural Case in *p*-projections project the head p_{tr}, and so forth.

5.4.4   *Transitivity*

If the approach to structural ACC Case developed in this section is correct, then it, like structural nominative Case, cannot be merely an uninterpretable feature that must be valued and eliminated in order to render syntactic representations legible to the CI systems. Rather, it must be the morphological marker of some interpretable syntactic feature. I propose to term this feature *transitivity*. That the transitivity relation between a predicate and a nominal is not the same as the relation between a predicate and a thematic argument is shown by the fact that the nominal to which a predicate bears the transitivity relation may have a variety of different thematic roles. In that way the transitivity relation is similar to the subject relation, which may also hold between a predicate and a nominal, independent of what type of argument it is. One way to tease out the semantic property of transitivity is to compare transitive active sentences with unaccusatives and passives:

(69)   a. John rolled the ball down the hill.
       b. The ball rolled down the hill.
       c. The ball was rolled down the hill by John.

The transitivity relation between an activity such as 'rolling down the hill' and an ACC Case-marked argument such as 'the ball' in (69) cannot be reduced to the relation between the verbal root √roll and its v_{th} argument *the ball*. The latter clearly holds in all three of the sentences in (69), whereas the former only holds in (69a). In a transitive sentence such as (69a), the nominal expression *the ball* is in some sense the focus of the activity of 'rolling down the hill,' independent of agency. This relation of transitivity can hold quite independently of the presence of an agentive v_{pred} argument, as is demonstrated by languages such as Russian that have impersonal sentences such as (70), in which the thematic argument is marked with ACC Case despite the fact that there is no v_{pred} argument in the sentence at all (not even an "understood" one):

(70)   Rabočego   ubilo   oskolkom   plity.
       worker-ACC   killed-3P.SG.NEUT   shard-INSTR   of.concrete.slab
       'A worker was killed by a shard of concrete slab.'

Similarly, there is a subtle difference of interpretation between the prepositional dative sentence and the double object sentence illustrated in (62a,b) due to the fact that in the former the focus of the activity of giving something to someone is the entity referred to by *the book*, whereas in the latter it is the entity referred to by *her*.

Still another way to tease out the property of transitivity is to compare two closely related, but not identical, sentences such as *John believes that she is nice* and *John believes her to be nice*. In the first sentence the focus of the state of 'believing' is the proposition 'she is nice,' whereas in the second sentence the focus of the (complex) state of 'believing to be nice' is the entity 'she.' Both sentences are transitive, but the state/action is quite different in the two cases, as are the entities they focus on.

Finally, it is worth noting that in many languages the feature of transitivity is morphologically marked with an affix attached to the verbal stem. This is easily accounted for in relational terms by assuming that the v_{tr} head in such languages is phonologically realized as an affix rather than as an illegible symbol v, as it is in English.

I propose, then, that the selection features (49) and (57a) are differentially associated with v_{tr}, depending on whether it has the feature [+trans] or [−trans]:

(71)   a. $v_{[+trans]}$: [___ n_{det}]
                          Case: ACC
         b. $v_{[-trans]}$: [___ n_{det}]

ACC will therefore be selected if and only if v_{tr} has the feature [+trans]. Like the feature [+/−fin], the feature [+/−trans] is interpretable. Hence the function of structural ACC Case is to make visible at PHON the interpretable syntactic feature of transitivity.

5.5   Conclusion

It has been argued in this chapter that no new primitives are needed in the relational theory proposed here in order to account for morphological alternations at PHON. In particular, the systems of Case (both inherent and structural) and subject–verb agreement commonly found in natural language are selected in the course of applying FR to pairs of LIs α and β on the basis of their intrinsic features, without the necessity of introducing a new primitive operation Agree. It has also been argued that it is possible to eliminate entirely the need for valuing and deleting uninterpretable features in order to produce representations at SEM legible to the CI systems. It has been proposed instead that morphological Case and agreement should be conceptualized as a means of making interpretable features visible at PHON, as is true of morphological alternation generally.

6 *Operators*

I show next that the theory developed in the preceding chapters is sufficient to cover the various processes involved in the formation of operator construc- tions. I first analyze question formation within single root clauses and *wh*- complements, demonstrating that apparent instances of head movement and constituent movement can once again be explained in terms of basic selection relations, together with legibility conditions at PHON. I then show that the proposed architecture provides a typology of word order variation in operator constructions attested in the world's languages. I conclude by showing how the relational version of phase theory introduced in Chapter 2 can be minimally extended to account for most of the well-known island constraints governing displacement of *wh*-expressions in complex sentences.

6.1   *Lexical Projection: Auxiliary Inversion and* **do-support**

Let us start by comparing the formation of questions in English in root clauses and *wh*-complements with respect to the projection relation. As is well known, auxiliary verbs in English must appear before the subject of yes/no questions in root clauses, but not in *wh*-complements and, conversely, *wh*-complements require an overt complementizer that is disallowed in root clauses:

(1)   a. Will/did/does he eat?
       b. *Whether/if he will eat/ate/eats.

(2)   a. I wonder whether/if he will eat/ate/eats.
       b. *I wonder will/did/does he eat.

This complementary distribution can be accounted for in relational terms in the following way. Let us assume that the category v_{comp} comes with various features, including at least [D] and [Q], the former the type of declarative clauses, the latter the type of interrogative clauses. In declarative clauses in English, v_{comp} is lexicalized as *that* in embedded clauses and as Ø in root clauses. Interrogative v_{comp}, in contrast, is more complex. When embedded as a complement of verbs such as *wonder, ask, doubt*, etc., v_{comp} may be lexicalized as either *if* or *whether*, whereas in root clauses it is realized as the phonetically uninterpretable symbol v, which must be replaced with the phonetic form of the verbal element in the v_{tns} heads that selects it. This will produce derivations such as the following:

(3)   a. if_{comp}

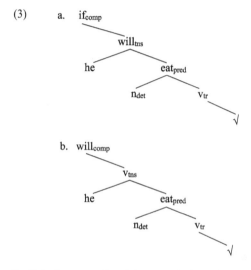

b. $will_{comp}$

In (3a) the v_{comp} head is occupied by the phonetically interpretable word *if*, yielding automatically the correct linear order: ... (wonder)-if-he-will-~~he~~-eat-~~eat~~-√eat. In (3b), in contrast, v_{comp}, like v_{ag}, v_{tr}, and other heads we have investigated has no phonetic content of its own that is readable by SM. Hence FR must provide it with an occurrence of the phonetic form of the head it is selected by, in this case will, producing the correct order at PHON: will-he-~~will~~-~~he~~-eat-~~eat~~-√eat. The appearance of T-to-C movement in the syntax can thus be explained, as have other apparent instances of head movement, by the interaction of FR and the legibility conditions at PHON.

However, matters are more intricate than this, as has been known since the earliest work in transformational generative grammar. To begin with, notice that while the main verb in Modern English in finite clauses is inflected for tense and φ-features (person and number), in the corresponding negative and interrogative sentences these features must appear on the auxiliary *do*, rather than on the main verb:

(4)   a. He eats/ate.
       b. He does/did not (doesn't/didn't) eat.
       c. *He dĭd eat.
       d. *He eats/ate not.
       e. Does/did he eat?
       f. *Eats/ate he?

As has been shown by Emonds (1978), Pollock (1989), and others, the reason for this is that in English (unlike in French, for example) the inflected verb does not raise to T, requiring instead that the special auxiliary *do* be provided to "carry the tense" in interrogative and negative sentences. This particular property of English has proven to be quite awkward to deal with under the otherwise well-motivated assumption that tense and agreement features are associated with T, necessitating that these features be lowered onto the main verb in blatant violation of the extension condition. In the theory proposed here, it is impossible to even define such an operation.[1] Hence it is essential to show that there is some other way of accounting for the data in relational terms.

To begin with, let us assume that all the possible inflected forms of a lexical item are available in LEX and that one of these forms is selected at the start of each v-projection. Obviously, not every inflectional form of a root can be used in every derivation; rather, their distribution is dependent on what syntactic categories are projected. To be more specific, a given verb form inflected for tense and φ-features can only be used if it projects a v_{tns} head with matching features and feature values. To ensure that this condition is met, let us simply build the matching condition into the lexical projection feature of v_{pred}. For example, suppose the form *eats* is selected from the LA with the following feature values: [tns:pres, per:3, num:sg]. In order to be licensed, a v_{pred} projection containing the form *eats* must select a v_{tns} head with matching features and feature values.

However, the special property of English that has to be accounted for is that the phonetic form of *eats* is actually pronounced at the position of v_{pred}, not at the position of v_{tns}. This can be described without introducing any new theoretical apparatus under the assumption that the v_{tns} head in English has as one of

---

[1] Another alternative proposed in the literature, namely, delaying V to T movement in the case of lexical verbs until after Spell-out, i.e. covert movement, is likewise impossible to formulate in the relational framework proposed here, as is also the case in the Minimalist Program.

its possible lexical realizations the form $\emptyset[\text{tns},\varphi]$. Now all that needs to be stipulated is that v_{pred} containing an inflected lexical verb is required to select $\emptyset[\text{tns},\varphi]$ in standard English:[2]

(5)

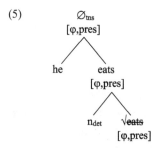

Since $\emptyset_{\text{tns}}$ is a legible LI, the phonetic form of *eats* remains at the position where v_{pred} is spelled out at PHON.

Consider next the negative forms in (4b). Here the lexical root is uninflected, while v_{tns} must have the shape of an inflected form of the verb *do*. Let us assume, first, that there is a morphological form of the root *eat* lacking tense and φ-features altogether and, second, that v_{tns} in English has another possible lexical realization of the form $do[\text{tns},\varphi]$. Now we need only specify that v_{pred} containing an uninflected root of this form must select the projection $do[\text{tns},\varphi]$.

This is not sufficient, however, because such forms only occur with the negative element *not*, as shown by the fact that (4c) with unstressed *do* is impossible. To solve this problem, let us assume, as proposed in earlier chapters (cf. §3.1.3 and §4.2.4), that there is a head v_Σ projected between v_{pred} and v_{tns} that has a polarity feature with two values [pos] and [neg]. We must now determine (i) what possible phonetic forms v_Σ may have, (ii) which forms of v_Σ are selected by different kinds of roots, and (iii) what selection properties each form of v_Σ has.

Consider first positive, declarative sentences such as (4a) in which the lexical root is inflected. The polarity head can only have the value [pos] for such sentence types, as shown by the ungrammaticality of **He not eats*. Let us therefore assume that v_Σ has tense and φ-features, together with the phonetic form $\emptyset$, just in case its polarity feature has the value [pos]. A more complete derivation of (4a) would then be as follows:

---

[2] In this and subsequent derivations, I refrain from specifying all the φ-features and their values, assuming that they are identical throughout.

(6)

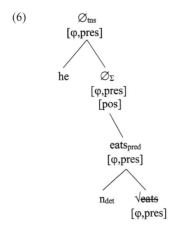

The tense and φ-features of the verbal root *eats* are now licensed by selecting the positively valued $\varnothing_\Sigma$ head with matching tense and φ-features with the same values, rather than by selecting v_{tns} directly. I assume that the tense and φ-features of the $\varnothing_\Sigma[pos]$ head are in turn licensed by selecting a $\varnothing_{tns}$ head with matching tense and φ-features with the same values.

Returning now to the negated sentences in (4b), let us assume that an uninflected verbal root such as *eat* in English must select v_Σ whose polarity feature is valued [neg].[3] This head in turn must select a v_{tns} head with an inflected form of the auxiliary *do*. Hence (4b) may be derived as follows:

(7)

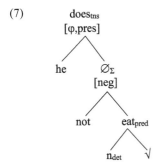

We have thus derived the basic form of positive and negative sentences in English solely from the different forms of roots and heads, together with their selection properties.[4]

---

[3] This requirement will be modified shortly.
[4] Theoretically, there could be a language or a dialect of English in which $\varnothing_\Sigma[\varphi,pres,pos]$ selects *do*[φ,tense], producing examples such as *he does likes me, he didn't liked me*, etc. Interestingly,

There is, however, another set of lexical elements that can occur in the v_{tns} projection in English, namely, the modals *will, shall, can, may, might*, etc. If there is a modal in v_{tns}, then the verbal root is in its default uninflected form in both positive and negative sentences and is pronounced in the v_{pred} position:

(8)   He will (not) eat.

Noting that the modals are inflected for tense/modal features, but not for φ-features, let us assume a third possible realization of v_{tns} that has only the feature [tense]. Such heads may be selected by $\varnothing_\Sigma$, regardless of the value of its polarity feature. Likewise, an uninflected v_{pred} is free to select uninflected $\varnothing_\Sigma$ regardless of the value of its polarity feature. The examples in (8) can then be derived as follows:[5]

(9)

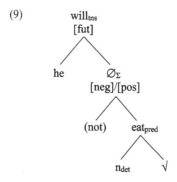

We must consider next how to produce all the possible forms of both declarative and question sentences in English. To do so, we must first determine the possible lexical realizations of the v_{comp} head. For the moment I will assume there are three: (a) $\varnothing$[D]; (b) $\varnothing$[Q]; (c) v[Q]. As before, the task facing us is to specify which of these possible lexical realizations of v_{comp} are selected by each of the possible forms of v_{tns}. Clearly, (a) must be selected by $\varnothing_{tns}$[tns,φ] and may be selected by v[tns], resulting in declarative clauses such as *He eats* and *He will eat*:

---

examples of precisely this kind are spontaneously produced by children at early stages of language acquisition (cf. Radford 1997: 80) and, as readers can verify for themselves, numerous such examples are found in internet postings, especially in online conversations on Instagram and the like. I leave it to future investigation to discover whether there are languages that regularly require an auxiliary verb and a root, both of which are inflected for tense and φ-features. My bet is that there are such languages. At the same time, however, we might expect them to be comparatively rare, since tense and φ-features would be redundantly marked on both the main verb and a semantically empty auxiliary element.

[5] Since stressed (or contrastive) *dó* behaves exactly like a modal, I treat it in the same way.

(10)

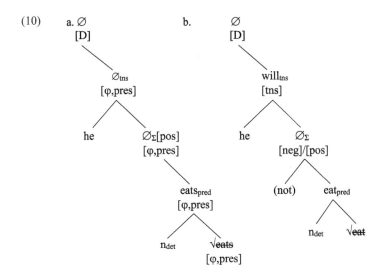

On the other hand, (c) may not be selected by $\varnothing_{tns}[\varphi,tns]$, but may be selected by $v[tns]$, producing interrogatives such as *Will he eat?*

Turning to the head do_{tns}, it may *not* select either (a) or (b), excluding **He does eat*, interpreted as either a declarative or an echo question, but may, if projected from $\varnothing_{\Sigma}[neg]$, select (a), (b), or (c), producing declarative *He does not eat*, echo question *He does not eat?*, and interrogative *Does he not eat?* (*Doesn't he eat?*, if contracted). Earlier, we only allowed do_{tns} to be selected by $\varnothing_{\Sigma}[neg]$. Notice, however, that *do* also appears in positive interrogative sentences such as *Does he eat?*, suggesting that do_{tns} can, in fact, be projected by $\varnothing_{\Sigma}[pos]$, but if so, *must* select (c), as follows:

(11)

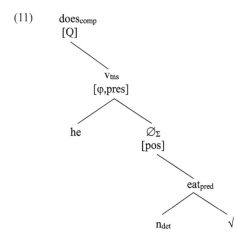

Because inflected do_{tns} selects $v[Q]$, where v is phonetically illegible, the latter must be supplied with the phonetic form of its selector (in this instance *does*), resulting in the correct question form of a simple present or past tense sentence.

This raises a problem, however, for at the point where do_{tns} projects v_{comp} [Q], there is no way to tell whether it was projected by positive or negative $\varnothing_{\Sigma}$. A possible solution is to assume that both v_{Σ} and v_{tns} have a polarity feature which must agree in value when the former selects the latter. It can then be stipulated that $do_{tns}[pos]$ obligatorily selects $v_{comp}[Q]$, whereas, as mentioned earlier, $do_{tns}[neg]$ may select either (a), (b), or (c). In support of this proposal, it might be suggested that if the [neg] feature is spelled out in v_{Σ}, the full negative morpheme *not* results, whereas if it is spelled out in v_{tns}, the negative morpheme must combine phonologically with whatever else is spelled out in that position, producing contracted forms such as *didn't, won't, can't, isn't*, etc. In addition, if the polarity feature is present in both v_{tns} and v_{Σ}, that would explain the not uncommon phenomenon of double negation, such as *ne ... pas* in French, the first part (often non-obligatory) being spelled out in v_{tns}, the second part being spelled out in v_{Σ}.[6] It is important, in any case, to observe that the complementary distribution of the lexical items do_{tns} and $\varnothing_{tns}$ follows directly from the fact they do not share any selection features, whereas modals such as *will* share selection properties with both.

To conclude this section, I show that the behavior of the auxiliary verbs *be* and *have* can also be accounted for in this system by adding just one further logically possible type of lexical realization of the categories v_{Σ} and v_{tns}. As is well known, the auxiliaries *be* and *have*, as well as copular *be*, in Modern English behave like main verbs in French in that they raise to T rather than remaining in the v_{pred} position like lexical verbs:

(12)   a. He is (not) there.
        b. Is he there?
        c. *Does he be there?
        d. He will (not) be there.
        e. Will he be there?

Examples (12d,e) show that when *be* selects a modal, it behaves exactly like a lexical verb such as *eat*. However, when it is in simple present or past tense form, it is pronounced at v_{tns} in declarative sentences and at v_{comp} in interrogative sentences. To account for this apparently anomalous behavior, we need only add a fourth possible lexical realization of v_{Σ} and v_{tns} to the list,

---

[6] See §4.2.4 for further discussion of French negation, as well as supporting evidence from other languages.

namely, $v_\Sigma[\text{tns},\phi]$ and $v_{\text{tns}}[\text{tns},\phi]$. Because both v_Σ and v_{tns} in this instance are phonetically uninterpretable, each must be provided with an occurrence of the phonetic form of the head that selects it. In English, this possibility is severely limited by the fact that these forms of v_Σ and v_{tns} can *only* be selected by the specific roots *be* and *have*, whereas in French *all* lexical verbs select these forms, and the special forms $\varnothing[\text{tns},\phi]$ and *do*$[\text{tns},\phi]$ simply do not exist. Once the phonetic form $v[\text{tns},\phi]$ has been selected, it behaves exactly like modals with respect to its projection possibilities. Hence it may either project $\varnothing[\text{D}]$, producing (10a), or it may project $v[\text{Q}]$, producing example (10b).

To conclude, then, we have succeeded in accounting in purely relational terms for the distribution of inflected main verbs, modal auxiliaries, "raising" *be* and *have*, as well as the special auxiliary *do* in declarative, interrogative, and negative clauses and in both embedded and root clauses, without having to add any new theoretical apparatus whatsoever. All that is needed are language-specific LIs and their projection features. This in turn makes it unnecessary to appeal to any kind of *ad hoc* device such as a lowering operation to account for the fact that all inflected main verbs in English apart from *be* and *have* are pronounced at the v_{pred} projection rather than at the v_{tns} projection, despite the fact that the relevant tense and agreement features universally originate in the latter.

6.2   wh-*selection*

Having accounted for the basic properties of simple declaratives and interrogatives, let's consider next the form of *wh*-questions in root clauses and *wh*-complements. To begin with, look at the following data:

(13)   a. What will he eat?
         b. *What he will eat?
         c. *Will he eat what?

(14)   a. *I wonder what will he eat.
         b. I wonder what he will eat.
         c. *I wonder will he eat what.

The examples in (13) illustrate the well-known fact that in root clauses in English both displacement of a non-subject *wh*-expression to initial position and inversion of the auxiliary are obligatory; those in (14) show that in *wh*-complements, in contrast, displacement of the *wh*-expression is obligatory, while inversion of the auxiliary is impossible. In order to account for this data, we must assume, first of all, that v_{comp} may contain another feature

[wh], in addition to the [Q] feature, which is obligatorily present in both *wh*-root clauses and *wh*-complements. We already have at our disposal the means of accounting for the fact that inversion of the auxiliary is obligatory in *wh*-root clauses but impossible in *wh*-complements. The contrast is easily explained under the assumption that the phonetic form of v_{comp} in the former is illegible (hence has the form $v[Q,wh]$), whereas in the latter it is legible but null (hence has the form $\varnothing[Q,wh]$).

Consider next the fact that the phonetic form of the *wh*-expression *what* is pronounced at PHON to the left of the auxiliary in both root and embedded clauses. To explain this, it must be assumed that there is a selection relation between $v[Q,wh]_{comp}$ and *what*$_{det}$. Since the only syntactic property that the selection feature in v_{comp} imposes on the selected head is that it must bear a matching [wh] feature, such *wh*-selection features may be represented quite generally in the following form: [_wh].[7] Also, since the projection selected by a $[Q,wh]_{comp}$ head is obviously not a new argument or modifier, the *wh*-selection feature must be athematic, hence seeking a head with the required [wh] feature that has already been interpreted as an argument or modifier at SEM. Given these assumptions, a copy of the phonetic form of the selected argument or modifier will then be automatically placed by Spell-out to the left of the phonetic form of the $[Q,wh]_{comp}$ head in PHON, thereby deriving (13a) as follows:

(15)

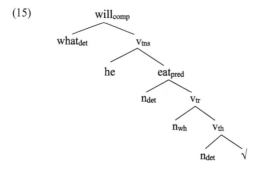

---

[7] Note that the [wh] feature in v_{comp} that distinguishes *wh*-clauses from other types of clauses is distinct from the *wh*-selection feature [_wh] that causes leftward displacement of the phonetic form of some *wh*-expression at PHON. Suppose that in English the selection feature [_wh] is optional in *wh*-root clauses, but obligatory in *wh*-complements. This accounts nicely for the fact that both echo questions and non-echo *wh in situ* questions of the kind discussed in §6.2.3 are possible in the former but not the latter, e.g. *He read which book?*, **I wonder he read which book?* Clearly, the *wh*-selection feature can be parameterized: cf. the remarks at the end of this paragraph.

A wh-argument such as that in (14b) is derived identically, except that the head of v_{comp} has the null phonetic form $\emptyset$. Note that the presence or absence of a wh-selection feature in v_{comp}, like that of the selection feature in v_{tns}, is subject to parametric variation, since, as is well known, there are languages such as Japanese, Chinese, etc., in which the pronunciation of wh-phrases is never displaced leftwards but remains *in situ*. I return to this topic shortly.

6.2.1   Displacement from Within the v_{pred} Phase

A problem much discussed in the recent literature is posed by the fact that the wh-selection feature must be able to search for a head with the required [wh] feature inside the projection v_{pred}, which was argued in Chapter 2 to be a phase. The difficulty is that by the time v_{comp} is projected, the material contained inside the head v_{tr} that selects v_{pred}, will no longer be accessible, making it impossible for the wh-selection feature to find a head with a matching [wh] feature. The standard minimalist solution to this problem is to assume that the vP phase head may optionally have a so-called "edge feature" which licenses Merge of a second specifier with v. If a constituent containing a wh-expression is merged with v to satisfy this edge feature, it is accessible, by the Phase Impenetrability Condition, to the wh-probe in C, thereby providing a way for the wh-expression to "escape" from the vP phase. Clearly, such a solution is not available in the relational theory proposed here, since neither the notion of a constituent nor the operation Merge are primitives of the theory. More importantly, any attempt to create the relational equivalent of a second specifier is disallowed by the theory. It would be impossible, for example, to add an optional second argument selection feature to the phase head v_{pred}, because, as was shown in Chapter 1, IG limits the number of possible selection features of a head to a maximum of one argument selection feature and one lexical projection feature.

There is, however, another way of addressing the problem in relational terms. Recall that in Chapter 3 it was argued that the heads v_{pred} and n_φ are recursive in English, in order to account for the fact that there can be an unbounded number of v_{pred} modifiers, as well as an unbounded number of prenominal modifiers. Suppose, then, that the phase head v_{pred} may optionally select another v_{pred} projection with a selection feature [_wh].[8] As proposed in Chapter 3, I assume that whenever a head α_1 projects another head α_2 of the

---

[8] I assume that v_{pred} with the selection feature [_wh] *must* select v_{tns} (or v_Σ, assuming the analysis of negation discussed earlier), thereby ensuring that it is the highest of a sequence of recursive v_{pred} heads.

same type, the lexical projection feature [_β] of α_1 is automatically transferred to α_2. Technically, this means that v_{pred} has a second projection feature [_v_{pred}] that might be termed a "recursion feature." No violation of IG results, however, because the projection feature [_β] of the first v_{pred} projection is transferred to the new v_{pred} projection. Since the new v_{pred} projection has, by hypothesis, a *wh*-selection feature [_wh] of its own, that feature must be satisfied first, after which the transferred projection feature [_β] can be satisfied. Note also that if a head α has both a lexical projection feature [_β] and a recursion feature [_α], IG dictates that the latter must be satisfied first. If the lexical projection feature were satisfied first, then by IG the selection feature of the new lexical projection β would have to be satisfied immediately, making it impossible to ever satisfy the recursion feature of α. If, however, the recursion feature [_α] is satisfied first, no violation of IG results because, by hypothesis, the lexical projection feature [_β] is transferred to the new head α. Finally, let us assume that in the special case in which a phase head α_P is "extended" by selecting another phase α_P' of the same category, the sealing off of the head γ that selected α_P is delayed until the new phase head α_P' is saturated. This seems quite natural given our previous assumption that the projection feature of α_P is transferred to α_P'.

If these assumptions are correct, example (13a) can then be derived straightforwardly as follows:

(16)

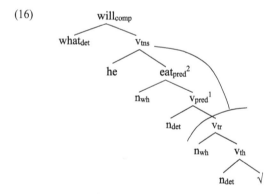

As indicated in (16), the projection v_{tr} that selects the phase head v_{pred}^1 is not closed off until v_{pred}^2, the extension of v_{pred}^1, is saturated, i.e. when it selects *will*$_{\text{tns}}$. This ensures that the *wh*-expression *what* is still accessible at the point in the derivation where the *wh*-selection feature of v_{pred}^2 must be satisfied. The new occurrence of *what* selected by *eat*$_{\text{pred}}^2$ is in turn available to satisfy the *wh*-selection feature of v_{comp}. We have thus succeeded in accounting for the fact that a *wh*-expression may escape from a phase without having to add anything new to the theory, apart from an optional wh-selection feature of a kind that is needed anyway.

Note that if the subject is a wh-expression, v_{pred} need not be extended in order to ensure that there is a wh-expression accessible to the wh-selection feature in v_{comp}.[9] This immediately explains classic superiority effects of the following kind:

(17)   a. Who ate what?
       b. *What did who eat?

(18)   a. Who went where?
       b. *Where did who go?

(19)   a. What was bought by whom?
       b. *By whom was what bought?
       c. *Who was what bought by?

(20)   a. Who bought books when?
       b. *When did who buy books?

(21)   a. Who gave books to whom?
       b. *To whom did who give books?
       c. *Who did who give books to?

To see that this is so, consider the following derivation:

(22) $[Q,wh]_{comp}$

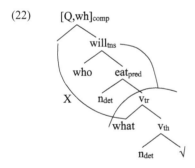

At the point in the derivation where $[Q,wh]_{comp}$ is attempting to satisfy its [_wh] selection feature, the v_{th} argument *what* will already be inaccessible, since eat_{pred} is saturated as soon as its projection feature is satisfied by selecting

---

[9] Technically, nothing would prevent v_{pred} from being extended in this case also. However, the only effect would be for the [_wh] feature in the extension to redundantly select the wh-subject. I will assume that the Vacuous Movement Hypothesis (VMH) discussed in §6.2.2 can be extended to rule out string-vacuous displacement in this instance as well.

will$_{tns}$, thereby sealing off v_{tr}. Consequently, only the subject *who* is available to satisfy the *wh*-selection feature of v_{comp}.

6.2.2   wh-*subjects and the Vacuous Movement Hypothesis*

This, however, raises a new question, namely, whether displacement of the *wh*-expression and the auxiliary takes place at all in sentences containing a *wh*-subject, given that the output of these two operations is string-identical to the input. Chomsky (1986: 48–54), following George (1980), argues that when the *wh*-expression is the subject, neither the *wh*-subject nor the auxiliary move to CP, but simply remain *in situ*. This is what he terms the "Vacuous Movement Hypothesis" (VMH). Restated in relational terms, the VMH prohibits the formation of a relation between $[Q,wh]_{comp}$ and a head containing a [wh] feature selected by v_{tns}:

(23) $[Q,wh]_{comp}$

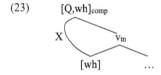

Why should the VMH exist? Chomsky suggests that "the language learner assumes there is syntactic movement only when there is overt evidence for it. We might suppose that the unmarked case for a language with overt *wh*-movement is that it always takes place at S-structure, so that non-movement of subject in English would have a somewhat marked character." But one might question whether lack of overt evidence for movement (multi-attachment in this framework) provides a sufficient reason for tolerating a feature of this "somewhat marked" character.

I would like to approach the question from a slightly different angle. The feature of English that seems somewhat unusual (hence more "marked," in one sense of the term) is that lexical verbs morphologically inflected for tense and agreement fail to be pronounced at v_{tns}, despite the fact that the syntactic features of tense and agreement are located there. Accounting for this property requires, as was shown in §6.1, positing a null lexical item $\varnothing[\varphi,tense]_{tns}$ that must be selected by $\varnothing[\varphi,tense]_{\Sigma}$, which in turn must be selected by v_{pred}, just in case it contains an inflected form of a verbal root. Once these null heads are available, it is necessary to assume that there also exists a null head $\varnothing[Q, wh]_{comp}$ lacking a [_wh] selection feature, in order to account correctly for the form of sentences such as the following:

(24)   a. Who ate the apple?
        b. *Who did eat the apple?
        c. *Did who eat the apple?

Given all these assumptions, example (24a) can then be derived as follows:[10]

(25)

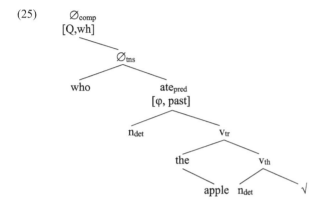

If this analysis is correct, there is no reason why sentences with a modal auxiliary such as the following should not be derived in exactly the same way, namely, by simply allowing *will*$_{tns}$ to select $\emptyset$[Q,wh]$_{comp}$:

(26)   a. Who will eat the apple?
        b. *Will who eat the apple?

But notice that there are now two entirely different ways of deriving subject *wh*-questions in English! The first involves successive displacement of the auxiliary and the *wh*-subject, while the second simply requires selection of a null v_{comp} projection by v_{tns}. One might imagine that such a situation would run afoul of a general economy principle prohibiting redundant derivations. If that were the case, then one of the two derivations would have to be ruled out. Obviously the second derivation cannot be ruled out on account of the English-specific property requiring lexical verbs to be pronounced at v_{pred}. Consequently, the only choice is to rule out derivations of the first kind. The VMH could then be regarded as a language-specific strategy for satisfying such an economy principle while at the same time avoiding a multi-attachment structure for which there is no direct evidence in the data the child is exposed to.

I will therefore assume that the VMH is correct, at least for languages such as English. However, this still leaves the question of why (24b) is ruled out, since

---

[10] Henceforth I omit reference to the intermediate polarity head v_Σ in derivations unless it is germane to the point at issue.

there is apparently nothing to prevent do_{tns} from projecting $v[Q,wh]$ regardless of whether the *wh*-word is a subject or non-subject. In the latter case, examples such as *What did he eat?* will be correctly derived exactly as shown in (16), parallel to *What will he eat?* But in the former case, (24b) will be incorrectly derived. I propose to account for the peculiar and rather limited distribution of the unstressed auxiliary *do* in English purely in terms of its own special selection and projection features. The first property of *do* to be noted, as was observed in §6.1, is that unlike modal auxiliaries such as *will*, it *must* be pronounced at v_{comp} in questions and may never be pronounced at v_{tns} in positive declarative sentences.[11] This can be accounted for by assigning *do* the following projection feature:

(27) do_{tns}: $[\_v[Q,(wh)]_{comp}]$ (projection feature)

Since *do* always selects a form of v_{comp} that is illegible, it follows that it will always be pronounced at v_{comp}, never at v_{tns}. If *do* selects $v[Q]$, the result will be yes/no questions of the form *Did he eat a bagel?* If it selects $v[Q,wh]$, the result will be *wh*-questions of the form *What did he eat?*, derived as shown in (16). To rule out (24b), however, we must also restrict the argument selection feature of do_{tns} in such a way that it can only select a non-*wh*-expression:

(28) do_{tns}: $[\_n_{det}[-wh]]$ (selection feature)

This selection feature embodies the second peculiarity of *do*, namely, that it only appears in *wh*-questions when the *wh*-expression is not the subject, that is to say, when it is not selected by v_{pred}. Unstressed *do* again differs markedly from the modal auxiliaries (and stressed *do*), which are subject to no such restriction, as shown in (26a).

It is interesting to speculate as to why English should tolerate an LI like unstressed *do* with such odd and idiosyncratic properties. One possible answer is that once the language has, as it were, committed itself to pronouncing the tensed forms of lexical verbs at v_{pred}, there is simply no alternative consistent with general principles of syntactic uniformity and morphological simplicity. If there were no unstressed *do* at all, then the phonetic form of questions for non-subject *wh*-expressions would be markedly different in morphologically tensed sentences and sentences with a modal auxiliary, i.e. *What [will] he eat?* but *What [?] he ate?* On the other hand, if unstressed *do* had the same distribution as modal auxiliaries, then there would be two different ways of expressing tense, namely,

---

[11] This is only true, of course, of unstressed *dŏ*. Stressed *dó* behaves exactly like a modal auxiliary: cf. note 4.

with an auxiliary in yes/no questions and *wh*-questions with a *wh*-non-subject, e.g. *Did he eat the apple?* and *What did he eat?*, parallel to *Will he leave?* and *What will he eat?*, respectively, but without an auxiliary in *wh*-questions with a *wh*-subject, e.g. *Who ate the apple?* and in declaratives, e.g. *He ate the apple.* It would thus seem that considerations of syntactic uniformity and morphological simplicity outweigh the disadvantage of having a lexically idiosyncratic auxiliary *do.* It seems clear, in any case, that though these idiosyncratic properties of the unstressed auxiliary *do* in English are highly language-specific, they can nevertheless be formally characterized in terms of the primitive operations available in a relational theory of the sort proposed here.

6.2.3   *Non-echo* in situ wh-*questions in English*

The analysis of clauses with *wh*-subjects just proposed makes the interesting prediction that there should be sentences of the following form interpretable as non-echo questions:

(29)   He ate what?

The reason is that in derivations such as (25), there is simply nothing to prevent *wh*-expressions from being in non-subject positions as well as in subject position. Now the received wisdom in the literature is that a sentence with a *wh*-expression *in situ* can only be interpreted as an echo question, but that assumption is in fact false. This can be seen quite clearly in certain kinds of contexts, one example of which is an interview situation, in which a sentence such as *And then you did what?* can be used as a straightforward non-echo *wh*-question. Such *in situ wh*-questions are distinguished phonologically from echo questions in having the normal final rise-fall contour characteristic of questions rather than the rising contour characteristic of echo questions:

(30)

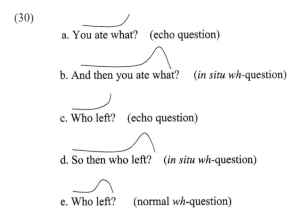

a. You ate what?   (echo question)

b. And then you ate what?   (*in situ wh*-question)

c. Who left?   (echo question)

d. So then who left?   (*in situ wh*-question)

e. Who left?   (normal *wh*-question)

The proposed analysis of *wh*-questions in relational terms thus turns out to reap an unexpected dividend, correctly predicting that there is a three-way distinction in English between normal *wh*-questions (with displacement of non-subject *wh*-expressions), echo questions, and *in situ wh*-questions, where the latter two of course do not have displacement of the *wh*-expression.[12] Note, incidentally, that because of the VMH, normal *wh*-questions and *in situ wh*-questions are identical in phonetic form when the *wh*-expression is in subject position, as shown in (30d,e).

It was mentioned earlier that the proposed analysis of *wh*-questions based on a relational version of phase theory predicts strong superiority effects of the kind illustrated in examples (17)–(21). With the VMH in hand, we can now complete the explanation proposed in (22), the details of which were left somewhat up in the air. Thus (17b) will be ruled out as follows:

(31)

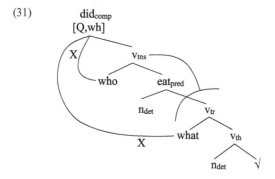

The VMH prevents $v[Q,wh]_{comp}$ from selecting a *wh*-expression in subject position. At the same time, $v[Q,wh]_{comp}$ is prevented from selecting any non-subject *wh*-expressions because they are inside the v_{pred} phase and therefore become inaccessible as soon as v_{pred} is saturated. This rules out superiority violations such as (17b). Even if *what* is left *in situ*, the VMH will still prevent $v[Q,wh]_{comp}$ from selecting the subject *who*, ruling out **Who did eat what?* Since every possible means of satisfying the *wh*-selection feature of $v[Q,wh]$ has been disallowed, the derivation crashes.[13]

---

[12] It appears, then, that English is more similar than has been assumed to languages such as Indonesian (cf. Saddy 1991, 1992) and Malay (cf. Cole and Hermon 1998), in which *wh*-expressions can either be displaced or remain *in situ*.

[13] Note that projecting another v_{pred} would not help either, since the second v_{pred} has, by hypothesis, a *wh*-selection feature. Then, regardless of whether *who* or *what* is selected by the athematic argument feature in do_{tns}, the VMH will rule out the resulting structure.

The only option left in such a case is to project $\emptyset[Q,wh]_{comp}$ instead of $v[Q,wh]_{comp}$, producing a derivation similar to (25) containing an inflected lexical verb (or a modal auxiliary such as *will*), but pronouncing both *wh*-expressions *in situ*:

(32)

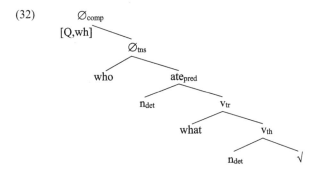

As we would predict, it is perfectly possible for such sentences with multiple *wh*-words to be either echo questions or *wh*-questions depending on intonation:

(33)

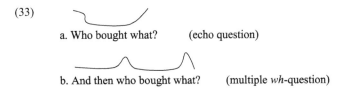

    a. Who bought what?   (echo question)

    b. And then who bought what?   (multiple *wh*-question)

In sentences in which both *wh*-expressions are in non-subject positions, in contrast, $v[Q,wh]_{comp}$ should have no problem forming a relation with one of the *wh*-expressions, and we predict at worst mild superiority violations depending on which expression is closer:

(34)   a. What did you give to whom?
       b. ?To whom did you give what?
       c. ?Who did you give what to?

(35)   a. What did he put where?
       b. ?Where did he put what?

(36)   a. Who did you give what?
       b. ?What did you give who.

(37)   a. Who did Brutus stab with what?
       b. ?With what did Brutus stab who?
       c. ??What did Brutus stab who with?

Depending on precisely what analysis is assumed of the argument structures involved, the b.- and c.-examples in (34)–(37) will have at most one or two more relational links between $v[Q,wh]_{comp}$ and the selected *wh*-expression than the a.-examples. Finally, if $\varnothing[Q,wh]_{comp}$ is projected instead of $v[Q,wh]_{comp}$, it is correctly predicted that there exist non-echo multiple *wh*-questions such as the following:

(38)   a. So then you gave what to whom?
        b. At that point, he put what where?
        c. After that, you gave who what?
        d. Then Brutus stabbed who with what?

Contrary to what has usually been assumed, then, English, has both *in situ wh*-questions and questions with displaced *wh*. The former, as has often been noted, are not subject to island constraints whereas the latter are.

6.2.4   More on Phases: Bare Infinitive and Participial Small Clauses
Returning to *wh*-selection, I provide next further evidence in support of the idea that v_{pred} in English can be extended by selecting another instance of v_{pred} with a *wh*-selection feature. Recall that in §2.2.1.3 it was argued that bare infinitive complements, as well as progressive and passive participial phrases, are all different types of small clause arguments, that is to say, v_{pred} projections. As such, they are phases, which entails that the content of the head from which they are projected should become inaccessible as soon as v_{pred} is saturated. Since they are also maximal, which means they do not project any further, that would seem to imply that the head that projects v_{pred} should become inaccessible as soon as the selection feature of v_{pred} is satisfied, making it impossible for a *wh*-expression ever to be selected by v_{comp}. If, however, it is possible for a *wh*-expression to escape from within a v_{pred} phase by extending v_{pred}, we predict that there should be no problem with displacing a *wh*-expression from such small clause arguments. That prediction is fully confirmed, as the following data shows:

(39)   a. Who did you see __ give the book to Mary?
        b. What did you see John give __ to Mary?
        c. Who did you see John give the book to __?

(40)   a. Who did you see __ giving the book to Mary?
        b. What did you see John giving __ to Mary?
        c. Who did you see John giving the book to __?

(41)   a. What did you see __ given to Mary by John?
        b. Who did you see the book given to __ by John?
        c. Who did you see the book given to Mary by __?

Furthermore, since progressive and passive sentences are, as argued in Chapter 2, participial small clause complements of *be*, the same prediction should hold for them as well:

(42)   a. Who is giving the book to Mary?
          b. What is John giving __ to Mary?
          c. Who is John giving the book to __?

(43)   a. What was given __ to Mary by John?
          b. Who was the book given to __ by John?
          c. Who was the book given to Mary by __?

Putting all this together, then, an example similar to (42b) can be derived as follows:

(44)

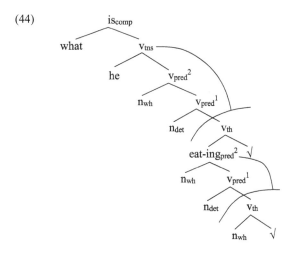

The progressive participial complement of *be* is headed by v_{pred}, hence is a phase. However, it can be extended by projecting another v_{pred} head with a *wh*-selector, permitting *what* to be selected by v_{pred}^2 before v_{th} is closed off. The next phase is is_{pred}, which can also be extended, allowing *what* to be selected again by is_{pred}^2 before is_{th} is closed off. Finally, *what* can be selected again by the *wh*-selector in v_{comp}, where it is finally pronounced in PHON to the left of *is* in v_{comp}.

6.2.5   *More on Word Order Variation in* wh-*questions*

One of the strongest pieces of evidence adduced in support of the antisymmetric approach to word order variation is the claim that *wh*-movement is universally leftward, never rightward:

(45)   a. How many books did John steal from the library?
          b. *Did John steal from the library how many books?

This asymmetry is predictable on the antisymmetric view, so the argument goes, because specifiers are universally leftward, whereas this restriction is a complete accident under any standard version of the head direction parameter. We have already seen in Chapter 4, however, that question particles exhibit both leftward and rightward selection, with both sometimes occurring in the same language. It is therefore not too surprising to find that the claim that *wh*-words are universally leftward is false. In English, for example, *wh*-words can occur at the right edge of a clause in both echo and non-echo questions. In the latter case, they are most felicitous in the same kind of contexts as the *in situ* non-echo questions discussed in §6.2.3.

(46)

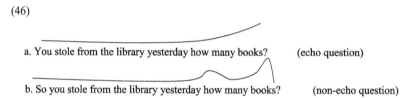

    a. You stole from the library yesterday how many books?   (echo question)

    b. So you stole from the library yesterday how many books?   (non-echo question)

It might be countered that such examples can be derived antisymmetrically by first doing leftward *wh*-movement, followed by leftward movement of the entire TP complement of C to some higher specifier position:

(47)

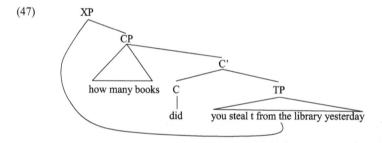

However, because raising of the auxiliary to C is obligatory in both echo and non-echo *wh*-questions,

(48)   *How many books you stole from the library yesterday?

this proposal will incorrectly leave the auxiliary behind in rightward position:

(49)   **You steal from the library yesterday how many books did?

If instead we try to move C′ rather than TP (violating the ban on moving non-maximal projections) or CP itself (requiring that the *wh*-expression in Spec,C be first raised to yet another hypothetical projection), we predict incorrectly that raising of the auxiliary must occur with rightward wh-movement (whether echo or non-echo):

(50)   *Did you steal from the library yesterday how many books?

Notice, incidentally, that displacement of the auxiliary to C, unlike wh-movement, is indeed always leftward and never rightward (in both echo and non-echo questions):

(51)   a. *How many books you steal from the library yesterday did?
         b. *You steal from the library yesterday did how many books?

However, this follows automatically in the relational theory from the fact that projection is uniformly leftward in English.

As has just been shown, leftward displacement of the auxiliary in English occurs obligatorily in both echo and non-echo questions when selection of the wh-word is leftward. Conversely, rightward selection of the wh-word is incompatible with displacement of the auxiliary. These dependencies are easily expressed in the relational framework by making the directionality parameter contingent on the form of the v_{comp} head. Assuming, as proposed in Chapter 4, that a selection feature is always linearized leftward unless specially marked with the subscript "R," the dependencies in question can be built into the lexical entries for v_{comp} as follows:

(52)   a. v[Q,wh]
            [_[wh]]

         b. Ø[Q,wh]
            ([_[wh]]$_R$)

Notice that by making the rightward selection feature in (52b) optional, we automatically account for the fact that displacement of the auxiliary is also disallowed with *in situ* wh-questions, both echo and non-echo:

(53)   a. You bought what?   (echo)
         b. *Did you buy what?

(54)   a. So then you bought what?   (*in situ* wh-question)
         b. *So then did you buy what?

One might of course still wonder whether the dependencies could be reversed, i.e. is there a possible language in which rightward wh-selection requires displacement of the auxiliary, whereas leftward wh-selection prohibits it? That is a question I leave for future research. The main point of relevance here is that the observed dependency in English cannot even be described correctly in the antisymmetric framework, whereas it is easily stated in the relational framework without adding any new apparatus at all.

6.2.6   *Parametric Variation in* wh-*selection*

It is often noted in the literature that there are three different types of languages: (i) *wh in situ* languages, in which no *wh*-expressions are displaced; (ii) single *wh*-movement languages, in which at most a single *wh*-expression is displaced; (iii) multiple *wh*-movement languages, in which any number of *wh*-expressions are displaced. Strikingly, there are no known languages in which a maximum of just two, three, or *n* *wh*-expressions are displaced. I argue that this important observation concerning the possible parameters of *wh*-selection is predicted by the relational approach to phase theory proposed earlier.

Recall that in §6.2 it was suggested that the reason non-subject *wh*-expressions can escape from a v_{pred} phase in English is that v_{pred} may optionally select another v_{pred} projection with a *wh*-selection feature [_wh]. By hypothesis, the argument selection feature of v_{pred} is transferred to this recursive v_{pred}, preventing a violation of IG. At the same time, closing off the selector of v_{pred} is delayed until the new v_{pred} has been saturated. Now suppose that there are languages in which v_{pred} simply lacks a recursive projection feature altogether. In such a language, displacement of *any* *wh*-expression from within the v_{pred} phase would be prohibited. Consequently, any and all *wh*-expressions (with the possible exception of a subject *wh*-expression, about which more shortly) would necessarily remain *in situ*. Schematically, such a language would look as follows:

(55)

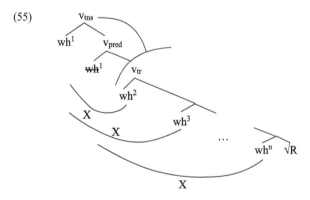

As indicated in (55), the head v_{tr} that projects the phase head v_{pred} becomes inaccessible as soon as v_{pred} is saturated by selecting v_{tns}. Hence none of the *wh*-expressions inside v_{tr} can be displaced.

It has already been shown how a language such as English with just one extension of v_{pred} works, so let us consider next a third possibility. Imagine a language that is similar to English in that v_{pred} can select another v_{pred} with a wh-selector, but which differs in that the second v_{pred} with wh-selector can itself optionally select a third v_{pred} with a wh-selector. Obviously, the third v_{pred}, being identical to the v_{pred} that selected it, can in turn select a fourth v_{pred} with a wh-selector, and so on, with no upper bound on the number of such v_{pred} phases with wh-selectors that can be projected. Schematically, such a language would look as follows:

(56)

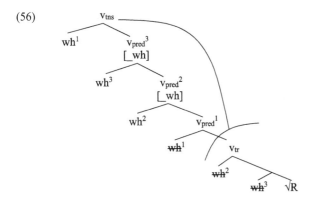

As indicated in (56), none of the wh-expressions in v_{tr} become inaccessible until the topmost $v_{pred}{}^{n}$ becomes saturated by projecting v_{tns}, leaving all of them free to be selected by a wh-selector in one of the v_{pred} projections. Significantly, once the second $v_{pred}{}^{2}$ projection is permitted to be recursive, there is no longer an upper bound on the number of v_{pred} heads that can be projected. Hence the pronunciation of any number of wh-expressions may be displaced, but there is no way of restricting the number of such displacements to just 2, 3, or n.

In languages such as English that allow just a single wh-expression to be displaced, that wh-expression cannot remain inside the extended v_{pred} phase but must be selected again by a wh-selector in v_{comp}, where it is ultimately pronounced. Similarly, in well-studied languages with multiple wh-displacement such as Serbian, Bulgarian, and Russian, all the displaced wh-expressions are pronounced on the left periphery. Hence in these languages the v_{comp} phase must also be recursive. It was reported in early work (cf. Rudin 1988) that in some multiple wh languages such as Bulgarian, the order in which the elements in question occur in declarative sentences must be preserved on the left periphery (examples from Tasseva-Kurktchieva 2001):

(57)   [$_{CP}$ Koj$_1$ kakvo$_2$ na kogo$_3$ [$_{TP}$ t$_1$ kaza t$_2$ t$_3$]]?
       [$_{CP}$ who$_1$ what$_2$ to who.$_{DAT}$.$_3$ [$_{TP}$ t$_1$ said t$_2$ t$_3$]]
       'Who told what to whom?'

Such data, if correct, can be explained rather neatly in the framework proposed here if multiple *wh*-expressions are first selected by the *wh*-selectors in a sequence of recursive v_{pred} phases in accordance with a principle of shortest distance, in the manner indicated in (56), and then selected again in the same fashion by the *wh*-selectors in a sequence of recursive v_{comp} phases:

(58)

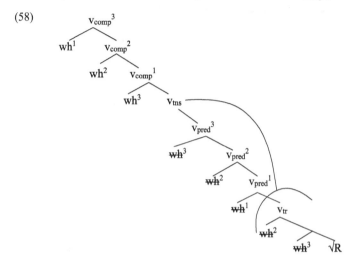

The result, as can be seen, is to preserve the initial order of *wh*-expressions on the left periphery.

Later work, however, has shown that the facts are probably more complicated. For a start there are languages such as Serbian and Russian in which virtually any ordering of *wh*-expressions is possible on the left periphery (Bošković 2002). It has also been suggested that *wh*-expressions in these languages are focused, leading many to argue that *wh*-expressions are selected by focus heads rather than by v_{comp} (cf. Tasseva-Kurktchieva 2001, Bošković 2002). Moreover, recent work on Bulgarian has revealed that while the position of the first *wh*-element is fixed, the order of the following ones is much freer. This kind of data is actually more in line with what the relational theory proposed here would predict, since, as shown in Chapter 2, the heads available for selection inside a phase are not generally constrained by a distance principle. Thus it might be the case that in languages like Serbian, *wh*-expressions are simply selected in any random order by a recursive focus head v_{foc}. Multiple *wh*-constructions in Bulgarian, on the other hand, might start out in much the same way but require in addition that the nearest focused *wh*-expression also be selected by v_{comp}; cf. Tasseva-Kurktchieva (2001) and Bošković (2002) for analyses along these lines.

Rather than trying to provide a detailed analysis of these languages, which would go well beyond the scope of this work, I conclude this discussion by focusing on a somewhat different problem having to do with SOV languages in which *wh*-expressions are attracted to a position immediately to the left of the verb.

6.2.6.1 *wh*-selection in SOV Languages   It is well known that in many languages such as Hungarian, Turkish, and Basque, as well as a number of African languages, including Aghem, Chadic, and Kirundi, question words must occur immediately to the left of the verb. I focus attention here on the data from Malayalam provided by Jayaseelan (2001). To see the nature of the problem, consider the following two examples (Jayaseelan's examples (10) and (44), respectively):

(59)   a. ñaan   innale   Mary-k'k'ə   oru   kattə   ayaccu
          I   yesterday   Mary-dat.   a   letter   sent
          'I sent a letter to Mary yesterday.'
       b. [ii kaaryam aarə   aar-ooDə   eppooL   paRaññə   ennə]   eni-k'k'ə   aRiy-illa
          this matter   who   whom-to   when   said   COMP   I-dat.   know-neg.
          'I don't know who told this matter to whom, when.'

As can be seen in (59b), the *wh*-expressions are arrayed immediately to the left of the verb, which is in final position, while any non-*wh*-expressions are to the left of them. Working within an antisymmetric framework, Jayaseelan (2001) proposes to account for this data by assuming stacked F(ocus)Ps above *v*P into which the *wh*-expressions move, after which any remaining arguments and *v*P internal adjuncts such as manner, time, and location adverbials, move into specifiers of higher functional categories above the FPs. This leaves the entire *v*P vacated and its contents moved leftwards, apart from the verb which remains in final position, with the *wh*-expressions arrayed to the immediate left of the verb.

Rather than assuming the massive number of movement operations required by an antisymmetric analysis, I propose instead that a relatively simple ordering parameter combined with recursion of the v_{pred} phase will suffice to explain this data. Let us consider first the order of elements in declarative clauses. Following the analysis of SOV languages proposed in Chapter 4, I assume that Malayalam has rightward projection and leftward selection. I also assume, following the analysis of circumstantial C_{event} modifiers proposed in Chapter 4, that adjuncts such as *innale* 'yesterday' are modifiers of a v_{time} head above v_{pred} and below v_{tns}. This leads to the following derivation of (59a):

(60)

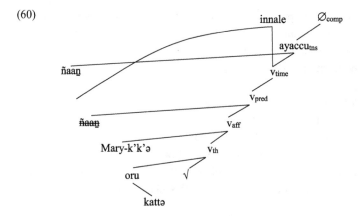

Assuming that modifiers are also linearized leftward in Malayalam, for the reasons discussed in Chapter 4, the time adverbial *innale* 'yesterday' will be ordered between the subject and dative arguments, producing the order of elements shown in (59a).

I propose next that a distinctive feature of Malayalam is that the *wh*-selection features of the recursively extended v_{pred} phase are parameterized *rightward*. Furthermore, I assume that in a derivation with multiple v_{pred} phases, the closest *wh*-argument is selected first and that *wh*-modifiers are also parameterized rightward. Finally, I will assume that in Malayalam v_{comp} has no *wh*-selection features at all. With these assumptions in hand, the embedded multiple *wh* complement of (59b) can be derived as follows:

(61)

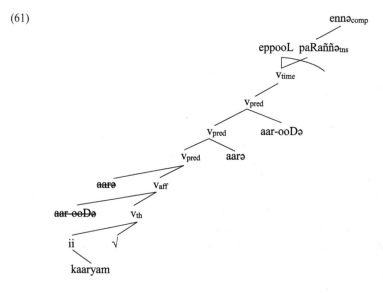

As can be seen, all the *wh*-expressions end up to the left of the verb, while any remaining arguments or adjuncts that are not *wh*-expressions end up to the left of them. Malayalam, then, and other languages like it, is a typical SOV language with three distinctive parameters. First, it has multiple *wh*-selection rather than *wh-in-situ*. Second, the *wh*-selection features are confined to the v_{pred} phase (i.e. v_{comp} has no *wh*-selection features). Third, *wh*-selection, in contrast to argument selection, is rightward. These parameters are sufficient to ensure that *wh*-expressions cluster immediately to the left of the verb in final position with only minimal displacement, contrasting sharply with the anti-symmetric analysis which requires multiple leftward movement of *wh*-expressions to stacked focus positions, followed by multiple leftward movement of any remaining arguments or adjuncts into stacked positions of some kind below topic phrases and above focus phrases, all of which movement operations are independently motivated only weakly, if at all.

6.3   *Island Effects*

I take up next a variety of constraints that limit how far away from a *wh*-selector a selected *wh*-item may be. This discussion does not in any sense constitute a complete overview of island effects, nor will I be concerned at all with any of the semantic properties of selected *wh*-items that have been shown in the recent literature to affect extractability. Rather, I will focus on the most important syntactic constraints that play a role in island effects. My aim will be to show that in every case the relational theory provides an account at least as descriptively adequate as a theory based on constituents, and that in a number of significant cases it provides a superior one. It will also emerge from this discussion that both the relational version of phase theory proposed here and the VMH, as formulated in §6.2.2, are required in order to provide an explanatory account of the island constraints.

6.3.1   *Long-distance* wh-*selection*

Let us consider first how far away a *wh*-expression may be from the *v*[Q,wh] head that selects it. As is well known, any *wh*-argument or *wh*-modifier may be selected in a non-finite complement:

(62)   a. What do you believe him to have cooked __?
       b. Who do you believe __ to have cooked the steaks?
       c. When/how/how rare/how carefully do you believe him to have cooked the steaks __?

(63)   a. What do you want him cooking __?
       b. Who do you want __ cooking the steaks?
       c. When/how/how rare/how quickly do you want him cooking the steaks __?

The same is true of finite complements without a *that*-complementizer:

(64)   a. What do you believe he cooked __?
        b. Who do you believe __ cooked the steaks?
        c. When/how/how rare/how quickly do you believe he cooked the steaks __?

However, the situation is more complicated in English when the finite complement has an overt complementizer. Basically, non-subjects can be selected in
such complements but subjects may not. The latter phenomenon, often referred
to in the literature as the "*that*-trace effect," is illustrated as follows:

(65)   a. What do you believe that he cooked __?
        b. *Who do you believe that __ cooked the steaks?
        c. When/how/how rare/how carefully do you believe that he cooked the
           steaks __?

To account for (62)–(64), I will assume that infinitival complements without
for, ACC-ing complements, and finite complements without *that* are maximal
v_{tns} projections that do not project v_{comp}. It follows that *wh*-expressions of any
kind may be selected from such complements because they are not contained in
a v_{comp} phase.

    As for the data in (65), let us assume, first, that finite complements with a *that*-
complementizer do project v_{comp} and, second, that v_{comp} is a phase. By the
definition of phase proposed in Chapter 2, this entails that the head that projects
v_{comp} and everything in it become inaccessible as soon as v_{comp} is saturated. In
contrast to the case of v_{pred}, however, v_{comp} does not itself have a projection
feature that must be satisfied, since there is no higher *v*-projection than v_{comp}. It
follows, then, that everything in v_{tns} becomes inaccessible as soon as the selection
feature of v_{comp}, if it has one, is satisfied. Notice that this difference between v_{comp}
and v_{pred} phases follows automatically from general principles in the relational
framework without having to be specially stipulated. The result is that anything
within the v_{tns} head that projects a v_{comp} phase will be inaccessible to a *wh*-selector
in a higher projection. In diagrammatic terms, the situation would look as follows:

(66)

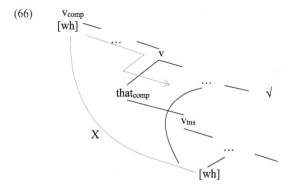

The *wh*-selector in the higher v_{comp} traces back through the previous relational links to find a head with a [wh]-feature. However, when it comes to v_{tns}, the head from which *that*$_{comp}$ is projected, it is barred from searching any further, because *that*$_{comp}$ is a phase. Hence it is unable to form a relation with any *wh*-head inside the domain of v_{tns}. Notice, by the way, that a *wh*-expression within the root v_{tns} projection is not inaccessible to the *wh*-selector in v_{comp}, because at the point where the *wh*-selection feature must be satisfied, v_{comp} has not yet been saturated. The definition of a phase thus correctly predicts that an example such as *What will he eat?* is perfectly grammatical.

Given what has been proposed so far, any *wh*-expression inside a finite clause headed by *that* will be inaccessible to a *wh*-selector in a higher v_{comp}, thus incorrectly ruling out (65a) and (65c) along with (65b). Let us therefore suppose that a *that*$_{comp}$ head selected as an argument, which obviously cannot contain an intrinsic [wh]-feature (and hence no *wh*-selector), can, if needed, be provided with an optional *wh*-selector that can act as a "rescue link." To be more specific, consider the following derivation of (65a):

(67)

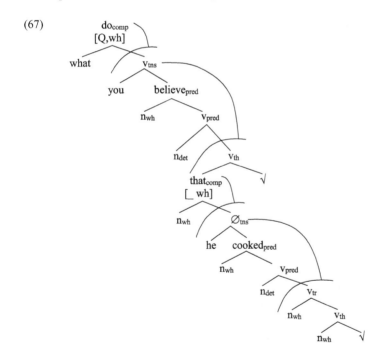

In this relational diagram the *wh*-selector in the upper *do*$_{comp}$ traces back through the previous links in the derivation to the lower *that*$_{comp}$, at which point it would normally be able to search no further within $\emptyset_{tns}$ because v_{comp} is a phase. If, however, *that*$_{comp}$ forms a link with *what* by virtue of its optional added *wh*-selector, then the inaccessibility of *what* can be circumvented. The *wh*-expression *what* is thus able to escape successively from the v_{pred} phase in the complement clause, from the *that*$_{comp}$ phase, and from the v_{pred} phase in the matrix clause, its phonetic form finally being spelled out and pronounced to the left of *do*$_{comp}$. I assume that *what* cannot be pronounced to the left of *that*, producing the ungrammatical sentence **I believe what that he cooked*, because a *wh*-expression can only be pronounced in a displaced position if it is selected by a head with an *inherent wh*-selector, i.e. one that is licensed by a [wh] feature. Since the *that*-complement selected by *believe* does not contain an inherent *wh*-selector, a *wh*-word selected by a "rescue" feature must be selected again by an inherent [wh] feature in some higher v_{comp} projection before it can actually be pronounced.

It might be argued that permitting *that*$_{comp}$ to have an optional *wh*-selection feature is nothing more than a notational variant of the optional "edge feature" assigned to *v* in the Minimalist Program. I reject that criticism, however, and maintain that the two devices are not at all equivalent. An edge feature essentially stipulates that some LI may undergo an additional Merge operation above and beyond the maximum of two applications of Merge that are normally allowed to an LI. Adding an edge feature to an LI thus produces a totally new structure, one that has no empirical or theoretical motivation, apart from the fact that it makes it possible to escape the consequences of phase theory, if necessary. Edge features are thus essentially *ad hoc*. In contrast, specifying that *that*$_{comp}$ has an optional *wh*-selection feature does not add any new type of operation or any new kind of structure to relational derivations. On the contrary, it is simply an ordinary selection feature of a type that is independently motivated. An edge feature is a powerful device that creates new structure, whereas assigning *that*$_{comp}$ an optional [wh] feature is simply a lexical specification of a perfectly normal kind that does not go beyond what is needed in the system anyway.

Given what has been proposed so far, it appears that though we have found a way of deriving (65a) and (65c), we have inadvertently permitted the ungrammatical (65b) to be derived as well. That is not so, however, because the VMH will rule it out! To see that this is so, consider a structure identical to (67) in which the subject *he* of the *that*-complement is replaced with *who* (and the object *what* with *it*). This is exactly the configuration that is ruled out by the VMH. Therefore, even though *that*$_{comp}$ can have a "rescue" *wh*-selector, it is barred from selecting *who* in this case, because it is the subject. Since the escape route making it possible for *who* to form a relation with the *wh*-selector in *do*$_{comp}$ is no longer available, the derivation breaks down. In further support of this analysis, I note that because the VMH, as argued earlier, is a language-specific constraint of English, it is not surprising to find, as is well known, that languages such as Italian which are not subject to the VMH also do not exhibit *that*-trace effects (cf. Rizzi 1990).

6.3.2   wh-*islands*
It is a well-established fact that *wh*-complements are strong islands when the specifier of C is occupied by a *wh*-expression:

(68)   a. *To whom do you wonder what he gave ___ ___?
       b. *What do you wonder who he gave ___ to___?
       c. *What do you wonder when/how he cooked ___ ___?
       d. *When/how do you wonder what he cooked ___ ___?
       e. *How well do you wonder what he cooked___ ___?
       f. *What do you wonder how well he cooked___ ___?

This is immediately explained under the assumption that v_{comp} is a phase, because as soon as the *wh*-selector in the *wh*-complement has formed a relation with one of two (or more) *wh*-expressions contained in it, everything remaining in v_{tns} becomes inaccessible:[14]

(69)

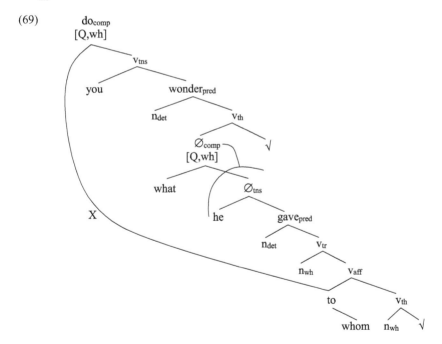

---

[14] In the interests of clarity, I henceforth omit from derivations the steps involving the displacement of *wh*-expressions through v_{pred} phases unless they are relevant to the issues under discussion.

I assume that once a *wh*-expression has been selected by a head with an inherent *wh*-selection feature, it is inert and can no longer be selected by any other *wh*-selector, thus preventing the *wh*-expression selected by $\varnothing_{comp}$ in the *wh*-complement in (6) from being selected again by the *wh*-selector in do_{comp}:

(70)   a. *What do you wonder he gave to whom?
        b. *What do you wonder he cooked when/how.

On the other hand, if there are additional *wh*-expressions in the complement, they can perfectly well be left *in situ*, producing well-formed multiple *wh*-complements:

(71)   a. I wonder what he gave to whom.
        b. I wonder what he cooked how/when.

Consider next *wh*-complements with the overt complementizers *if* and *whether*. Such complements, as is well known, are weak islands. Displacement of *wh*-arguments from weak islands are degraded only slightly, if at all, while displacement of *wh*-modifiers produces violations that are quite mild compared to displacement from the strong *wh*-islands discussed in §6.3.2:

(72)   a. Which books do you wonder whether/if he read__?
        b. Where do you wonder whether/if he went __?
        c. How rare do you wonder whether/if he cooked the steaks__?
        d. ?By what method/??how do you wonder whether/if he cooked the steaks__?
        e. ?For what reason/??why do you wonder whether/if he cooked steaks__?

To account for this data, we need only assume, first, that *whether* and *if* are lexical realizations of v_{comp} with an inherent [Q] feature (cf. §6.1) and, second, that the v_{comp} phase, as proposed earlier, may have an optional *wh*-selector. If there are no *wh*-expressions in the *wh*-complement, then the *wh*-selector is not needed, e.g. *I wonder whether he cooked the steaks.* If, however, there is a *wh*-expression in the *wh*-complement, then the optional *wh*-selector is available to provide an escape route for it, since v_{comp} is, by hypothesis, a phase:

(73)

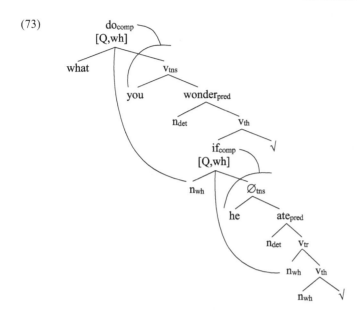

In short, *wh*-expressions can escape from weak *wh*-islands for exactly the same reason they can escape from *that*-clauses.

There is, however, a surprising exception to this generalization. If the *wh*-expression is the subject of the *wh*-complement, then extraction is extremely degraded:

(74)   *Who do you wonder whether/if ___ cooked the steaks?

But now observe that this is precisely the configuration to which VMH is applicable! Predictably, then, the fact that subject *wh*-expressions are prevented from escaping from weak *wh*-islands falls together with the *that*-trace effect under the VMH.

In conclusion, all the major syntactic properties of both strong and weak islands, as well as the *that*-trace effect, follow directly from the relational version of phase theory proposed in this chapter, combined with the VMH and the theoretically benign assumption that a non-*wh* v_{comp} may, if necessary, be provided with an optional *wh*-selection feature.

6.3.3   Nominal Islands

I take up next a variety of nominal island effects, all of which can be explained under the following assumptions: (i) nominal projections headed by n_K are phases; (ii) n_K, in contrast to v_{comp}, never has a [wh] feature; (iii) the n_K phase in most languages does not allow a "rescue" *wh*-selection feature. If n_K is a phase, then by definition anything within the n_{det} projection that selects it becomes inaccessible as soon as n_K is saturated:

(75)

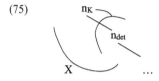

By (ii) and (iii), n_K is saturated as soon as it is projected. Hence maximal *n*-projections are, generally speaking, islands. Some cases where a *wh* escape hatch is found in nominals have been reported in the literature, notably Hungarian (cf. Szabolcsi 1983), but these appear to be rare. There is, however, a set of apparent violations of the islandhood of nominals that are quite systematic, to which I turn next.

6.3.3.1   Specificity Effects   It has frequently been observed in the literature that extraction from nominals in English improves notably if the nominal is indefinite rather than definite:

(76)   a. Who did you buy (??those) pictures of?
       b. Who did you read a/*that story about?
       c. What have you read (*John's) many reports about?
       d. Which crimes do you think they have (*the) evidence of?

Recall, however, that in this framework it is perfectly possible for projections to stop short of the highest possible projection, producing various sizes of "small nominal." In particular, it was shown in Chapter 2 that nominals need only project as far as $n_{\#}$, or even n_{nom}. Now suppose that the feature of definiteness is universally associated with n_{det} and that an indefinite nominal is simply one that projects only as far as $n_{\#}$. Since such an expression does not project n_{def}, it will *ipso facto* be unable to project n_K. That in turn means that indefinites are not phases, hence are predicted not to be barriers to displacement. The existence of specificity effects, then, far from being a counterexample to the claim that nominals are islands, simply reinforces the conclusion reached earlier that different sizes of nominal can be projected.

6.3.3.2   Factive versus Non-factive Complements   I take up next an issue much discussed in the literature, namely, the contrast in extractability between factive and non-factive complements, illustrated as follows:

(77)   a. How rare do you think John cooked the steaks?
        b. *How rare do you regret that John cooked the steaks?

I will argue that whereas non-factive *that*-complements are ordinary v_{comp} projections which may, as shown in §6.3.1, have an optional *wh*-selection feature, factive *that*-complements, reformulating slightly in relational terms a line of thought first proposed by Kiparsky and Kiparsky (1971), are headed by an n_K projection and are therefore phases which do not have such a rescue mechanism available to them.

I start by reviewing some important but often overlooked observations of Kiparsky and Kiparsky.

A   Only factive predicates allow as complements the full range of gerundive nominalizations:

(78)   a. John's having been found guilty is interesting/bothers me/*is likely/ *seems to me.
        b. I regretted/deplored/ignored/*supposed/*believed/*asserted John's having been found guilty.

B   Only factive predicates allow as arguments adjectival nominalizations in -*ness*, -*ity*, etc.:

(79)   a. The peacefulness/tranquility of the countryside bothers me/is significant/ *is likely/*turns out.
        b. I regretted/ignored/cared about/*believed/*supposed/*maintained/*claimed the peacefulness/tranquility of the countryside.

To this we may add that action nominals in -*al* (and other morphological forms) are only permitted in factive complements:

(80)   a. John's removal of the sink/descent into folly bothers me/is odd/matters/ *seems/*is true.
        b. I regretted/ignored/deplored/was aware of/*believed/*supposed/*concluded John's removal of the sink/descent into folly.

C   Conversely, only non-factive complements may appear in raising constructions:

(81)   a. He is likely/seems/appears/*is odd/*is tragic/*amuses me to be there.
        b. I believed/supposed/assumed/*regretted/*ignored/*resented him to be there.

D   Likewise, only non-factive complements can be pronominalized with *so*:

(82)   John supposed/regretted that Bill had done it, and Mary supposed/*regretted so, too.

Given these observations, the simplest possible hypothesis as to the syntactic difference between factive and non-factive complements is the following:

(83)   Factive complements are nominal; non-factive complements are sentential.

In Kiparsky and Kiparsky (1971), this possibility was effectively ruled out in advance, because they assumed without discussion that *both* factives and non-factives were NPs, differing only in that the former contained the noun *fact*:

(84)

If the conjecture in (83) is correct, however, it ties in with the often noted fact that topic and focus are impossible in factive complements. Much of the recent literature (cf. De Cuba 2006, Basse 2008) has attempted to account for this by assuming that factive CPs are somehow "reduced" in comparison to non-factive complements, or, to put it differently, that non-factive complements have an additional layer of structure that is missing in factive complements. If, however, factive complements are a type of nominal, then this additional complication is simply unnecessary. The reason is that nominals quite generally lack left periphery elements such as topic and focus, as can be seen in both derived nominals and gerundives:

(85)   *Mary regrets [the sink John's removal of/removing].

Likewise, speaker-oriented adverbs are quite generally prohibited in nominals:[15]

(86)   *Mary resents [obviously/probably John's removal of/removing the sink].

Similarly, the fact that T-to-C movement is disallowed in factive complements in Hiberno-English simply follows from the fact that nominals quite generally do not permit any operation analogous to T-to-C. In short, all the properties that have been adduced in support of the claim that factive complements belong to a special kind of reduced CP can be derived from independently motivated properties of nominals, if it can be maintained that factives are simply nominals of some kind.

---

[15] Example (86) is fine, of course, if the adverbs are parenthetical modifiers of the main verb *resents*.

Returning now to the relational perspective, let us simply combine hypothesis (83) with the assumption discussed earlier that the highest nominal projection n_K is a phase. One immediate piece of evidence in support of this approach comes from the fact that derived nominals and gerundives are weak islands:

(87)   *How/when did Mary resent John's removal of/John's removing the sink?

Again, this is simply a general property of nominals. Therefore, if factive *that*-complements are nominals, it follows automatically that they are weak islands.

Likewise, the fact that raising is impossible out of factive complements follows from the assumption that n_K is a phase, as shown again by the impossibility of raising out of nominals:[16]

(88)   *Mary resents him removal of the sink.

Conversely, the fact that raising out of infinitive complements *is* possible follows from the fact that they are small *v*-projections, as argued in Chapter 2, and are therefore not phases.

Assuming, then, that hypothesis (83) is correct, all that remains is to explain how it is possible for finite *that*-complements to be structurally either nominal or sentential. The latter possibility is no problem: it has been assumed all along that *that* belongs to the category v_{comp}, which is the highest possible *v*-projection. As such, it is a phase, which renders everything in its selecting category v_{tns} inaccessible as soon as it is saturated. However, as was shown earlier, *that*$_{comp}$ may have a rescue *wh*-selection feature that permits a *wh*-element to be displaced to v_{comp} before it becomes inaccessible, whereas n_K quite generally lacks such a rescue feature.

One possible way of cashing out the idea that factive complements are simply nominals, following the spirit of Kiparsky and Kiparsky (1971), would be to assume that factive *that*-complements are sentential complements of an unpronounced N having the same meaning as the noun *fact*:

---

[16] Examples of ACC-ing constructions such as *Mary resents him removing the sink* are not instances of raising. Rather, as was shown in Chapter 5, ACC Case here is assigned to the subject of the complement by non-finite T. Note, for example, that the ACC Case-marked subject cannot be passivized: **He was resented removing the sink.*

(89)

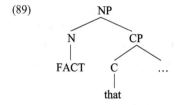

However, while this approach is able to account for the extraction facts, it fails completely to explain the "reduced" nature of factive complements, i.e. the absence of topic and focus constituents, speaker-oriented adverbs, and other features of the left periphery. On the contrary, since factive complements under this analysis are CPs, there is every reason to expect them to have all of these left periphery properties.

The second approach is to assume that *that* is simply lexically ambiguous in that it can belong either to the category v_{comp} or to the category n_K. It is well known that there are different "cut-off" points for nominalization. Gerundives, for example, are widely assumed to be verbal projections up to the v_{pred} projection, but to project the nominal category n_{det} above that. Suppose, then, that factive *that*-complements are verbal in nature all the way up to the v_{tns} projection, but nominal above that, so that the cut-off point for nominalization is even higher than it is for gerundives:

(90)

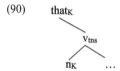

We can assume that while v_{tns} may select either *that*$_{comp}$ or *that*$_K$, n_{det} only has the option of projecting $\varnothing_K$. Similarly, while v_{tns} may optionally project other left peripheral categories such as v_{top}, v_{foc}, etc., there are no equivalents of these in the nominal system that may be selected by n_{det}. Finally, we know that even though v_{comp} is a phase, it may have a rescue *wh*-selection feature under certain conditions, whereas n_K cannot. Therefore extraction from non-factive *that*-complements is possible, while extraction from factive *that*-complements is not.

To conclude, let us consider briefly the fundamental semantic difference between factive and non-factive complements, namely, that the former are presupposed, while the latter are not. If factive complements are simply nominals, it becomes possible to provide a straightforward explanation, based on the fact that nominalized sentences, like all nominals, are referential. Let us assume that while ordinary common nouns refer to individuals, nominalizations refer to what Melvold (1991) calls an "event argument," in which the open event-argument is bound by an ι-operator. A nominalized sentence thus presupposes the existence of an event in exactly the same way that an ordinary referential nominal presupposes the existence of an individual. The truth of a nominalized complement is therefore not at issue in the same way that the truth of a sentential complement is.

6.3.4   Adjunct Islands

I conclude this survey of island phenomena with a brief discussion of so-called "adjunct islands." I shall not address here the question of whether subordinate clauses of various kinds should be treated as arguments or as modifiers. Instead, I will show that the island status of subordinate clauses can be explained purely in terms of their internal selection properties.

Typical examples of adjunct islands are the following:

(91)   a. *What did John leave before/after he ate__?
         b. *Who did Bill faint while he was talking to__?
         c. *What joke did John laugh when/because Mary told him __?
         d. ?What will Bill get annoyed if we drink__?

Consider first the subordinate clause introducers *before* and *after*. Observing that they are homophonous with the prepositions *before* and *after* in examples such as *John left before/after dinner*, Emonds (1969) suggested that they were in fact simply prepositions with a clausal complement. Recasting this proposal in relational terms, (91a) might then be derived as follows:

(92)   before$_{rel}$

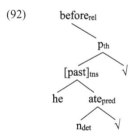

The problem with this analysis is that the clausal complement is clearly headed by a v_{tns} lacking a v_{comp} projection, since it is impossible for it to occur with the complementizer *that*:

(93)   *John left before/after that he ate.

Since unprojected v_{tns} is not, as was shown earlier, a phase, there is nothing to prevent a *wh*-expression inside it from being selected by a higher *wh*-selector, thereby producing the very examples in (91a) that we are trying to rule out. Another problem is that this analysis does not generalize to other subordinate conjunctions, none of which can be used as prepositional phrases:

(94)   *John left while/when/because/if the party.

Another possibility would be to analyze all of these subordinate conjunctions as v_{comp} heads:

(95)

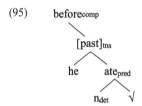

The problem with this proposal is that there is nothing to prevent such a v_{comp} head from having an optional "rescue" *wh*-selector of exactly the sort that was posited for complements headed by *that*, predicting incorrectly that there should be no adjunct island violations such as those in (91). The third, and final, possibility is to assume that v_{comp} in these subordinate clauses is a null head that selects the subordinators *before, after, when, because, etc.*:

(96)

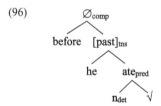

This yields exactly the right result. Recalling that IG prevents any head from having more than one argument selection feature, it will be impossible for the null v_{comp} head to have a "rescue" [wh] feature because it is required to select a subordinator. Notice that if we wanted to distinguish the prepositional subordinators *before* and *after* from the others, they could be analyzed as very small intransitive p_{rel} arguments, thereby claiming, in effect, that they are *both* prepositions and complementizers:

(97)

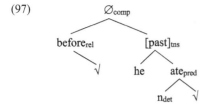

Finally, it is worth noting that examples such as (91d) with the subordinate conjunction *if* are considerably less degraded than the others, reminding one of the weak island violations discussed in §6.3.2. This can be accounted for nicely by assuming that *if*, unlike the other subordinate conjunctions, is actually in the v_{comp} head, as was assumed in the case of *wh*-complements, thereby allowing the possibility of an optional *wh*-selector to provide an escape route.

6.4   Conclusion

Summarizing briefly, I have shown in this chapter that the relational theory is able to account for the basic properties of operator constructions without the addition of any new theoretical assumptions. It is also at least as adequate in terms of descriptive and explanatory adequacy as theories based on constituent structure, and in some cases is demonstrably superior. I have shown, for example, that edge features of the sort posited in the Minimalist Program in order to account for the fact that *wh*-expressions can be displaced from inside a phase are not only unnecessary, but in fact impossible in the relational theory. The same results can be achieved with the simpler, as well as independently motivated, assumption that v_{pred} is a recursive head. I have also shown that the relational theory, together with a parametric approach to *wh*-displacement, correctly predicts a wider range of cross-linguistic and language-internal variation than antisymmetric approaches based on constituent structure. Finally, it has been shown that the major island effects can be explained at least as well in relational terms as they can in traditional constituent-based terms, and that in a number of cases the relational approach is demonstrably superior. In particular, I have argued that the explanation proposed here for the contrast of extractability from factive versus non-factive arguments is better than any that has been put forward within the framework of constituent-based theories, as is my suggested explanation for the existence of adjunct islands.

7 Ellipsis

I conclude this work by showing that the relational theory proposed here makes it possible to construct a novel approach to ellipsis. I show, first of all, that ellipsis is optimally formulated in terms of the primitives of the relational theory, and secondly, that the relational approach makes it possible to develop a unified theory of ellipsis, contrasting sharply with the rather piecemeal descriptions found in the recent literature. I finish up by analyzing two potential counterexamples to the proposed theory of ellipsis discussed in the recent literature, concluding that they are in fact only apparent, albeit for quite different reasons.

7.1 The Standard Theory of Ellipsis

The standard theory of ellipsis, following in the footsteps of Lobeck (1995), Merchant (2001), and others, has basically the following form. Suppose H is a head whose complement is XP. Traditionally, H was said to license the deletion of XP under identity with an antecedent XP'. Restating this basic idea in minimalist terms, we may assume there is a feature [E] that may be attached to H. The feature [E] is an instruction to the phonetic system to elide (i.e. to not pronounce) XP, subject to an identity constraint that must hold between XP and an antecedent XP'. Following standard practice, I henceforth abbreviate the elided constituent and the antecedent constituent as follows:

(1)   a. XP_E = elided constituent;
        b. XP_A = antecedent constituent.

There are a number of issues with this general conception of ellipsis that will become clear as we go forward, but one immediate problem is that in order to meet the identity condition, any and all parts of XP_E that do not have identical counterparts in XP_A must first be moved out of both XP_A and XP_E. The difficulty is that there are a potentially indefinite number of such non-identical parts, as can be seen most clearly in sentences involving pseudogapping:

(2)   Mary will read stories to the children on Mondays as often as Sue will ~~read~~ poems to the adults on Tuesdays.

It is not too hard to make a case for moving one or two NP- or PP-constituents out of vP_A and vP_E (see Lasnik 1999 and Takahashi 2004, for example), but, as the number and different kinds of such constituents goes up, it becomes increasingly difficult to find independent motivation for moving all of these elements out of both vP_A and vP_E, leaving only the main verbs behind, and, worse yet, to find a plausible location to move them to (see Bowers 1998 for discussion).

Suppose we think about ellipsis in an entirely different way. Rather than moving all the non-identical parts out of the elided constituent and its antecedent, let's leave everything *in situ* and simply elide those parts of XP_E that are identical to the corresponding parts of XP_A, leaving those parts of XP_E that are not identical to the corresponding parts of XP_A to be pronounced. One immediate advantage of conceiving of ellipsis in this way is that all of the various (and potentially unbounded number of) pseudogapping possibilities can be derived in a simple and unified fashion, as indicated in the following examples:

(3)   Mary will [$_{vP}$ read stories to the children on Mondays] as often as Sue will
        a. [$_{vP}$ ~~read~~ poems to the adults ~~on Mondays~~].
        b. [$_{vP}$ ~~read~~ poems ~~to the children on Mondays~~]
        c. [$_{vP}$ ~~read~~ poems ~~to the children~~ on Tuesdays]
        d. [$_{vP}$ ~~read stories~~ to the adults on Tuesdays]
        e. [$_{vP}$ ~~read stories~~ to the adults ~~on Mondays~~]
        f. [$_{vP}$ ~~read stories to the children~~ on Tuesdays]
        g. [$_{vP}$ ~~read stories to the children on Mondays~~]

Notice, in particular, that in the special case where all the elements of vP_E are identical to corresponding parts of vP_A, the result is simply verb phrase ellipsis (VPE), as shown in (3g). Making this work will obviously require a notion of *parallel structure* between XP_A and XP_A, which I will have more to say about in §7.6.

7.2   *Why Pseudogapping and VPE Should be Formulated in Relational Terms*

It is interesting to observe that in the examples in (3) the only element that is *obligatorily* elided is the lexical verb *read*. If the verb in vP_E can elide, by virtue of being identical to the verb in vP_A, then any other elements that have identical counterparts in $v\text{P}_A$ are licensed to elide also. If, on the other hand, the main verb in $v\text{P}_E$ is not elidable (because it is not identical to the corresponding verb in $v\text{P}_A$), then *none* of the other elements in $v\text{P}_E$ are licensed to elide either:

(4)   John PRES [<u>tells</u> stories to the children] as often as Mary
    a. [<u>reads</u> *(them/stories) *(to them/the childen)]
    b. [<u>reads</u> *(them) to the <u>adults</u>]
    c. [<u>reads</u> <u>poems</u> *(to them)
    d. [<u>reads</u> <u>poems</u> to the <u>adults</u>]

Various strategies are possible in sentences of this kind, including repeating the relevant elements of $v\text{P}_A$ in $v\text{P}_E$, pronominalizing them, or combining the two in various ways, but none of the elements of $v\text{P}_E$ can be elided even if they are identical to the corresponding elements of $v\text{P}_A$. It seems almost paradoxical that the lexical verb, which is the only obligatory element in a vP constituent, is obligatorily elided in ellipsis structures, while none of the other constituents of vP are obligatorily elided! How can this be explained?

The problem is that this pattern is not in any way predicted by the standard theory of ellipsis based on constituent structure. There is no reason why it should be the head of $v\text{P}_E$ that is obligatorily elided rather some other element of vP. Why, for example, could it not be the case that the v_{th} argument is always obligatorily elided and that elision of other elements is dependent on its being elidable? We would then predict the following pattern:

(5)   John PRES [tells stories to Sue] more often than Bill
    a. reads ~~stories~~ to Mary
    b. does ~~tell stories~~ to Mary
    c. reads ~~stories to Sue~~
    d. does ~~tell stories to Sue~~
    e. *does ~~tell~~ jokes ~~to Sue~~

Such a pattern is of course totally impossible. Only (5b) and (5d), in which the lexical verb is elided, are valid instances of ellipsis, while (5a) and (5c) are totally impossible. Furthermore, (5e), which should be bad, is perfectly OK.

The culprit here is once again the fact that a theory of syntax based on constituent structure fails to express the fundamental relations between words. The problem is that there is no inherent connection between the ellipsis feature [E] attached to the licensing head H and any one of the constituents that compose the ellipsis domain XP_E. All the licensing conditions for ellipsis are capable of telling us is that some part(s) of the vP constituent should elide under identity with the corresponding parts of the antecedent. There is nothing in these conditions that would lead us to expect the pattern of elision observed in

(3) and (4), as opposed to the one shown in (5). The standard theory of ellipsis posits that the feature [E] on a head (e.g. T) that selects the elided constituent (e.g. vP) somehow licenses ellipsis within its complement, but the head T, as we have just seen, is irrelevant. What really matters is whether the head of the ellipsis domain itself has an identical antecedent.

I show next that in a theory based on relations rather than constituents, the pattern of elision observed above follows directly from the assumption that ellipsis is a property of the *head* of the v-projection that is the domain of ellipsis. To be more specific, suppose that the feature [E] may be added to a projection α_{pred} just in case there is an antecedent projection β_{pred} which is parallel in structure to α_{pred}. The feature [E] is understood as an instruction to PF to not pronounce the head α_{pred} if it is identical to its antecedent β_{pred}, together with any other heads in the α_{pred} projection that are identical to the corresponding heads in the β_{pred} projection, plus any dependents or modifiers of heads in α_{pred} that are identical to their counterparts in β_{pred}. The elision of any other heads, dependents, or modifiers contained in an α_{pred}[E] projection that are identical to their counterparts in β_{pred}[A] is thus *dependent* on there being an elidable lexical head in v_{pred}[E]. Looked at from this point of view, the primary element in ellipsis of this sort (i.e. VPE with pseudogapping) is the lexical head v_{pred} rather than the VP constituent, and ellipsis should be thought of as non-pronunciation of a particular head in the ellipsis domain rather than of a VP constituent that happens to be the complement of some other head such as v_{tns}. It is entirely natural, in fact unavoidable, within a relational theory of the sort proposed here to conceptualize the phenomenon of ellipsis in terms of a relation of identity between a particular lexical projection and its antecedent. In a theory based on constituent structure, in contrast, there is no obvious reason why identity between the head of a VP constituent and its antecedent should have priority over any other of its parts.

This approach immediately predicts that we should expect to find similar effects with predicate adjectives, which are, like verbs, lexical predicates:

(6)   a. Mary is more often [angry$_A$ at Sue] than $\left\{ \begin{array}{l} \text{she *(is) [angry}_E\text{ at John]} \\ \text{Sam is [angry}_E\text{ at Sue]} \end{array} \right\}$

       b. Mary is more often [delighted$_A$ with Sue] than she is [furious$_E$ *(with her/Sue)].[1]

       c. Mary is more often [delighted$_A$ with Sue] than I am [delighted$_E$ with Sue].

---

[1] Note that the sentence *Mary is more delighted with Sue than she is furious* is grammatical, but cannot be construed as meaning *Mary is more delighted with Sue than she is furious at Sue/her.*

As (6a) shows, a lexical adjective $\alpha_{prop}[E]$, just like a lexical verb, obligatorily elides if it is identical with an antecedent β_{prop}, along with any other dependents in the $\alpha_{prop}[E]$ that are identical with the corresponding dependents in the β_{prop}. On the other hand, (6b) shows that if $\alpha_{prop}[E]$ is not elidable, then no other elements in its projection can be elided either, even if they are identical to the corresponding elements in β_{prop}, just as in v_{pred} ellipsis. Finally, in the limiting case (shown in (6c)) where everything in the a-projection headed by *delighted*[E] is identical to everything in its antecedent, we get a form of ellipsis similar to VPE. Van Craenenbroeck and Merchant (2013) classify this type of ellipsis as "predicate phrase ellipsis," but do not have any concrete explanation for its existence or any account of how it relates to other types of ellipsis. If my approach is correct, however, exactly the same mechanisms apply in both VPE and predicate phrase ellipsis, the only difference being that the domain of ellipsis is v_{pred} for the former and a_{prop} for the latter.

It is worth pointing out, as an interesting aside, that the behavior of prepositions under ellipsis shows that they are *not* predicates in this sense, and that p_{rel} is therefore not a domain of ellipsis. Thus the equivalent of (6a), in which the head of a p-projection elides under identity with its antecedent, is impossible, as (7a) shows:

(7)   a. *John drives [from$_A$ NC] as often as Mary drives [~~from~~$_E$ NY].
        b. John [drives$_A$ from NC] as often as Mary does [~~drive~~$_E$ from NY].
        c. John [drives$_A$ from NC] as often as Mary does [~~drive~~$_E$ ~~from NC~~].

Rather, the only possible form of ellipsis, as seen in (6b) and (6c), is v_{pred} ellipsis.

7.3   Gapping

Consider next the type of ellipsis known in the literature as gapping, illustrated by examples such as the following:

(8)   John ate/will eat/has eaten/is eating/has been eating the beans and Mary ~~ate/ will eat/ has eaten/is eating/has been eating~~ the hotdogs.

This data immediately poses a problem. As we have just seen, it is the lexical verb that elides in pseudogapping and VPE, while auxiliaries do not. But in gapping any and all auxiliaries are elided, along with the lexical verb. Rather than trying to find a unified approach capable of encompassing both types of ellipsis, Johnson (2009) and Toosarvandani (2013) argue that the apparent elision of the auxiliary in gapping is an illusion, brought about by "low conjunction" of vP beneath T, plus elision of the main verb in the second conjunct. However, there are at least two serious problems with this solution, as both authors acknowledge. One is that it will only work if a violation of the Coordinate Structure Constraint (CSC) is countenanced, since the internal subject of the first vP conjunct must raise to Spec,T, while the internal subject of the second vP conjunct must remain *in situ*. Another is that it requires nominative Case to be assigned in Spec,v rather than Spec,T, contrary to what is standardly assumed in the literature.

I propose instead that the mechanisms involved in gapping are identical to those involved in VPE, the only difference being that the domain of gapping is v_{tns} rather than v_{pred}. More concretely, suppose that the [E] feature in gapping is added to v_{tns} rather than v_{pred}. Given the mechanisms proposed above, it follows immediately that the lexical material contained in α_{tns}[E] must elide if it is identical to its antecedent β_{tns}[A], together with any other heads, dependents, or modifiers in the α_{tns}[E]-projection that are identical to their counterparts in the β_{tns}. Example (8) can then be derived straightforwardly as follows:

(9)   John [will$_A$ eat the beans] and Mary [~~will$_E$ eat~~ the hotdogs]

In this example, the head of the ellipsis domain *will$_E$* is identical to its antecedent *will$_A$*. Hence the former may be elided. In this case, however, since the v_{pred} heads are also identical, *eat$_{pred}$* may be elided as well. Note that the main verb in the v_{tns}[E]-projection need not be identical to its antecedent, but v_{tns}[E] will nevertheless elide, yielding the grammatical sentence (10):

(10)   John [will$_A$ eat the beans] and Mary [~~will$_E$~~ devour the hotdogs]

Furthermore, this analysis explains why *all* the auxiliary elements must elide in gapping, since by hypothesis any lower heads in the v_{tns}[E] projection which are identical to the corresponding heads in its antecedent must be elided along with v_{tns}[E] itself. Hence we will get examples of gapping such as the following:

(11)   John [has$_A$ been eating the beans] and Mary [~~has$_E$ been eating~~ the hot dogs]

Strong evidence in support of this analysis comes from the fact that gapping can be combined with pseudogapping, producing examples such as the following:

(12)   a. John [will$_A$ give <u>some books</u> to Mary] and Sam [~~will$_E$ give~~ some records ~~to Mary~~].
        b. John [will$_A$ give some books <u>to Mary</u>] and Sam [~~will$_E$ give some books~~ <u>to Sue</u>].

c. John [will$_A$ give <u>some books</u> <u>to Mary</u>] and Sam [~~will$_E$~~ ~~give~~ <u>some records</u> <u>to Sue</u>].[2]

d. John [will$_A$ give some books to Mary] and Sam [~~will$_E$~~ ~~give some books to Mary~~] too.

The point is that we find exactly the same range of pseudogapping possibilities as in VPE, the only difference being that the domain of ellipsis is the v_{tns} projection instead of the v_{pred} projection. In this case, however, the licensing procedure of the standard approach to ellipsis fails even to account for the basic properties of gapping, much less for the fact that pseudogapping can combine with gapping in exactly the same way that it combines with VPE.

As we would predict, exactly the same range of ellipsis plus pseudogapping possibilities is found in structures with a predicate adjective plus an infinitival complement:[3]

(13)   a. John is [likely$_A$ to give <u>books</u> to Sam] more often than he is [~~likely$_E$~~ ~~to give~~ <u>records</u> ~~to Sam~~].

b. John is [likely$_A$ to give books <u>to Sam</u>] more often than he is [~~likely$_E$~~ ~~to give~~ ~~books~~ <u>to Sue</u>].

c. John is [likely$_A$ to give <u>books</u> <u>to Sam</u>] more often than he is [~~likely$_E$~~ ~~to give~~ <u>records</u> <u>to Sue</u>].

Note that in these examples, not only is the head *likely*$_{prop}$ of the [E] domain elided but also the *to*$_{inf}$ and *give*$_{pred}$ heads as well, since they also are identical to their counterparts in the antecedent domain.

7.4   *Sluicing*

The next type of ellipsis to be considered, exemplified in (14), is usually referred to in the literature as "sluicing":

(14)   [[D]$_A$ John bought something for Mary], but I don't know what [[~~wh~~]$_E$ ~~John bought <what> for Mary~~].

Let's assume that exactly the same mechanisms operate in sluicing as in other cases of ellipsis, except that the domain in this case is v_{comp}. Since both $\varnothing$[Q, wh]$_{comp}$ and its antecedent $\varnothing$[D]$_{comp}$ are null in (14), the latter is redundantly elided, along with whatever material in its projection is identical to the corresponding material in the projection of its antecedent. In this case, everything in the ellipsis domain has an identical counterpart in the antecedent domain, apart from the displaced element *what*, which is unpronounced at PHON anyway for

---

[2] Examples similar to (12c) are often marked in the literature as degraded, but with the appropriate focus intonation, they seem fine to me.

[3] Of course it is also possible for the domain of ellipsis in examples such as those in (11) to be v_{tns} rather than a_{prop}, resulting in examples such as *John is likely to give books to Sam more often than Mary is records*, *John is likely to give books to Sam more often than Mary is to Sue*, etc.

independent reasons. Hence everything is unpronounced except for the displaced *wh*-word *what*.

It should hardly come as a surprise at this point to find that sluicing can also be combined with pseudogapping to produce examples such as the following:

(15)   a. What [did$_A$ John buy <u>for Mary</u>] and what [~~did$_E$ John buy~~ for Sue]?
          b. For whom [did$_A$ John buy <u>the books</u>] and for whom [~~did$_E$ John buy~~ the records]?
          c. Why [did$_A$ John buy <u>the books</u> <u>for Mary</u>] and why [~~did$_E$ John buy~~ the records <u>for Sue</u>?
          d. When [did$_A$ John buy the books for Mary] and why [~~did$_E$ John buy the books for Mary~~?

Note particularly that it is impossible *not* to elide the fronted auxiliary in $v_{comp}[E]$,

(16)   *What [did$_A$ John buy <u>for Mary</u>] and what [did$_E$ ~~John buy~~ <u>for Sue</u>]?

unless of course all the other identical elements in its c-command domain are also pronounced:

(17)   What did John buy for Mary and what did John/he buy for Sue?

This shows once again that it is the *head* of the relevant ellipsis domain (in this case v_{comp}) that is the locus of ellipsis: if it elides under identity with its counterpart in the antecedent, then and only then can other heads and their dependents or modifiers in $v_{comp}[E]$ be elided under identity with their counterparts in the antecedent.

Sluicing examples such as (14) in which the first clause is declarative and the second interrogative appear to exhibit some restrictions that I do not fully understand at this point. For example, it seems possible to construct examples such as the following in which the fronted *wh*-phrase is an adjunct (cf. example (83) in Toosarvandani 2013),

(18)   [[D]$_A$ John is buying a book for Mary], but I don't know why [[~~wh~~]$_E$ ~~John is buying a book for Mary~~ now/this week/etc.]

but similar examples in which the fronted *wh*-phrase is an argument range from significantly degraded in some cases to clearly bad in others:

(19)   a. ??[[D]$_A$ John gave something to Mary], but I don't know what [[~~wh~~]$_E$ ~~John gave~~ to Sue].
          b. *[[D$_A$ John gave a book to someone], but I don't know to whom [[~~wh~~]$_E$ ~~John gave~~ a record <to whom>]

I leave this as a problem for future research.

7.5   *Focus Sluicing*

Consider next a rather surprising type of ellipsis which is predicted by the approach to ellipsis proposed here, though it has not, as far as I am aware, been previously noticed in the literature:[4]

(20)   a. The book John gave to Mary,/and the record ~~John gave~~ to Sue.
      b. The poems John wants to read to the children, the novels ~~John wants to read~~ to the adults.
      c. The book John will give <u>to Mary</u> on Thursday, the record ~~John will give~~ to Sue on Friday.
      d. The poems John often reads to the children <u>on Thursdays</u>, the novels ~~John often reads to the children~~ on Fridays.
      e. The poems John reads <u>to the children</u> on Thursdays, the novels ~~John reads~~ to the adults ~~on Thursdays~~.
      f. The poems John read to the children, the novels Bill ~~read to the children~~.
      g. The book John gave to Mary,/and the record ~~John gave to Mary~~, too.

Here the elided elements follow a nominal in focus position at the beginning of a clause and, as can be seen from the examples, the elision has all the characteristics discussed earlier. In particular, any amount of material can be elided, as shown in (20b). It can also be combined with pseudogapping, with any number of identical elements elided, even if discontinuous, and any number of non-identical elements retained. Finally, as shown in (20g), all the material following the topic in the second clause can be elided if identical with the material in the antecedent.

This type of ellipsis is easily accounted for by the mechanisms proposed already, under the assumption that the head to which the [E] feature attaches is a focus head v_{foc} above v_{tns}:

(21)   The book $[\varnothing_{foc}[A]$ John gave <u>to Mary</u>] and the record $[\varnothing_{foc}[E]$ ~~John gave~~ <u>to Sue</u>].

Once again, it is the identity of the head of the ellipsis domain—in this case v_{foc}—with the head of the antecedent domain that crucially makes elision possible, even though elision of the head in this case is vacuous, since the head of v_{foc} is null in English.

---

[4] The notation ",/and" in (20a,g) is intended to indicate that the antecedent and ellipsis clauses can typically be separated either by a conjunction such as *and* or by comma intonation.

7.6   Syntactic Parallelism

If the approach to ellipsis developed in the preceding sections is correct, then there is a single uniform mechanism involved in every case, namely, elision (that is, non-pronunciation) of the head $v_H[E]$ of an ellipsis domain under identity with the corresponding v_H head in its antecedent domain, together with elision of any other material in the $v_H[E]$ projection that happens to be identical to the corresponding material in the v_H projection of the antecedent domain. Different types of ellipsis arise simply and solely from the fact that different heads in a v-projection can be targeted as ellipsis domains, including at least v_{pred}, v_{tns}, v_{comp}, and v_{foc}. As has already been mentioned, it is crucial, if this approach is to work properly, that the ellipsis domain and the antecedent domain be syntactically parallel in all their parts. Chung (2013) suggests that the syntactic identity constraint on ellipsis requires identity of argument structure and Case. If the approach developed here is correct, these conditions are certainly necessary but by no means sufficient. In addition to having parallel argument structures, the antecedent and ellipsis domains must have parallel modification structures as well. Furthermore, ellipsis domains such as v_{tns} and v_{comp}, which do not have thematic arguments at all, must also be strictly parallel in structure.

Fortunately, the necessary parallelism constraint can be stated quite straightforwardly in the relational framework. Suppose $\alpha_H[E]$ is an ellipsis domain and $\beta_H[A]$ its antecedent. Then $\alpha_H[E]$ and $\beta_H[A]$ are parallel if and only if: (i) they have the same set of categories in their respective projections, (ii) each category in their respective projections has the same selection and projection features, and (iii) each category is modified (if at all) in the same way. To illustrate, consider the antecedent and ellipsis domains that may give rise to example (12a), a combination of gapping and pseudogapping:

(22)

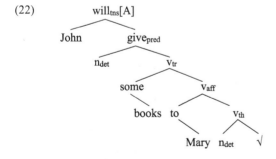

(23)

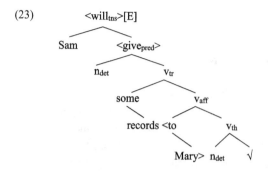

As is evident, the antecedent and ellipsis domains are strictly parallel in structure, since they have the same projections, i.e. v_{tns}, v_{pred}, v_{tr}, v_{aff}, and v_{th}, and each head has the same selection and projection features. Moreover, since the head of the ellipsis domain *will*$_{tns}$ and the lexical verb *give*$_{pred}$ are identical to their counterparts in the antecedent domain, both may be unpronounced, along with the argument *to Mary* selected by v_{aff}, which is also identical to its counterpart in the antecedent domain. The result at PHON is the string *John will hand the books to Mary and Sam the records*, interpreted to mean 'John will hand the books to Mary and Sam will hand the records to Mary.'

7.7   *Voice Mismatches in VPE*

Returning now to VPE, consider voice mismatches such as the following::

(24)   a. The garbage is taken out whenever the janitor wants to ~~take out the garbage~~.
        b. The janitor takes out the garbage whenever it needs to be ~~taken out~~.

Surprisingly, such voice mismatches are not tolerated in gapping:

(25)   a. *John will eat the beans and the hot dogs ~~will be eaten~~ by Mary.
        b. *The beans will be eaten by John and Mary ~~will eat~~ the hot dogs.

Merchant (2013) argues that this contrast can be explained by the fact that the voice head containing the syntactic features [+/−act] is higher than the elision site for VPE, whereas it is lower than the elision site for gapping. I will argue, however, that the approach to ellipsis proposed here makes it unnecessary to assume such a special voice head.

Consider first the case of VPE. The domain of elision for VPE is, as we have seen, v_{pred}. Therefore, given the analysis of passive proposed in Chapter 2, the examples in (24a) can be derived as follows (with the pronoun *it* substituted for *the garbage* in the interests of brevity):

(26)

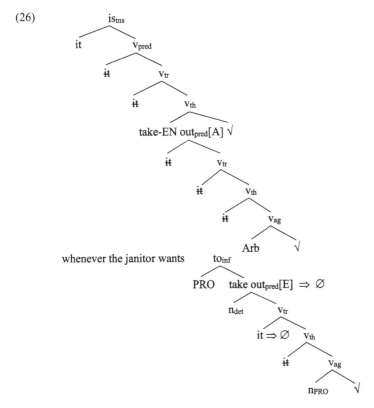

Since, as Merchant has shown, the identity requirement in ellipsis quite generally ignores purely morphological distinctions, the active form of the verb in $v_{pred}[E]$ can be elided under identity with the participial form in its antecedent, or vice versa. Similarly, though unpronounced copies of displaced elements are generally simply ignored by elision, the v_{th} argument *it* in the ellipsis domain in (24b) can be elided under identity with the copy of the displaced v_{th} argument in the corresponding position in its passive antecedent. Finally, the null elements PRO and Arb are simply invisible as far as ellipsis is concerned. The important point here is that the domain of elision is the same, namely v_{pred}, in both the antecedent and elided clauses and, crucially, they are strictly parallel in structure. Hence the head *take out*$_{pred}$ in the ellipsis domain may be elided, along with any other elements (in this case only *it*) that are identical to the corresponding elements in the antecedent domain.

Consider next the derivations that would be involved in an attempted gapping structure such as (27):

(27)

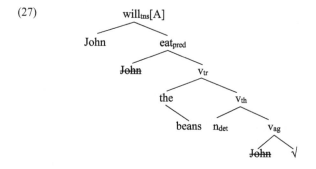

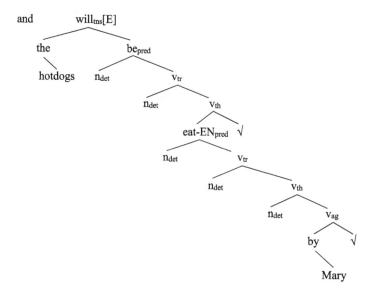

Here the domain of elision is *will*$_{tns}$ in both clauses, as required. The problem is that these domains are not at all parallel in structure, hence ellipsis is correctly predicted to be impossible.

It was shown in §7.2 that VPE and pseudogapping are derived in essentially the same way, the former simply being the special case in which all the elements in the v_{pred}[E] projection are identical to the corresponding elements in the antecedent v_{pred}[A] projection. A potential problem arises from Merchant's (2008, 2013) claim that voice mismatches are impossible in pseudogapping constructions. Since the domain of ellipsis is identical for both pseudogapping and VPE, voice mismatches should be possible in both. However, Tanaka (2011) has proposed an alternative explanation of the examples cited by Merchant in terms of a discourse factor discussed in Kehler (2000, 2002), in spite of which it is possible to construct examples that do not sound too degraded. Thus consider the following cases where the antecedent is passive and the ellipsis site is active:

(28)   a. Roses are planted by Sam more often than Bill does lilies.
       b. Klimt is admired by such collectors more than they do Klee.
       c. Hundertwasser's buildings will be remembered by architects far longer than they will his paintings.
       d. The arms were hidden by the rebels as carefully as a woman would (do) her most precious jewels.[5]

Examples in which the antecedent is active and the ellipsis site passive are more difficult for the reasons discussed by Tanaka, but even so the following do not seem impossible:

(29)   a. ?Mary plants roses more often than lilies are by John.
       b. ?The critics have always admired the German Expressionists far more than they have been by the public.
       c. ?Professional architects are likely to remember Hundertwasser's work far longer than it will be by the general public.
       d. ?The rebels hid the arms as carefully as a woman's most precious jewels would be. [constructed example—JSB]

I conclude, therefore, that voice mismatches are tolerated, subject to the identity conditions discussed by Merchant, just in case the antecedent and ellipsis domains are parallel, though the discourse factors discussed by Tanaka also play a role in determining acceptability judgments.

7.8   *Some Apparent Counterexamples*

I conclude this chapter by discussing two potential counterexamples to my claim that it is identity between the head of an elision domain and its antecedent that is the crucial condition for ellipsis. The first case comes from Irish, in which the verb apparently survives ellipsis even though it is identical in both the antecedent and the elided clause. The second case, which is from Malagasy, is similar in that the verb survives despite being identical, but appears to be even more problematic in that indefinite arguments and adverbial modifiers obligatorily survive ellipsis whereas definite arguments do not.

---

[5] This sentence is adapted from an example in Miller (1991: 94) cited by Merchant (2008).

7.8.1   *Ellipsis in Irish*

Consider the following examples of ellipsis from Irish (McCloskey 2005):

(30) a. Sciob   an   cat   an   t-eireaball   de-n   luch.
         snatched   the   cat   the   tail   from-the   mouse
         'The cat cut the tail off the mouse.'

      b. A-r   sciob?
         INTERR-PAST   snatched
         'Did it?'

      c. Creidim   gu-r   sciob
         believe.1s   C-PAST   snatched
         'I believe it did.'

In these examples, which are generally assumed to be instances of VPE, the whole verb is repeated, while all the other elements in the ellipsis domain identical to their counterparts in the antecedent domain disappear, apparently contradicting my assertion that the head of the domain of ellipsis must be unpronounced when identical to the head of its antecedent. It has been argued, however, that in order to account for VSO word order in languages such as Irish, main verbs must be raised to T and subjects must remain in vP. Restated in relational terms, main verbs in Irish project v_{tns} and v_{tns} has no athematic argument selection feature. An example such as (30a) would thus be derived as follows:

(31)

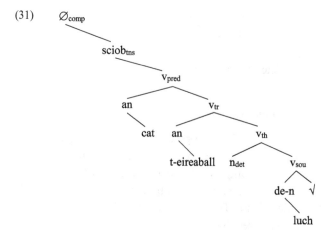

Now suppose that (31) is the antecedent of a potential ellipsis site of the following form:

(32)

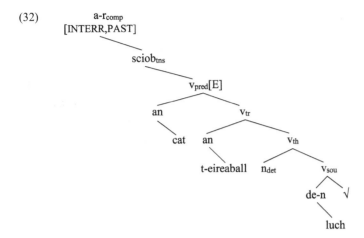

The head of the domain of elision ~~sciob~~_{pred} is identical in both clauses, despite the fact that it is already slated for non-pronunciation due to the displacement of the main verb to v_{tns}. Hence the conditions for ellipsis are still met, permitting the head to be (redundantly, in this case) elided, along with all other elements in the domain of ellipsis that are identical to their counterparts in the antecedent domain, including of course the subject *an cat* 'the cat.'

It is interesting to contrast verbal ellipsis briefly with ellipsis in predicative copular clauses in Irish. Consider first an example with a predicate adjective (McCloskey 2005):

(33) a. An   cosúil le   taibhse é?
        INTERR.COP like   with   ghost   him
        'Is he like a ghost?'

      b. Is   cosúil.
        COP   like
        'He is.'

Since adjectives, just like verbs, survive ellipsis, it seems reasonable to assume that they too are pronounced at v_{tns}. However, the somewhat surprising appearance of the subject at the right edge of these copular constructions has engendered speculation that it is not the adjective that is moved but the whole predicate phrase. Such an analysis, as McCloskey rightly points out, makes it very difficult to explain the pattern of ellipsis, which depends crucially on the assumption that both adjective and verbs are pronounced at v_{tns}. Recalling the discussion of word order variation in Chapter 4, I propose that it is simply a language-specific property of Irish that the selection feature of a_{prop} is rightwards rather than leftwards, a fact that can be represented in the lexical entry of a_{prop} by means of the selection feature $[\_n_{det}]_R$. I also adopt the assumption, implicit in many analyses of Irish, that the various forms of the copula are phonetic realizations of the tense features of v_{tns} combined with the clause-typing features of v_{comp}. Finally, let us assume that in main clauses in Irish the non-verbal predicational heads a_{prop}, n_{nom}, and p_{rel} directly select the tense head, thereby adapting in essence the ideas in Bowers (1993, 2001b, 2002) to the relational framework.[6] Example (33a) can then be derived as follows:

(34)

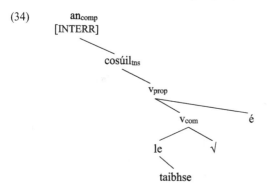

The declarative copular form *Is cosúil le taibhse é* is identical, apart from the fact that *is*[DECL] occupies the v_{comp} position, permitting the elided form (33b) to be derived in a manner completely parallel to verbal ellipsis. This analysis hearkens back to a proposal first put forward by Doherty (1996), withdrawn in later work, though I believe there is much to be said in its favor.

   Consider next nominal predicates. The question in (35a) can only be answered as in (35b), not as in (35c):

(35)   a. An   duine   de   na   fearaibh   é?
           INTERR.COP   person   of   the   men   him
           'Is he one of the men?'

        b. Is ea.
           DECL.COP
           'He is.'

        c. *Is   duine.
           DECL.COP   person
           'He is.'

---

[6] In this respect, Irish differs considerably from English, which only permits direct projection of a predicational head in small clauses. In main clauses English requires adjectival, prepositional and nominal predicates to be selected as arguments by a copular verb such as *be*.

No part of the nominal predicate, even its head, survives ellipsis. Instead the v_{tns} head is filled in with an invariant element *ea(dh)*. To account for this pattern, we may assume that a nominal predicate n_{nom} projects $\varnothing_{tns}$ instead of v_{tns}. If n_{nom} has the feature [E], then it selects ea_{tns}. Finally, prepositional predicates, which I shall not discuss here (cf. McCloskey 2005 for details), pattern in some cases like adjectives, but in other cases like nouns.

7.8.2   Apparent Ellipsis in Malagasy

Travis (2005) discusses data from Malagasy for certain speakers for whom it is impossible to freely drop internal arguments:

(36)   a. Mametraka   ny   boky   eo   ambonin'ny   latabatra   Rakoto.
              PRES-AT-put   DET   book   there   top' DET   table   Rakoto
         b. *Mametraka eo ambonin'ny latabatra Rakoto.
         c. * Mametraka ny boky Rakoto.

This is true even in an appropriate discourse environment such as the following:

(37)   a. Natao   inona   ilay   boky?
              PST-TT-do   what   DET   book
         'What happened to the book?'

         b. *Nametraka __   teo   ambonin'ny   latabatra   Rakoto.
              PRES-AT-put   PST-there   on' DET   table   Rakoto

Travis then goes on to show that in environments that typically allow VPE, internal arguments apparently can be unexpressed. Furthermore, if one of the obligatory arguments is unexpressed, both must be:

(38)   Mametraka   ny   boky   eo   ambonin'ny   latabatra   ve   Rakoto?
            PRES-AT-put   DET   book   PST-there   top' DET   table   Q   Rakoto
         'Does Rakoto put the book on the table?'

(39)   Nilaza   Rasoa   fa . . .
            PST-AT-say   Rasoa   that
         a. . . . nametraka   ~~ny~~   ~~boky~~   ~~teo~~   ~~ambonin'ny~~   ~~latabatra~~   Rabe/izy
              PST-AT-put   DET   book   PST-there   top' DET   table   Rabe/he
         b. . . . nametraka ny boky teo ambonin'ny latabatra Rabe.
         c. . . . *nametraka ny boky ~~teo ambonin'ny latabatra~~ Rabe.
         d. . . . *nametraka ~~ny boky~~ teo ambonin'ny latabatra Rabe.

So far, the facts look very similar to Irish. However, Travis goes on to discuss further data which seems to indicate that while definite objects and PPs can be elided, agents and indefinite objects can't, exactly the opposite of what would be expected under an approach to ellipsis similar to that proposed for Irish:

(40)   Empon-dRakoto   ve   ny   savoka?
       TT-melt-Rakoto   Q   DET   wax
       'Does Rakoto melt the wax?/Is the wax melted by Rakoto?'

(41)   Nilaza   Rasoa   fa
       PST-AT-say   Rasoa   that...
       'Rasoa said that ...'
       a. ... empon-dRakoto ny savoka.
       b. ... *empona (-~~dRakoto~~) ny savoka.

(42)   Nanosotra   menaka   ny   latabatra   ve   Rabe?
       PST-AT-polish oil   DET   table   Q   Rabe
       'Did Rabe polish the table with oil?'

(43)   Nilaza   Rasoa   fa
       PST-AT-say   Rasoa   that ...
       'Rasoa said that ...'
       a. * ... nanosotra   ~~menaka ny latabatra~~   izy.
            PST-AT-polish   he
       b. ... nanosotra   menaka ~~ny latabatra~~   izy.
            PST-AT-polish   oil   he

Stranger still is the fact that both manner adverbs and adverbial modifiers of v_{pred} are required to survive ellipsis and may not be elided:

(44)   Mandraraka tsara ny rano foana ao   anatin'ny vilany ve Rakoto?
       PRES-AT-pour well DET water always there in DET   pot   Q Rakoto
       'Does Rakoto always pour the water into the well?'

(45)   Nilaza   Rasoa fa
       PST-AT-say   Rasoa that ...
       'Rasoa said that ...'
       a. ... nandraraka tsara foana Rakoto
       b. ... nandraraka Rakoto[7]

Travis then goes on to argue that the only way this ellipsis data can be understood is by an intraposition-type analysis which involves iterative predicate fronting into specifiers of adverbial phrases (see Travis 2005 for details).

---

[7] NB: (45b) is a grammatical sentence but does not include the meaning of either 'well' or 'always.'

Clearly, if this data is to be explained by an ellipsis process of the sort discussed here, then it is incompatible with the clause structure proposed for Malagasy in Chapter 4, which is identical in all relevant respects, apart from the direction of selection, to the clause structure of Irish. I do not believe, however, that the examples cited by Travis are in fact instances of ellipsis. Notice, first of all, that in contexts such as those in (37), it is impossible to drop arguments in English, just as it is in Malagasy:

(46)   a. What happened to the book?
       b. *John put ~~the book~~ on the table.

At the same time, in ellipsis environments such as those in (38), though it is possible in English (as it always is) to elide the whole VP, it is also possible to retain the verb, in which case the pattern is identical to Malagasy, namely, the agent cannot be elided and at the same time retain the elliptical meaning:

(47)   Was the wax melted by John?

(48)   Mary said that
       a. ... it was.
       b. ... *the wax/it was melted ~~by John/him~~.

Similarly, if a clause contains both a definite and an indefinite argument, it is impossible to elide both arguments if the verb is retained or to elide only the indefinite, but it seems much more acceptable to elide the definite alone:

(49)   Did John polish the table with oil?

(50)   Yes, Mary said that
       a. ... *he polished ~~the table with oil~~.
       b. ....*he polished the table ~~with oil~~.
       c. ... he polished ~~the table~~ with oil.

Even more striking is the fact that in English, just as in Malagasy, neither manner adverbs nor v_{pred} modifiers can ever be dropped if the verb is retained:

(51)   a. Does John throw baseballs well?
       b. *Yes, John/he throws baseballs ~~well~~.

(52)   a. Does John always throw curve balls?
       b. *Yes, John/he ~~always~~ throws curve balls.

(53)   a. Does John always throw curve balls well?
       b. *Yes, John/he ~~always~~ throws curve balls ~~well~~.

In fact, the contrast between dropping definite arguments and dropping indefinite arguments becomes even clearer if there is also an adverb present:

(54)   a. Does John sing arias perfectly?
         b. *Yes, he sings ~~arias~~ perfectly.

(55)   a. Did John sing the aria perfectly?
         b. Yes, he sang ~~the aria~~ perfectly.

I do not fully understand the discourse conditions that make it possible to drop definite arguments in English and there are certainly contexts in which it seems to be impossible:

(56)   a. Did John hit the ball?
         b. *Yes, he hit ~~the ball~~.

Nevertheless, it seems clear that dropping of internal arguments and adverbs (or not) when the verbal head of v_{pred} is retained is quite independent of true ellipsis, and that the discourse conditions under which it takes place may even be to a large degree the same cross-linguistically.

7.9   *Conclusion*

The main claim of this chapter is that the essential requirement for ellipsis is identity and elision of the head of the ellipsis domain under identity with its counterpart in the antecedent domain. Elision of any other elements of the ellipsis domain under identity with their counterparts in the antecedent domain is dependent on identity of heads, and can only take place under conditions of strict syntactic parallelism. This provides strong support for a relational theory of the sort proposed here in which the primitives of syntax are relations between words rather than constituents, because the only possible approach to ellipsis in this framework is one in which ellipsis is solely driven by the properties of heads of ellipsis domains. Furthermore, the requisite notion of syntactic parallelism is one that is naturally definable in the relational framework. Empirical support for the relational approach is provided by the fact that it is able to account for all known types of ellipsis by means of a single unified procedure and by the fact that a potentially unbounded number of elements can be pseudogapped in every ellipsis domain. It was also shown that two potential counterexamples in the literature from Irish and Malagasy are only apparent, albeit for entirely different reasons.

8 *The DNA of Language*

If the approach developed in this book is on the right track, the basic structure of language—its DNA, as it were—is constructed out of nothing more than a set of LIs, plus the three fundamental syntactic relations of projection, argument selection, and modification. There is just one syntactic operation FR that forms a network of binary relations between lexical items based on selection properties that the head of a relation imposes on its dependent. The three fundamental types of relation are strictly defined in terms of the inherent selection properties of heads. Specifically, given a relation $<\alpha,\beta>$, where α is the head of the relation and β is the dependent, a relation of *lexical projection* holds between α and β, just in case α is itself selected by another head and β still has selection properties that remain to be satisfied. The relation of *argument selection* holds just in case α is itself selected by another head and β has no selection properties that remain to be satisfied. The relation of *modification* holds just in case α has unsatisfied selectors but is not itself selected as an argument by any other head. Within a given lexical subarray, we may define a head with no lexical projection selectors of its own as the *root* of the derivation/tree constructed from that subarray, while a root with no lexical projection features of its own that is not itself selected as an argument by any other head is defined as the root of an entire LA. Finally, a head that has unsatisfied selectors but is not selected by any other head is defined as a *lexical root*. The operation FR is regulated by a general condition termed Immediate Gratification (IG), which requires that when a head is selected from an LA (or a subarray of an LA), its selectors must be satisfied immediately, i.e. as soon as possible. IG ensures that a network of relations formed from a lexical array or lexical subarray is formed in strict bottom-up fashion, starting with a lexical root, while at the same time determining a strict order in which the selection conditions of a given head must be satisfied.

I have tried to show in the course of this work that a relational theory of this form not only equals the major achievements of mainstream generative syntax, but surpasses them in significant respects. Among the broad features common to both approaches are the universality of the central computational component, localization of cross-linguistic variation within a finite, learnable lexicon, the capacity to illuminate diachronic syntactic change, and so forth. Conspicuously absent from the relational approach, however, is an operation equivalent to Merge that combines syntactic entities to form constituents. I have argued that eliminating constituent structure in favor of syntactic relations between words not only provides a conceptually simpler basis for syntactic theory, but has numerous empirical and explanatory advantages as well. I have shown, for example, that a relational theory makes it possible to formulate a simple and general Spell-out algorithm which, combined with a small set of language-specific parameters, is able to explain the limits of word order variation in natural language. Combined with the basic operation FR, Spell-out also explains the existence of "displacement" phenomena without having to posit syntactic operations such as head raising or internal Merge. Another advantage of the strictly bottom-up relational approach advocated in this work is that it directly generates the "extended projection" of an LI in a non-*ad hoc* manner, as well as explaining, not merely stipulating, the existence of "defective" categories. Finally, with regard to accessibility constraints, I have argued that a relational theory makes possible a more natural, less stipulative formulation of phase theory than does a theory based on constituent structure.

The approach to modification developed in this work is quite distinct from previous attempts and, I believe, more promising. It explains why modifiers are always optional, why modifiers are classified in terms of type of projections they modify, and why it is generally the case that only one modifier of a given type can occur within a given projection. At the same time, taken in conjunction with the independently motivated assumption that certain heads are recursive, the theory explains why there is also a certain degree of freedom in the co-occurrence and ordering of modifiers. Specifically, I have shown that more than one type of v_{pred} modifier may occur in a given projection, and that the order in which these modifiers are introduced may vary in a way that correlates precisely with differences of scope, whereas other types of modifiers that select non-recursive heads exhibit no such freedom of occurrence. I have also shown that because the modification relation is fundamentally independent of projection and argument selection, the linearization algorithm simply does not specify the direction of selection for modifiers in the unmarked case. Hence the linear order of a modifier with respect to the PF of the head it modifies is basically free, providing still another source of word order variation not as readily available to the other two basic relations.

With respect to the more general issue of word order variation, I have shown that the relational theory, in conjunction with a measure of transparency, provides the basis for a parametric approach that is superior to X-bar parameterization, on the one hand, and antisymmetry, on the other. The former is too permissive, producing a far wider range of cross-linguistic variation than is found in natural language, while the latter is too restrictive, forcing all word order variation to be described in terms of complex and unmotivated movement operations. It emerges very clearly from the approach advocated here that the reason that quite a wide range of word order variation is permitted in natural language is that the one property of syntactic derivations that is universally preserved under Spell-out is the order of projection. From this point of view, the added assumption of antisymmetry that there is a fixed universal word order from which all cross-linguistic variants must be derived by syntactic movement operations is not only unnecessary but makes incorrect predictions about the relative frequency of occurrence of different word order types. More fundamentally, the antisymmetric approach obscures the fact that the only truly universal features of natural language are syntactic relations between words.

Morphology is another area where a relation-based theory of syntax of the kind advocated here pays unexpected dividends. The current minimalist approach to Case and subject–verb agreement rests on two dubious assumptions. The first is that there is a primitive relation Agree in addition to Merge. The second is that derivations are driven by the need to value and delete "uninterpretable" features such as Case and the φ-features of heads such as T and v in order to render syntactic representations legible to the CI systems. I have shown that neither assumption is necessary or desirable in a relational framework. Instead, the role of morphology is conceived of in an entirely different way, namely, as an (optional) means of mapping the interpretable features and relations of syntax onto morpheme alternates at PHON legible to the SM systems. I have argued, in particular, that so-called structural NOM Case is not in fact an uninterpretable feature that must be eliminated, but rather is the visible manifestation at PHON of the *relation* between a v_{tns} head containing the interpretable syntactic feature of finiteness and a selected n_{det}, as are the φ-features of v_{tns}. I have also shown that the distribution of Case and agreement morphology can be accounted for without adding any new apparatus to the syntax beyond what is already available in the relational theory, namely, LIs consisting of sets of features and selection features governing the formation of relations between LIs. Importantly, there is new data concerning long-distance agreement in expletive constructions with *there* in English that argues decisively against the existence of Agree and in support of the more constrained approach required by the relational theory.

With regard to operator constructions, I have shown that relational theory is not only equal in descriptive power to theories based on constituent structure, but superior in significant respects. For example, edge features of the sort posited in the Minimalist Program to account for displacement of *wh*-expressions that apparently violate phase theory are not only unnecessary, but in fact impossible in the relational theory. The same results can be achieved with the simpler, as well as independently motivated, assumption that v_{pred} is a recursive head. Furthermore, the relational theory, together with a parametric approach to *wh*-displacement, correctly predicts a wider range of cross-linguistic and language-internal variation than antisymmetric approaches based on constituent structure. Finally, not only can the major island effects be explained at least as well in relational terms as in traditional constituent-based terms, but, I have argued, the relational approach is demonstrably superior in a number of cases. In particular, the explanation proposed here for the contrast in extractability from factive versus non-factive arguments is simpler and more straightforward than any that has been put forward within constituent-based theories. Likewise, I have proposed a relational explanation for the existence of adjunct islands that relies solely on the internal structure of subordinate clauses.

Finally, I have argued that the phenomenon of ellipsis, much studied in the recent literature, provides surprising evidence in support of relational syntax. The basic problem with current constituent-based approaches is that in pseudo-gapping structures there is no limit to the number and different types of constituents that must be raised out of the ellipsis domain before it can be elided under identity with its antecedent. Not only is there little or no independent motivation for the required movement operations, but it is extremely difficult to find a plausible landing site for these constituents in all but the simplest cases. This is a general problem, since, as I have shown, pseudogapping is not restricted to VP-ellipsis but is found in every type of ellipsis. The relational theory proposed in this work makes it possible to construct an entirely different approach to an ellipsis that requires no movement at all in pseudogapping structures. The basic idea is that the primary requirement for ellipsis is simply that the *head* of the ellipsis domain must be identical with the head of the antecedent domain. If, however, the two domains are strictly parallel in syntactic structure, then any other elements in the ellipsis domain that are identical with their counterparts in the antecedent domain may be unpronounced as well, while those elements that do not have identical counterparts in the antecedent domain must be pronounced. This procedure gives rise to a wide variety of pseudogapping structures in every possible size of ellipsis domain, many of which have never been explicitly accounted for in the literature. Finally, I have shown that a notion of parallel structure required to make this theory work is easily defined in relational terms.

In conclusion, I hope to have made a strong case for the view that the fundamental building blocks of natural language syntax are not constituents, i.e. sets constructed out of LIs and previously formed constituents, but relations, or dependencies, between LIs, i.e. ordered pairs of LIs, determined by the selection properties of heads. Given the basic notion of selection, there are just three basic relations—projection, argument selection, and modification—from which a network of syntactic relations is constructed. No movement of any kind is required in this framework and a network of syntactic relations is directly mapped, in incremental and strict bottom to top fashion, onto linearly ordered strings of phonetic forms of LIs by the Spell-out algorithm, together with a highly restricted set of directionality parameters.

References

Abels, K. and A. Neeleman 2008. Universal 20 without the LCA. Manuscript, University of Tromsø and University College London.

Abney, S. 1987. *The English Noun Phrase in its Sentential Aspect.* Doctoral dissertation, MIT.

—— 1995. Dependency grammars and context-free grammars. Unpublished draft of a talk presented at the meeting of the Linguistic Society of America, January 1995.

Adam, L. 1897. *Matériaux pour servir à l'établissement d'une grammaire comparée des dialectes de la famille Kariri.* Bibliothèque Linguistique Américaine 20. Paris: J. Maisonneuve. Reprinted 1968, Nendeln, Lichtenstein: Kraus.

Andrews, A. 1982. A note on the constituent structure of adverbials and auxiliaries. *Linguistic Inquiry* 13, 313–317.

Bailyn, J. 1995a. *A Configurational Approach to Russian "Free" Word Order.* Doctoral dissertation, Cornell University.

—— 1995b. Underlying phrase structure and "short" verb movement in Russian syntax. *Journal of Slavic Linguistics* 3, 13–58.

—— 1995c. Configurational case assignment in Russian syntax. *Linguistic Review* 12, 315–360.

Baker, M. 1988. Theta theory and the syntax of applicatives in Chichewa. *Natural Language and Linguistic Theory* 6, 353–389.

Basse, G. 2008. Factive complements as defective phases. In N. Abner and J. Bishop (eds.), *Proceedings of the 27th West Coast Conference on Formal Linguistics*, 54–62. Somerville, MA: Cascadilla Press.

Bobaljik, J. 1999. Adverbs: the hierarchy paradox. *Glot International* 4 (9/10), 27–28.

Boisson, C. 1981. Hiérarchie universelle des spécifications de temps, de lieu, et de manière. *Confluents* 7, 69–124.

Borer, H. 1998. Deriving passive without theta roles. In S. Lapointe, D. Brentari, and P. Farrell (eds.), *Morphology and its Relations to Phonology and Syntax*, 60–99. Stanford, CA: CSLI.

—— 2005. *Structuring Sense: An Exo-Skeletal Trilogy.* New York: Oxford University Press.

Borthen, K. 2003. *Norwegian Bare Singulars.* Doctoral dissertation, Det Historisk-filosofiske Fakultet, Trondheim.

Bošković, Ž. 2002. On multiple wh-fronting. *Linguistic Inquiry* 33, 351–383.

2005. On the locality of left branch extraction and the structure of NP. *Studia Linguistica* 59, 1–45.

2008. What will you have, DP or NP? In E. Elfner and M. Walkow (eds.), *Proceedings of the Northeast Linguistic Society* 37, 101–114. Amherst, MA: GLSA.

2009. More on the no-DP analysis of article-less languages. *Studia Linguistica* 63, 187–203.

Bowers, J. 1973. *Grammatical Relations*. Doctoral dissertation, MIT. Reprinted 1985, Outstanding Dissertations in Linguistics, New York and London: Garland Publishing.

1991. The syntax and semantics of nominals. In S. Moore and A. Wyner (eds.), *Proceedings of the First Semantics and Linguistic Theory Conference*, 1–30. Cornell University Working Papers in Linguistics 10, Ithaca, NY: Cornell University.

1993. The syntax of predication. *Linguistic Inquiry* 24, 591–656.

1997. A binary analysis of resultatives. In R. Blight and M. Moosally (eds.), *Texas Linguistic Forum 38: The Syntax and Semantics of Predication*, 43–58. Austin, TX: Department of Linguistics, University of Texas at Austin.

1998. On pseudogapping. Unpublished paper, Department of Linguistics, Cornell University.

2000. Syntactic relations. Unpublished paper, Department of Linguistics, Cornell University.

2001a. Syntactic relations. Manuscript, Department of Linguistics, Cornell University.

2001b. Predication. In M. Baltin and C. Collins (eds.), *The Handbook of Contemporary Syntactic Theory*, 299–333. Malden, MA, and Oxford: Blackwell.

2002. Transitivity. *Linguistic Inquiry* 33, 183–224.

2008. On reducing control to movement. *Syntax* 11, 125–143.

2010. *Arguments as Relations*. Cambridge, MA: MIT Press.

Bresnan, J. and J. Kanerva 1989. Locative inversion in Chicheŵa: a case study of factorization in grammar. *Linguistic Inquiry* 20, 1–50.

Brody, M. 1994. Phrase structure and dependence. *UCL Working Papers in Linguistics* 6, 1–33.

Chomsky, N. 1970. Remarks on nominalization. In R. Jacobs and P. Rosenbaum (eds.), *Readings in English Transformational Grammar*, 184–221. Waltham, MA: Ginn.

1981. *Lectures on Government and Binding*. Dordrecht: Foris.

1986. *Barriers*. Cambridge, MA: MIT Press.

1995a. *The Minimalist Program*. Cambridge, MA: MIT Press.

1995b. Bare phrase structure. In G. Webelhuth (ed.), *Government and Binding and the Minimalist Program*, 383–439. Oxford: Blackwell.

2000. Minimalist inquiries. In R. Martin, D. Michaels, and J. Uriagereka (eds.), *Step by Step: Essays on Minimalist Syntax in Honor of Howard Lasnik*, 89–155. Cambridge, MA: MIT Press.

2001. Derivation by phase. In M. Kenstowicz (ed.), *Ken Hale: A Life in Language*, 1–52. Cambridge, MA: MIT Press.

2004. Beyond explanatory adequacy. In A. Belletti (ed.), *Structures and Beyond: The Cartography of Syntactic Structures* 3, 104–131. Oxford and New York: Oxford University Press.

Chomsky, N. and H. Lasnik 1977. Filters and control. *Linguistic Inquiry* 8, 425–504.

Chung, S. 2013. Syntactic identity in sluicing: how much and why. *Linguistic Inquiry* 44, 1–44.

Cinque, G. 1999. *Adverbs and Functional Heads*. Oxford: Oxford University Press.

2005. Deriving Greenberg's Universal 20 and its exceptions. *Linguistic Inquiry* 36, 315–332.

2006. *The Cartography of Syntactic Structures 4: Restructuring and Functional*. Oxford: Oxford University Press.

Cole, P. and G. Hermon 1998. The typology of wh-movement: wh-questions in Malay. *Syntax* 1 (3), 221–258.

Collins, C. 2002. Eliminating labels. In S. Epstein and T. Seely (eds.), *Derivation and Explanation in the Minimalist Program*, 42–61. Oxford: Blackwell.

2005. A smuggling approach to the passive in English. *Syntax* 8, 81–120.

Collins, C. and H. Ura 2001. Eliminating phrase structure. Unpublished paper, Cornell University and Kwansei Gakuin University.

Corver, N. 1990. *The Syntax of Left Branch Extractions*. Doctoral dissertation, Tilburg University.

1991. Evidence for DegP. *Proceedings of NELS* 21, 33–47.

1997. The internal syntax of the Dutch extended adjectival projection. *Natural Language and Linguistic Theory* 15, 289–368.

Covington, M. 2001. A fundamental algorithm for dependency parsing. In J. Miller and J. Smith (eds.), *Proceedings of the 39th Annual ACM Southeast Conference*, 95–102. Athens, GA: Institute for Artificial Intelligence, University of Georgia.

van Craenenbroeck, J. and J. Merchant 2013. Ellipsis phenomena. In M. den Dikken (ed.), *The Cambridge Handbook of Generative Syntax*, 701–745. Cambridge: Cambridge University Press.

Debusmann, R. 2000. An introduction to dependency grammar. Hausarbeit für das Hauptseminar Dependenzgrammatik SoSe 99, Universität des Saarlandes.

De Cuba, C. 2006. The adjunction prohibition and extraction from non-factive CPs. In D. Baumer, D. Montero, and M. Scanlon (eds.), *Proceedings of the 25th West Coast Conference on Formal Linguistics*, 123–131. Somerville, MA: Cascadilla Press.

Derbyshire, D. and G. Pullum 1981. Object-initial languages. *International Journal of American Linguistics* 47, 192–214.

Despić, M. 2011. *Syntax in the Absence of Determiner Phrase*. Doctoral dissertation, University of Connecticut.

2013. Binding and the structure of NP in Serbo-Croatian. *Linguistic Inquiry* 44, 239–270.

Dobashi, Y. 2003. *Phonological Phrasing and Syntactic Derivation*. Doctoral dissertation, Cornell University.

Doherty, C. 1996. Clausal structure and the modern Irish copula. *Natural Language and Linguistic Theory* 14, 1–46.

Dryer, M. 1988. Universals of negative position. In M. Hammond, E. Moravcsik, and J. Wirth (eds.), *Studies in Syntactic Typology*, 93–124. Amsterdam: John Benjamins.

1992. The Greenbergian word order correlations. *Language* 68, 81–138.

2007. Word order. In T. Shopen (ed.), *Clause Structure, Language Typology and Syntactic Description* 1, second edition. Cambridge University Press.

Emonds, J. 1969. *Root and Structure-preserving Transformations*. Doctoral dissertation, MIT. Distributed by the Indiana University Linguistics Club.

1978. The verbal complex V'-V in French. *Linguistic Inquiry* 9, 151–175.

2012. Blackjack!: 21 arguments that agreeing adjectives are derived nominals. In E. Torrego (ed.), *Of Grammar, Words, and Verses: In Honor of Carlos Piera*, 171–200. Amsterdam: John Benjamins.

Ernst, T. 2001. *The Syntax of Adjuncts*. Cambridge: Cambridge University Press.

Freidin, R., C. Otero, and M. Zubizarreta (eds.) 2008. *Foundational Issues in Linguistic Theory: Essays in Honor of Jean-Roger Vergnaud*. Cambridge, MA: MIT Press.

Frey, W. 2000. Syntactic requirements on adjuncts. In C. Fabricius-Hansen, E. Lang, and C. Maienborn (eds.), *Approaching the Grammar of Adjuncts*, 107–134. Berlin: ZAS Papers in Linguistics.

Gaifman, H. 1965. Dependency systems and phrase-structure systems. *Information and Control* 8, 304–337.

George, L. 1980. *Analogical Generalization in Natural Language Syntax*. Doctoral dissertation, MIT.

Givón, T. 1979. From discourse to syntax: grammar as a processing strategy. In T. Givón (ed.), *Discourse and Syntax*, 81–109. New York: Academic Press.

Goodall, G. 1997. Theta-alignment and the by-phrase. In K. Singer, R. Eggert, and G. Anderson (eds.), *Chicago Linguistic Society (CLS)* 33, 129–139. Chicago, IL: Department of Linguistics, University of Chicago.

Greenberg, J. 1963. Some universals of grammar with particular reference to the order of meaningful elements. In J. Greenberg (ed.), *Universals of Language*, 73–113. Cambridge, MA: MIT Press.

Grimshaw, J. 1990. *Argument Structure*. Cambridge, MA: MIT Press.

Haider, H. 2000. Adverb placement: convergence of structure and licensing. *Theoretical Linguistics* 26, 95–134.

Halle, M. and A. Marantz 1993. Distributed morphology and the pieces of inflection. In K. Hale and S. J. Keyser (eds.), *The View from Building 20: Essays in Linguistics in Honor of Sylvain Bromberger*, 53–109. Cambridge, MA: MIT Press.

Hays, D. G. 1964. Dependency theory: a formalism and some observations. *Language* 40, 511–525.

Higginbotham, J. 1987. Indefiniteness and predication. In E. Reuland and A. ter Meulen (eds.), *The Representation of (In)definiteness*, 43–70. Cambridge, MA: MIT Press.

Hinterhölzl, R. 2001. Event-related adjuncts and the OV/VO distinction. In K. Megerdoomian and L. Bar-el (eds.), *Proceedings of the 20th West Coast Conference on Formal Linguistics*, 276–289. Somerville, MA: Cascadilla Press.

2002. Parametric variation and scrambling in English. In C. J.-W. Zwart and W. Abraham (eds.), *Studies in Comparative Germanic Syntax*, 131–150. Amsterdam: John Benjamins.

Holmer, A. 2005. Antisymmetry and final particles in a Formosan VOS language. In A. Carnie, H. Harley, and S. Dooley (eds.), *Verb First: On the Syntax of Verb-initial Languages*, 175–201. Amsterdam: John Benjamins.

Hornstein, N. 1999. Movement and control. *Linguistic Inquiry* 30, 69–96.

2001. *Move! A Minimalist Theory of Construal*. Oxford: Blackwell.

Hornstein, N., J. Nunes, and K. Grohmann 2005. *Understanding Minimalism*. Cambridge: Cambridge University Press.

Hudson, R. 1990. *English Word Grammar*. Oxford: Blackwell.

Jackendoff, R. 1972. *Semantic Interpretation in Generative Grammar*. Cambridge, MA: MIT Press.

1977. *X' Syntax: A Study of Phrase Structure*. Cambridge, MA: MIT Press.

Jayaseelan, K. 2001. IP-internal topic and focus phrases. *Studia Linguistica* 55, 39–75.

Johnson, K. 2009. Gapping is not (VP-) ellipsis. *Linguistic Inquiry* 40, 289–328.

Julien, M. 2004. *The Syntax of Scandinavian Nominal Phrases*. Amsterdam: Elsevier.

2005. *Nominal Phrases from a Scandinavian Perspective*. Amsterdam: John Benjamins.

Kallulli, D. 1999. *The Comparative Syntax of Albanian: On the Contribution of Syntactic Types to Propositional Interpretation*. Doctoral dissertation, University of Durham.

Kayne, R. 1994. *The Antisymmetry of Syntax*. Cambridge, MA: MIT Press.

2010. Why are there no directionality parameters? Unpublished paper, New York University.

Keenan, E. 1976. Remarkable subjects in Malagasy. In C. Li (ed.), *Subject and Topic*, 247–301. New York: Academic Press.

Kehler, A. 2000. Coherence and the resolution of ellipsis. *Linguistics and Philosophy* 23, 533–575.

2002. *Coherence, Reference, and the Theory of Grammar*. Stanford, CA: CSLI Publications.

Keyser, S. J. 1968. Review of S. Jacobson, "Adverbial Positions in English" (Uppsala dissertation). *Language* 44, 357–374.

Kiparsky, P. and C. Kiparsky 1971. Fact. In D. Steinberg and L. Jakobovits (eds.), *Semantics: An Interdisciplinary Reader in Philosophy, Linguistics and Psychology*, 345–369. Cambridge: Cambridge University Press.

Koizumi, M. 1993. Object agreement phrases and the split VP hypothesis. *MIT Working Papers in Linguistics* 18, 99–148.

1995. *Phrase Structure in Minimalist Syntax*. Doctoral dissertation, International Christian University.

Krishnamurti, B. and B. Benham 1998. Konda. In S. Steever (ed.), *The Dravidian Languages*, 241–269. London: Routledge.

Kučerová, I. 2016. Long-distance agreement in Icelandic: locality restored. *Journal of Comparative Germanic Linguistics* 19, 49–74.

Laka, I. 1990. *Negation in Syntax: On the Nature of Functional Categories and Projections*. Doctoral dissertation, MIT.

Larson, R. 1988. On the double object construction. *Linguistic Inquiry* 19, 335–391.

Lasnik, H. 1999. On feature strength: three minimalist approaches to overt movement. *Linguistic Inquiry* 30, 197–217.

Li, C. and S. Thompson 1978. An exploration of Mandarin Chinese. In W. Lehman (ed.), *Syntactic Typology*, 223–266. Austin, TX: University of Texas Press.

Lobeck, A. 1995. *Ellipsis: Functional Heads, Licensing, and Identification*. New York: Oxford University Press.

Manzini, M. 1995. From Merge and Move to Form Dependency. *UCL Working Papers in Linguistics* 7, 323–345.

Manzini, M. and M. Savoia 2011. *Grammatical Categories: Variation in Romance Languages*. Cambridge: Cambridge University Press.

Marantz, A. 1997. No escape from syntax: don't try morphological analysis in the privacy of your own lexicon. *University of Pennsylvania Working Papers in Linguistics* 4, 201–225.

Matsuoka, M. 2013. On the notion of subject for subject-oriented adverbs. *Language* 89, 586–618.

May, R. 1985. *Logical Form: Its Structure and Derivation*. Cambridge, MA: MIT press.

McCloskey, J. 2005. A note on predicates and heads in Irish clausal syntax. In A. Carnie, H. Harley, and S. Dooley (eds.), *Verb First: On the Syntax of Verb-initial Languages*, 155–174. Amsterdam: John Benjamins.

McIntyre, A. 2001. Functional interpretations: borderline idiosyncrasy in prepositional phrases and other expressions. Manuscript, University of Leipzig.

Melvold, J. 1991. Factivity and definiteness. *MIT Working Papers in Linguistics* 15, 97–117.

Merchant, J. 2001. *The Syntax of Silence: Sluicing, Islands, and the Theory of Ellipsis*. Oxford: Oxford University Press.

2008. An asymmetry in voice mismatches in VP-ellipsis and pseudogapping. *Linguistic Inquiry* 39, 169–179.

2013. Voice and ellipsis. *Linguistic Inquiry* 44, 77–108.

Miller, P. 1991. *Clitics and Constituents in Phrase Structure Grammar*. Doctoral dissertation, Utrecht University.

Milsark, G. 1974. *Existential Sentences in English*. Doctoral dissertation, MIT.

Nilsen, Ø. 2000. *The Syntax of Circumstantial Adverbials*. Oslo: Novus Press.

Oseki, Y. 2015. Eliminating Pair-Merge. In U. Steindl et al. (eds.), *Proceedings of the 32nd West Coast Conference on Formal Linguistics*, 303–312. Somerville, MA: Cascadilla Press.

Pereltsvaig, A. 2006. Small nominals. *Natural Language and Linguistic Theory* 24, 433–500.

Perlmutter, D. 1970. On the article in English. In M. Bierwisch and K. Heidolph (eds.), *Progress in Linguistics*, 233–248. Mouton.

1983. *Studies in Relational Grammar* 1. Chicago, IL, and London: University of Chicago Press.

Perlmutter, D. and C. Rosen 1984. *Studies in Relational Grammar* 2. Chicago, IL, and London: University of Chicago Press.

Pesetsky, D. 1995. *Zero Syntax: Experiencers and Cascades*. Cambridge, MA: MIT Press.

Picallo, M. C. 1991. Nominals and nominalization in Catalan. *Probus* 3, 279–316.

Pollock, J.-Y. 1989. Verb movement, universal grammar, and the structure of IP. *Linguistic Inquiry* 20, 365–424.

Postal, P. (with D. E. Johnson) 1980. *Arc Pair Grammar.* Princeton, NJ: Princeton University Press.

Rackowski, A. 1998. Malagasy adverbs. In I. Paul (ed.), *The Structure of Malagasy* II, 11–33. Los Angeles, CA: UCLA Occasional Papers in Linguistics.

Rackowski, A. and L. Travis 2000. V-initial languages: X or XP movement and adverbial placement. In A. Carnie and E. Guilfoyle (eds.), *The Syntax of Verb Initial Languages*, 117–141. New York: Oxford University Press.

Radford, A. 1997. *Syntax: A Minimalist Introduction.* Cambridge: Cambridge University Press.

Ramchand, G. 2008. *Verb Meaning and the Lexicon: A First Phase Syntax.* Cambridge: Cambridge University Press.

Ritter, E. 1991. Two functional categories in noun phrases: evidence from Modern Hebrew. In S. Rothstein (ed.), *Syntax and Semantics* 26, 37–62. San Diego, CA: Academic Press.

Rizzi, L. 1990. *Relativized Minimality.* Cambridge, MA: MIT Press.

Robinson, J. J. 1970. Dependency structures and transformation rules. *Language* 46, 259–285.

Rudin, C. 1988. On multiple questions and multiple wh fronting. *Natural Language and Linguistic Theory* 6, 445–501.

Saddy, D. 1991. Wh-scope mechanisms in Bahasa Indonesia. In L. Cheng and H. Demirdash (eds.), *More Papers on wh-movement.* MIT Working Papers in Linguistics 15, 183–218. Cambridge, MA: Department of Linguistics and Philosophy, MIT.

   1992. A versus A-bar movement and *wh*-fronting in Bahasa Indonesia. Manuscript, University of Queensland, Australia.

Shlonsky, U. 2004. The form of Semitic noun phrases. *Lingua* 114, 1465–1526.

Siewierska, A. 1988. *Word Order Rules.* London and New York: Croom Helm.

Sigurðsson, H. 1996. Icelandic finite verb agreement. *Papers in Scandinavian Syntax* 57, 1–46.

Szabolcsi, A. 1983. The possessor that ran away from home. *Linguistic Review* 3, 89–102.

Takahashi, S. 2004. Pseudogapping and cyclic linearization. *Proceedings of NELS* 34, 571–586.

   2011. Voice mismatch and syntactic identity. *Linguistic Inquiry* 42, 470–490.

Tanaka, H. 2011. Syntactic identity and ellipsis. *Linguistic Review* 28, 79–110.

Tasseva-Kurktchieva, M. 2001. Multiple wh-movement in Bulgarian: What is still not explained. Paper presented at *Formal Descriptions of Slavic Languages (FDSL) 4.* Potsdam, Germany.

Tesnière, L. 1959. *Éléments de syntaxe structurale.* Paris, France: Klincksieck.

Toosarvandani, M. 2013. Gapping is low coordination (plus VP-ellipsis): a reply to Johnson. Unpublished manuscript, University of California at Santa Cruz.

Travis, L. 2005. VP-internal structure in a VOS language. In A. Carnie, H. Harley, and S. Dooley (eds.), *Verb First: On the Syntax of Verb-initial Languages*, 203–224. Amsterdam: John Benjamins.

Valois, D. 1991. *The Internal Syntax of DP*. Doctoral dissertation, UCLA.

Vikner, S. 1995. *Verb Movement and Expletive Subjects in the Germanic Languages*. Oxford: Oxford University Press.

Vilkuna, M. 1998. Word order in European Uralic. In A. Siewierska (ed.), *Constituent Order in the Languages of Europe*, 173–233. Berlin: Mouton de Gruyter.

Wall, R. 1972. *Introduction to Mathematical Linguistics*. Englewood Cliffs, NJ: Prentice-Hall.

Whitman, J. 2005. Preverbal elements in Korean and Japanese. In G. Cinque and R. Kayne (eds.), *The Oxford Handbook of Comparative Syntax*, 880–902. Oxford: Oxford University Press.

Index

CPSIA information can be obtained
at www.ICGtesting.com
Printed in the USA
LVHW011727170920
666365LV00012B/166

9 781107 480650